Deconstructing Europe

Deconstructing Europe: Postcolonial Perspectives engages with the question of what makes Europe postcolonial and how memory, whiteness and religion figure in representations and manifestations of European 'identity' and self-perception. To deconstruct Europe is necessary as its definition is now contested more than ever, both internally (through the proliferation of ethnic, religious, regional differences) and externally (Europe expanding its boundaries but closing its borders).

This edited collection explores a number of theoretical discussions on the meaning of Europe, and proposes analysing some of the deeds committed in the name of Europe, both today and in the past, by foregrounding a postcolonial approach. To deconstruct Europe as a postcolonial place does not imply that Europe's imperial past is over, but on the contrary that Europe's idea of self, and of its polity, is still struggling with the continuing hold of colonialist and imperialist attitudes. The objective of this volume is to account for historical legacies which have been denied, forgotten or silenced, such as the histories of minor and peripheral colonialisms (Nordic colonialisms or Austrian, Spanish and Italian colonialism), and to account for the realities of geographical margins within Europe, such as the Mediterranean and the Eastern border, while tracing alternative models for solidarity and conviviality. The chapters deal with social and political formations as well as cultural and artistic practices drawing from different disciplinary backgrounds and methodological traditions. As such it creates an innovative space for comparative and cross-disciplinary exchanges.

This book was previously published as a special issue of the journal *Social Identities*.

Sandra Ponzanesi is Associate Professor of Gender and Postcolonial Critique in the department of Media and Culture Studies/Gender Programme at Utrecht University, the Netherlands. Among her publications are *Paradoxes of Post-colonial Culture* (2004), *Migrant Cartographies* (2005) and *Postcolonial Cinema Studies* (2011).

Bolette B. Blaagaard is Research fellow at the Centre for Law, Justice and Journalism at City University London, UK. She has published articles and contributed to edited volumes on issues of Nordic colonialism and whiteness in the Nordic region as well as the ethics of journalistic practices, objectivity and freedom of speech.

Deconstructing Europe
Postcolonial Perspectives

Edited by
Sandra Ponzanesi and Bolette B. Blaagaard

LONDON AND NEW YORK

First published 2012
by Routledge
4 Park Square, Milton Park, Abingdon, Oxon OX14 4RN
605 Third Avenue, New York, NY 10017

First issued in paperback 2013

Routledge is an imprint of the Taylor & Francis Group, an informa business

© 2012 Taylor & Francis

This book is a reproduction of *Social Identities*, volume 17, issue 1. The Publisher requests to those authors who may be citing this book to state, also, the bibliographical details of the special issue on which the book was based.

All rights reserved. No part of this book may be reprinted or reproduced or utilised in any form or by any electronic, mechanical, or other means, now known or hereafter invented, including photocopying and recording, or in any information storage or retrieval system, without permission in writing from the publishers.

Trademark notice: Product or corporate names may be trademarks or registered trademarks, and are used only for identification and explanation without intent to infringe.

British Library Cataloguing in Publication Data
A catalogue record for this book is available from the British Library

ISBN 13: 978-0-415-69004-1 (hbk)
ISBN 13: 978-0-415-84695-0 (pbk)

Typeset in Times New Roman
by Taylor & Francis Books

Disclaimer
The publisher would like to make readers aware that the chapters in this book are referred to as articles as they had been in the special issue. The publisher accepts responsibility for any inconsistencies that may have arisen in the course of preparing this volume for print.

Contents

Notes on Contributors   vii

Introduction: In the name of Europe
Sandra Ponzanesi and Bolette B. Blaagaard   1

Part I: Outbound: geographical margins, historical cores

1. Negotiating white Icelandic identity: multicultural and colonial identity formations
Kristín Loftsdóttir   11

2. Asylum seekers as Austria's other: the re-emergence of Austria's colonial past in a state-of-exception
Brigitte Hipfl and Daniela Gronold   27

3. Spelling out exclusion in Southern Italy
Claudia Buonaiuto and Marie-Hélène Laforest   41

4. Whose freedom? Whose memories? Commemorating Danish colonialism in St. Croix
Bolette B. Blaagaard   61

Part II: Deconstructing Europe: conviviality and invisibility

5. Europe in motion: migrant cinema and the politics of encounter
Sandra Ponzanesi   73

6. Multiculturalism in a selection of English and Spanish fiction and artworks
Lourdes López Ropero and Alejandra Moreno Álvarez   93

7. Adrift on the black Mediterranean diaspora: African migrant writing in Spain
Esther Sánchez-Pardo   105

8. 'Rented spaces': Italian postcolonial literature
Manuela Coppola   121

9. 'Dubbing di diaspora': gender and reggae music inna Babylon
Sonia Sabelli   137

Workings of whiteness: interview with Vron Ware
Conducted by Bolette B. Blaagaard   153

   Index   162

Notes on Contributors

Bolette B. Blaagaard is Research fellow at the Centre for Law, Justice and Journalism at the City University London, UK. She holds a PhD degree in gender and ethnicity studies from Utrecht University, the Netherlands, and a MA in journalism from University of Southern Denmark, Denmark. She has published articles and contributed to edited volumes on issues of Nordic colonialism and whiteness in the Nordic region as well as the ethics of journalistic practices, objectivity and freedom of speech. Her research interests centre on how journalistic practices can be combined with cosmopolitanism, postcolonialism, and gender and ethnicity theories in order to challenge and change journalism to cope ethically with an increasingly globalised world.

Claudia Buonaiuto, teaches English postcolonial culture at the University of Naples 'L'Orientale'. She holds a MA in Cultural Studies from the University of East London, a PhD in Postcolonial Studies from the University of Naples 'L'Orientale', and is currently researching on multiculturalism and media with a post-doctorate fellowship from the University of Naples 'Parthenope'. She has researched extensively on contemporary African diaspora literature and visual arts, dedicating her PhD dissertation to the analysis of works by Derek Walcott, Caryl Phillips, Alice Walker and Keith Piper. She has edited a book on the Chicano music of protest in the US, *Canto Chicano* (Napoli: Marotta & Cafiero, 2007), has published articles on cross-cultural London, on the archive of the African diaspora, on Italian postcolonial literature, and has also translated into Italian a short story by Jackie Kay. She is active in intercultural promotion.

Manuela Coppola holds a PhD from the University of Naples 'L'Orientale' and teaches English literature at the University of Calabria. Her main interests focus on gender studies and postcolonial theory and literature. She has published articles on Shakespearean rewritings, South African and Caribbean women writers, and has co-edited with Katherine Russo *Middle Passages. English for Cultural and Postcolonial Studies* (Aracne 2007). She is currently researching on contemporary Caribbean women poets and on the 'literature of migration' in Italy.

Daniela Gronold is a media theorist and employing feminist and postcolonial methodology. Currently she is working on a concept of "gender democratic journalism" based on the analysis of contemporary media reports in Austria from a Critical Whiteness Studies perspective. She is located at the University of Klagenfurt, where she teaches at the media department and where she is involved in projects connected to the Centre of Peace Research and Peace Education.

Brigitte Hipfl is Professor at the Department of Media and Communication Studies at the University of Klagenfurt, Austria. Her areas of interest are media and identity, gender and identity, subjectivity and cultural studies. She is the co-editor of *Sündiger*

NOTES ON CONTRIBUTORS

Genuß? Filmerfahrungen von Frauen (1996 with Frigga Haug), *Bewegte Identitäten. Medien in transkulturellen Kontexten* (2001 with Brigitta Busch and Kevin Robins), *Identitätsräume. Nation, Körper und Geschlecht in den Medien. Eine Topografie* (2004 with Elisabeth Klaus and Uta Scheer) and *Media Communities* (2006 with Theo Hug).

Marie-Hélène Laforest, is a writer and Professor of Anglophone literatures at the University of Naples 'L'Orientale'. Her fields of research include postcolonial studies, gender studies, African diasporic literatures. She has published extensively on interculturality, hybrid identities, racial and gender issues, and Caribbean culture and literature. She has co-edited special editions of *Anglistica* and *Feminist Review*. Among her publications are two books of non-fiction, *Diasporic Encounters. Remapping the Caribbean* (2000) and *La magia delle parole. Omeros di Derek Walcott* (2007). She has been a John Simmons Short Fiction Awards semi-finalist and a James Michener fellow. Her collection of short stories *Foreign Shores* appeared in 2004.

Kristín Loftsdóttir is Professor in Anthropology at the University of Iceland. She received her Ph.D. in Cultural Anthropology from the University of Arizona, in 2000. Her doctoral dissertation is based on two years of ethnographic fieldwork among WoDaaBe in Niger from 1996 to 1998, and which focused on ethnicity, migrant work and global relations. More recently, Kristín Loftsdóttir has focused on issues regarding plurality in Icelandic society focusing on the historical formation of racism and national identity in Iceland in relation to ideas of 'others.' She has published the book: *The Bush is Sweet: Agency, Development and Power among WoDaaBe Pastoral in Niger* (The Nordic Africa Institute, 2008). Some of her other recent publications are: 'Shades of Otherness: Representations of Africa in 19th-century Iceland' in *Social Anthropology*, 2008, and 'Bounded and Multiple Identities: Ethnic Identities of WoDaaBe and FulBe' in *Cahiers d'Études Africaines*, 2007. She is a board member at the Institute of Anthropology at the University of Iceland and IMER (The Research Center on International Migration and Ethnic Relations) at the University of Iceland. Kristín has had a photo exhibition in relation to her work in Niger displayed in an art museum in Iceland.

Lourdes López Ropero holds an MA from the University of Kansas, and a PhD from the University of Santiago de Compostela. She has been a research fellow at the University of North Carolina and San Diego State University, among others. Currently, she is an Associate Professor in the English Department of the University of Alicante, Spain. Her research interests focus on Postcolonial and Children's Literature. She is the author of the volume *The Anglo-Caribbean Migration Novel: Writing from the* Diaspora (2004) and 'Homage and Revision: Zadie Smith's Use of E. M. Forster in *On Beauty*' (*Commonwealth Essays and Studies*, 32.2, 2010).

Alejandra Moreno Álvarez holds a PhD in Women's Studies from the University of Oviedo. She has been a research fellow at Rutgers University and Cornell University, among others. Currently, she is a Lecturer in the English Department of the University of Oviedo. Her teaching and research is centered in English Literature and Literatures in English Language, Feminist and Postcolonial Theory and in the subject of Body Politics in Literature and Cinema. She is the author of *Lenguajes* *comestibles: Anorexia, bulimia y su descodificación en la ficción de Margaret Atwood y Fay Weldon* (2009).

Sandra Ponzanesi is Associate Professor of Gender and Postcolonial Critique at Utrecht University (The Netherlands), department of Media and Culture Studies/ Graduate Gender Programme. She has been visiting professor at the University of California, Los Angeles and visiting scholar at the University of California, Riverside. Her recent research interests concern the reception of postcolonial literature in relation to the literary award industry and the exploration of digital literacies of migrant youth in transnational contexts. She is the coordinator of the European wide research network PEN (Postcolonial Europe Network) and of the PCI (Postcolonial Studies Initiative). She has published on post-colonial critique, transnational gender theories, Italian colonial history, visual culture and postcolonial cinema. Her publications include: *Paradoxes of Post-colonial Culture: Contemporary Women Writing of the Indian and Afro-Italian Diaspora* (Albany: Suny Press, 2004), *Migrant Cartographies New Cultural and Literary Spaces in Post-colonial Europe* (Lanham, MD,: Lexington Books, 2005) with Daniela Merolla and *Postcolonial Cinema Studies* (London: Routledge, 2011) with Marguerite Waller.

Sonia Sabelli graduated in Italian literature at Rome University, in 2000, with a dissertation on Italo Calvino's *Fiabe italiane*. In the same year she started her Ph.D. in Women's writings, that she finished in 2004, with a dissertation entitled *Eccentric women writers: transnational identities in the Italian literature*. This research focuses on literary texts written by migrant women, coming from different countries, now living in Italy, and writing in the Italian language. She has published several articles on journals and books (about Italian migration literature, women in reggae music and migrant musicians in Italy); and she has taught gender studies at Rome University, from 2005 to 2008. She currently works in the Italian Ministry for Internal Affairs, where she has been employed since 1997. She has been part of the crew of the Lionheart Sound (former Sattamassagana, one of the first sound systems active in Rome, from 1995); and she also presents a radio programme called *Attica Blues*, about black music and African American culture, broadcasting every week on Radio OndaRossa.

Esther Sánchez-Pardo is Professor of English at Universidad Complutense in Madrid. She works in a Comparative Literature framework with 20th century literatures in English focusing on poetics and theory. Her work in Modernist Studies, psychoanalysis and postcolonial and race theory took her to edit, *Women, Identities and Poetry* (1999), *Feeling the Worlds* (2001), and *Ophelia's Legacy* (2001, in Spanish). She has published *Cultures of the Death Drive. Melanie Klein and Modernist Melancholia* (2003), and her edited volume *History, Exile, Creation. W.H. Auden's Poetics Today* is forthcoming. Her sustained work in poetic translation shows in her recent bilingual critical Anthology of Mina Loy (2009). Recent publications include papers for the launch of the new book collection for European Avant-garde and Modernism Studies, *Europa! Europa?* (vol.1, Berlin & N.Y., 2009) and *The Great Divide?* (vol.2, forthcoming 2011), and to volumes such as, *(Un)Masking Bruno Schulz* (Rodopi, 2009), *The Popular Avant-garde* (Rodopi, 2010), *Visual Cultures* (Intellect, 2010), *Canadian Studies. The State of the Art* (ICCS, 2011) and *Henry James's Europe. Heritage and Transfer* (OpenBook, 2011).

INTRODUCTION
In the name of Europe

Sandra Ponzanesi[a] and Bolette B. Blaagaard[b]

[a]Department of Media and Culture Studies/Graduate Gender Programme, Utrecht University, Utrecht, The Netherlands; [b]Centre for Law, Justice and Journalism, City University London, London, UK

> Though that [imperial and colonial] history remains marginal and largely unacknowledged, surfacing only in the service of nostalgia and melancholia, it represents a store of unlikely connections and complex interpretative resources. The imperial and colonial past continues to shape political life in the overdeveloped-but-no-longer-imperial countries. (Gilroy, 2004, p. 2)

> 'Europe' in a sense is a phantom of the past, a name that 'is history' rather than society, political, or economics, since the flow of capitalization, population, communication and political action, cross its territory, invest its cities and workplace, but do not elect it as a permanent of specific site. Europe is not only de-territorialized, but also de-localized, put 'out of itself', and in the end deconstructed. It may be part of an imaginary, but less and less of the real. (Balibar, 2004, p. 10)

This special issue approaches feminist, postcolonial and race theory from different cultural, disciplinary and national backgrounds. The contributors engage with the question of what makes Europe postcolonial and how memory, whiteness and religion figure in representations and manifestations of European 'identity' and self-perception.

This intervention is necessary as the notion of Europe is now contested more than ever, both internally (through the proliferation of ethnic, religious, and regional differences) and externally (Europe expanding its boundaries but closing its borders). Is Europe a bulwark, an exclusionary and discriminatory fortress, or the last romantic ideal of a supra-national organization based on ideas of peace, justice and emancipation?

Many people still hold onto the notion that Europe is not simply a continent, a mere geographical space that continually redefines its boundaries and peripheries, but they want to see it as an ideal, the cradle of the Enlightenment and of scientific revolutions, and therefore of Western modernity and democracy. But as Gilroy writes in his epigraph, Europe is not innocent and does not reside beyond the disruptive forces of colonization; and as Benhabib states, the idea of Europe is an illusion instrumentalized to enforce new power dynamics:

> Contemporary Europe is facing the danger that its moral and political boundaries will be redefined via geographical borders. Geography once again will be used to cover the tracks of complex processes of political and moral inclusion and exclusion... [Europe] whether as an ideal or illusion, whom does it include and whom does it exclude? After the Cold War who are Europe's 'others'? (Benhabib, 2002, p. 155)

It is for these reasons that the Somali writer Nuruddin Farah accuses the European Union, often invoked as the political synonym for Europe, of being another scapegoat for 'postcolonial responsibility'. He argues that European nations do not want to take responsibility for their hazardous and short-sighted redefinition of national borders and ethnic allocations during colonial times that have brought about the recent mass migrations towards Europe. The European Union is, according to Farah, another empire of a more sophisticated order, which has taken the role of doing away with the imperial responsibilities of countries such as Britain, France, Portugal, the Netherlands and Italy. The people of this new empire are barricading themselves within an empty rhetoric of fear and helplessness. But as Farah (2000) forcefully puts it:

> If refugees are a challenge as well as a reproach to our humanity, if refugees are a lament raised, a cry spoken, if refugees are the bastards of the idea of empire, then how can one blame this highly disenfranchised, displaced humanity for all Europe's ills? (p. 55)

Farah addresses the responsibilities of the European Union, because he too has occupied the ambiguous territory of colonization and was forced to see himself as someone else's invention (Farah, 2000). As Graham Huggan writes, refugees and asylum seekers remind us of the limit of cosmopolitanism and of the contradictions of a 'euphoric' globalist worldview which should welcome migrants of every religion and ethnicity into the celebration of a world without borders (Huggan, 2008, p. 245). Conversely, Agamben (1994) states in 'We refugees' that:

> If in the system of the nation-state the refugee represents such a disquieting element, it is above all because by breaking up the identity between man and citizen, between nativity and nationality, the refugee throws into crisis the original fiction of sovereignty... For this reason – that is, inasmuch as the refugee unhinges the old trinity of state/nation/territory – this apparently marginal figure deserves rather to be considered the central figure of our political history. It would be well not to forget that the first camps in Europe were built as places to control refugees, and that the progression – internment camps, concentration camps, extermination camps – represents a perfectly real filiation. (1994, para. 5)

Following this line of thought, Passerini argues that we should perceive Europe less as a political program and more as an emotional project. The Europe that Passerini envisions is an imagined territory, rather than a self proclaimed and arrogant identity that is a locus for doubt, absences and shortcomings. The latter is an important analysis in order not to forget that Europe is not the cradle of civilization and humanity but the inheritance of many painful and violent connections (from the imperial past to Auschwitz, to the current resurgence of racism). These 'unwelcome' legacies need 'not be forgotten, but dismantled and uprooted' and addressed (Stråth, 2000, pp. 14–15).

In this new revaluation of where Europe is at the moment we should keep in mind that there has been a shift from Eurocentrism into what Philomena Essed has termed

Europism (Essed, 1995, p. 54) which has become even the more strident after 9/11. Eurocentrism refers to the old discourse of European superiority and domination over the south, through colonial expansion, imperialism and the civilising mission. Europism in contrast, is more introspective and characterized by the defensive discourse of constructing a pure Europe cleansed of foreign and uncivilized elements. Eurocentrism is therefore marked by Europe's movement towards the outside whereas Europism is marked by an inward looking position, and homogenizing process from the inside. Essed sees Fortress Europe as a form of Europism, operating both as an ideology and as a bureaucratic machinery to create legal, economic and political boundaries to protect Europe against the rest of the world, in particular the South. This idea of Western Europe goes well beyond an ideological construction, and is often implemented through a body of legislation whose objective is to close borders against refugees and immigrants.

As Wendy Brown (2008) has debated, the proliferation of borders or the creation of new walls is not resurgent expressions of nation-state sovereignty in late modernity but rather icons of its failure. The epidemic of building walls and strengthening borders is, in fact, testimony to the corrosion of the sovereign state instead of its authority. The borders that determine Europe have become, as Balibar writes, 'uncertain' and, despite the constant refencing of Fortress Europe, are vacilating. However, they are being replaced by multiple, invisible and internal borders that mark new forms of inclusion and exclusion based on linguistic, racial, ethnic and religious divisions. Balibar constructs his argument around what he terms 'European apartheid,' which makes reference to the types of exclusions that are implemented not only at the level of legislation but also as a way in which Europe is constructed as a concept. Balibar maintains that borders have not been eliminated but that there is a multiplication of borders in the form of 'internal borders', a myriad of new invisible borders that are ideological, radicalized and politicized (Balibar, 2003).

Borders are therefore moving from physical (the gate to European territories and citizenship) and symbolic (the myth of Europe and its idea of superiority) to material borders (the marked body of foreigners, immigrants and asylums seekers) which become 'border' figurations (construction of otherness, foreignness, alienness). These embodied borders come to signify a somewhat cohesive category that, pretty much in line with Said's notion of Orientalism, places the 'European subject', i.e. the host, in a position of definition by default. Instead of being the signifier, the European subject becomes the hollow referent, a kind of blind spot that needs the other for his/her/its self-definition. The European is what the other is not, therefore unmarked by race, ethnicity and religion but in reality implicitly constructed upon the idea of maleness, whiteness, and Christianity.

One of the best lessons of postcolonial thinking was precisely not the analysis of dichotomous relationships but the exploration of intertwinements, contaminations and condition of dependencies that allow for the undermining of the priority of one signifier above the other. Postcolonial cultural theorist, Iain Chambers, presents for example the Mediterranean as the hybrid product of cultural and material flows that resist the rigid mapping of borders and linear notions of progress. Chambers defines a geography without a real East or West, in which the 'Occident' and the 'Orient' are not guideposts but unwanted intrusions (Chambers, 2008). This special issue explores a number of theoretical discussions on the meaning of Europe and proposes configurations of Europe. To address anti-immigration issues means therefore to account for both the laws and regulations as well as for the ideological representations and symbolic order proposed by conflicting actors in Postcolonial Europe.

The essays deal with social and political formations as well as cultural and artistic practices, often focusing on women as the major site of interaction between conflicting loyalties, interests, legacies and rationales (Lutz, 1997). This issue draws from different disciplinary backgrounds and methodological traditions, and the collected essays create space for comparative and cross-disciplinary exchanges.

The first section of this special issue focuses on the submerged colonial legacies of marginal locations in Europe (i.e. Iceland, Denmark, Austria, Italy) and the second section analyzes the representations of migrant voices through different languages, genres and media (literature, cinema, music, art) across Europe.

The first section also focuses on how critical whiteness is developing as an important field to analyze the European context. Critical whiteness presents researchers with as many questions as the rest of the postcolonial field; and it does so while navigating different routes of analysis and uprooting the intricate issues of European postcolonialism. 'Whiteness studies' have come to Europe through American scholars' thorough investigations into the racial matters and debates in the US. However, when transposed into European history, political reality today and cultural memories of identities, nations and territories, the scholarly work done in the US is merely a platform for the re-evaluation of whiteness in terms of the particularities within and of Europe.

European colonial history depicts resemblances and differences from US racial history and politics. These are differences and resemblances that in each case need to be considered if critical whiteness studies are to make any sense in a European context. Being white or not white in Europe draws on discourses surrounding not only diaspora, slavery and segregation (though it does that too), but also religion, ethnicity, migrations and 'scientific' ambitions of phrenology and eugenics, national identities and territorial disputes. Whiteness constructed in the European context was not made up of legal structures, but of fluid structures of power relations, which have shifted throughout time and are still changing. Therefore critical whiteness studies in a European context raises issues of exclusion and inclusion, geographical and ethnic borders, migration and integration and assimilation. Critical whiteness is an aspect of this special issue and is elucidated in Kristín Loftsdóttir's article on the negotiations of white identity within the Icelandic population in a historical analysis that is expanded into a contemporary critique.

The intricate patterns of Nordic colonialism (see Charpentier et al., 2009) allow a country like Iceland to both assume a position as a former colony of Denmark and simultaneously textualize its position into that of a 'white' nation – on the political and genetic side of Britain, France and Belgium in the 'scramble for Africa' – producing unique opportunities to explore what 'whiteness' means in a European context and history and what postcolonial Europe may encompass.

Denmark's colonial history spread both in Nordic and southern directions. However, the issue of the Nordic colonies is often neglected or limited to discussions about Viking exploration and the vagueness of citizenship at the time of conquest. Or the issues are discussed in terms of the current financial situation in the colonies and their potential independence from Danish funding and politics. The former southern Danish colonies – Tranquebar, the Gold Coast (Ghana), and the Danish West Indies (the current US Virgin Islands) – are dealt with in archaeological and historical terms, and rarely engage with the present political and cultural situation in these places. However, looking at the converging space between journalism and cultural memory, when the past is allowed entry into the present it facilitates a historicized future. In this special issue Bolette B. Blaagaard examines how journalistic practices contribute to the continuous construction of cultural memory. Her article takes as a point of departure the argument that not only major events, but also everyday occurrences that are reported in the news media, help confirm who 'we' are in a given community. The question of 'collective' or 'cultural' memory is explored through journalistic representation and practices. The article addresses the issues of cultural and archival historical representations as they are presented in Danish journalism about historical events taking place in the former colonies of Denmark, the current US Virgin Islands.

The Austrian empire was of a magnitude that many of us have forgotten. In their article, Brigitte Hipfl and Daniela Gronold argue that the imperial past of Austria has not been excavated and has not become part of public consciousness. This omission prevents Austria from defining itself as a multicultural state in the present. However, the new immigrants and asylum seekers confront Austria with its past and challenge the comfortable and accessible view of the Habsburgian empire as an exemplary case of 'multiculturalism': combining nations, languages and people. The recent fluxes of immigration also renew a sense of loss that occurs in remembrance of the Austro-Hungarian Empire's glorious past, which loses its aura of nostalgia and touristy folklore.

In their piece on Naples as a porous city, Claudia Buonaiuto and Marie-Hélène Laforest refer not only to the forgotten legacy of Italian colonialism in Eastern Africa but also to the many forms of internal colonization within the nation. Buonaiuto and Laforest analyze the divisions between north and south, the city within the state, the ghettos within the city, and the multiple layers (both historical and geographical) of migrants and migrations claiming an identity within this most spectacularly complex city, which functions as a microcosm that illustrates the intersections between the many global souths of the world and the so-called 'center' (i.e. Europe).

In the second section the contributors specifically focus on how Europe has been revisioned, resignified and remoulded by its so-called strangers: postcolonial migrants, refugees and asylum seekers who see Europe as a transitory zone or as a final destination. This issue illustrates that it is not the outcasts and the ghosts from the underbelly but the strangers within who are now determining not only the configuration of European cities but also the renewed understanding of political citizenship, cosmopolitanism and human rights. This vision challenges ongoing or previous definitions of 'Europeanness' that has never been a static entity but an articulation of imaginations and belongings that needs to be unraveled and redrawn in its multiple layers of meanings, convergences and emotions.

The strangers within are part of the European discursive construction, rich in connotations and ambiguities, and as such operate in the name of Europe. These strangers are often pre-assigned, spoken for and relegated to the realm of victimhood in order to be entitled to the right of entrance, sojourn and protection in Europe. The dual politics of disenfranchisement while offering supposed 'solidarity', articulates an ambivalence that has been amply elaborated by Derrida in his notion of hospitality. This is textually, visually and aurally articulated in several recent European artworks, novels, songs and films which magnify the condition of the migrants as mirroring the violent benevolence of their hosts. From their perspective, before departure Europe is often a mirage, a paradise to be reached which is in stark contrast to the hostile reality of arrival, of borders that have been created within the nation between 'us' and 'them' that relegate 'them' to a uniform, homogenous history and geographical otherness.

In her article 'Europe in motion' Sandra Ponzanesi focuses on the contested notion of the (new) Europe from the vantage point of migrant cinema by analyzing how the politics of encounter is represented in three recent European migrant films: *Yasmin*, *Unveiled* and *The Unknown Woman*. These visual and ideological commentaries participate in the redefinition or abolition of the notion of Europe by presenting the representations of the strangers within. They do so not by depicting from original and unexpected positions but by highlighting the transformation of the 'European subject' through the politics of encounter. It explores how cinematic language offers alternative modalities of representation and subjectification in relation to migration, gender and identity.

Lourdes López Ropero and Alejandra Moreno Álvarez examine how the notion of conviviality takes shape in recent literary, cinematic and artistic productions, by paying attention to the dominant paradigm of British multiculturalism (through the work of Yinka Shonibare, Andrea Levy, Monica Ali) and how it connects and relates to other forms of emerging multiculturalism within Europe such as in the case of Spain (Lucía Etxebarría).

In her article 'Rented spaces', Manuela Coppola discusses how Italy recently acknowledged the presence of 'second generation' migrants, people of non-Italian origin who are still striving for recognition and who are increasingly gaining access to practices of self-representation. She analyzes the trend of migrant literature in Italy as a controversial site of self-representation, and suggests that women writers gain visibility through access to publication, but they still occupy ambiguous spaces of exotic objectification and limiting definitions. She refers to the concept of 'rented spaces' as a metaphor to investigate the politics of cohabitation in postcolonial Europe which can render the multiple signifiers of social, cultural, and linguistic practices.

Esther Sánchez-Pardo's article sketches the complexities of Spain's postcolonial reality and explores how the historically homogeneous emigrating country is transforming into a destination for members of several diasporas, many with their own legacies of colonialism and racism. Due to its European Union status and growing presence in the world economy, Spain is participating in a global phenomenon in which immigrants, asylum seekers, and refugees are looking towards the new Europe as an impenetrable fortress instead of a site of multicultural interaction. By analyzing the work of black African migrant writers who are residents of Spain (Inongo-vi-Makomé, Susan Akono and Donato Ndongo) her article explores the ways in which the self is reconstructed in diasporic situations through the various underpinnings and fragmentations of the migration experiences that are represented in narrative processes.

In her article on 'Dubbing di diaspora', Sonia Sabelli analyzes gender representations in reggae music in postcolonial Europe in the context of the processes of the global consumption of reggae music and the international appropriation – by white musicians – of a musical genre that historically had a black identity. She explores how reggae performers and audiences responded to the colonial strategy of legitimizing images that perpetuated European colonial governance through the exercise of command and subordination, whether identifying black liberation with virility, and male control of women's bodies, and therefore perpetuating sexist images and concepts and homophobic attitudes, or re-visioning their struggle for freedom in forms that do not support or perpetuate phallocentrism and patriarchal control.

As a coda to the issue we have included an original interview with Vron Ware, an important theorist of critical whiteness studies who explains the transitions from the dominant US paradigm to past and current European specificities and creates links and references to the issues addressed in Postcolonial Europe.

Postcolonial Europe is an ongoing project that requires continuous fresh perspectives and an account of untold or forgotten stories, told from both established institutional positions and more marginal ones. By collecting the efforts, voices and expertise of scholars, artists and independent thinkers throughout Europe, this issue is an attempt to map some of the possible routes for unthinking Europe in a global era.

Acknowledgements

We are particularly grateful to Rosi Braidotti and Vron Ware for their critical feedback and helpful suggestions on earlier drafts of these articles. We would also like to thank the anonymous reviewers for their comments and useful remarks.

This special issue is the output of the 'Postcolonial Europe' working group, coordinated by Sandra Ponzanesi and Bolette B. Blaagaard, operating under Athena3, the EU sponsored Advanced Thematic Network of Women's Studies in Europe (http://www.athena3.org/). We are particularly grateful to Athena and its coordination, in particular Berteke Waaldijk, for having provided the basis for regular annual meetings across Europe and for having financed the special workshop held in Utrecht in May 2008 in which Vron Ware participated as an invited guest. Another output of the working group is the online course 'Postcolonial Europe: Gender, Ethnicity and Migration' which can be found on www.postcolonialeurope.net

References

Agamben, G. (1994). We refugees (M. Rocke, Trans.). *Symposium, 49*, 114–119. Retrieved September 14, 2009, from http://www.egs.edu/faculty/agamben/agamben-we-refugees.html

Balibar, E. (2003). *We, the people of Europe? Reflections on transnational citizenship*. Princeton, NJ: Princeton University Press.

Balibar, E. (2004, November). *Europe as borderland*. Paper presented at the Alexander van Humboldt lecture in human geography, University of Nijmegen, The Netherlands. Retrieved September 14, 2009, from http://socgeo.ruhosting.nl/colloquium/Europe%20as%20Borderland.pdf

Balibar, E., & Wellerstein, I. (1991). *Race, nation, class: Ambiguous identities*. London: Verso.

Barker, F. (Ed.) (1985). *Europe and its others: Proceedings of the Essex Conference on the Sociology of Literature, July 1984*. Colchester: University of Essex.

Benhabib, S. (2002). *The claim of culture. Equality and diversity in the global era*. Princeton, NJ: Princeton University Press.

Brown, W. (2008, April). *Porous sovereignty, walled democracy*. Paper presented at the Katz Distinguished Lecture in the humanities, University of Washington, USA. Retrieved September 14, 2009, from http://dpts.washington.edu/uwch/katz/20072008/wendy_brown.html

Chambers, I. (2008). *Mediterranean crossings: The politics of an interrupted modernity*. Durham, NC: Duke University Press.

Charpentier, S., Keskinen, S., Tuori, S., & Mulinari, D. (Eds.) (2009). *Complying with colonialism: Gender, race and ethnicity in the Nordic region*. London: Ashgate.

Essed, P. (1995). Gender, migration and cross-ethnic coalition building. In H. Lutz, A. Phoenix & N. Yuval-Davis (Eds.), *Crossfires: Nationalism, racism and gender in Europe* (pp. 48–64). London: Pluto.

Farah, N. (2000). *Yesterday, tomorrow: Voices from the Somali diaspora*. London and New York, NY: Cassell Academic.

Gibson, S. (2006). 'The hotel business is about strangers'. Border politics and hospitable spaces in Stephen Frears' *Dirty pretty things*. *Third Text, 20*, 693–701.

Gilroy, P. (2004). *After empire: Melancholia or convivial culture?* London and New York, NY: Routledge.

Huggan, G. (2008). Perspectives on postcolonial Europe. *Journal of Postcolonial Writing, 44*, 241–249.

Lutz, H. (1997). The limits of Europeanness: Immigrant women in fortress Europe. *Feminist Review*, 57, 93–111.

Passerini, L. (2000). The last identification: Why some of us would like to call ourselves Europeans and what we mean by this. In B. Stråth (Ed.), *Europe and the other and Europe as the other* (pp. 45–65). Brussels: Peter Lang.

Ponzanesi, S. (2004). *Paradoxes of postcolonial culture: Contemporary women writings of the Indian and Afro-Italian diaspora*. Albany, NY: Suny Press.

Ponzanesi, S., & Daniela M. (Eds.) (2005). *Migrant cartographies: New cultural and literary spaces in postcolonial Europe*. Lanham, MD: Lexington.

Stråth, B. (Ed.) (2000). *Europe and the other and Europe as the other*. Brussels: Peter Lang.

Negotiating white Icelandic identity: multiculturalism and colonial identity formations

Kristín Loftsdóttir

Professor in Cultural Anthropology, Faculty of Social and Human Sciences, University of Iceland, Reykjavík, IS

> Post-colonial scholars have emphasized the need to explore the ways in which colonial contact shaped both the colonized and colonizers; that is, how European identities were formulated in relation to imperial projects. Colonial Europe itself has to be deconstructed, looking at similarities and variability within different countries.
>
> This article explores the construction of 'white' Icelandic identity in historical and contemporary discourses. The article shows that even though Iceland did not participate directly in the nineteenth century colonial project, the interwoven racial, gendered and nationalistic ideologies associated with the colonial project were very much a part of Icelandic identity in the nineteenth and early twentieth century as shaped by parallel discourses in Europe. Analysis of contemporary blog sites reflects the increasingly complex manifestations of racism in contemporary Iceland. Whiteness continues to be invisible as a position of power to many contemporary Icelanders. Interestingly, despite being few in numbers in Iceland, Muslims are increasingly constructed in the media as a threat in a similar way as in the rest of Europe.

Introduction

In the fall of 2007, the republishing of the book *Ten Little Negroes*, originally published in Icelandic in 1922 under the name *The Negro-boys* (*Negrastrákarnir*), caused enormous debates within Icelandic society. The existence of such debates can be seen as symbols of the great transformations that Icelandic society has undergone since I was growing up there in the 1970s. Contemporary Iceland is becoming increasingly connected with a globalized reality of migration and plurality. This particular debate was evident in different media forms, such as newspaper articles, talk-shows, radio programs and on-line blog sites. One blogger, expressing surprise over the fuss of republishing the book, states: '... these are just simple subtractions[1] placed forward in an amusing way, I for one look at it in that way rather than seeing it as some kind of racism'. What makes this comment particularly noteworthy is how it minimizes the racist character of the book – positioning it as a choice, i.e. the writer of the blog *chooses* not to see it as racist. The comment shows how those who have benefited historically and in the present from the social classification of people into different races often see racism as irrelevant, and in a sense such comments imply that Europe's colonial history had nothing to do with themselves or their current global and national reality.

As pointed out by Ann Stoler (1992), post-colonial theories have tended to see the 'West' as a collective whole, thus losing the particularities within the different countries and social groups located within this socially defined unit. Her arguments point to how we need to pay closer attention to the 'us' part of the dichotomy 'us' and 'other', destabilizing the normalization of whiteness as well as problematizing European identities within colonial and post-colonial contexts. The Nordic countries exemplify this. Very few studies have been conducted on colonialism in relation to these countries and some of which (such as Sweden and Denmark) were directly engaged in colonial enterprises in other parts of the world as well as having an ambiguous relationship with each other due to internal colonization (see still, for example, Jensen, 2005; Keskinen, Irni, Mulinari, & Tuori, 2009; also Freiesleben, 1998). These legacies can be seen as silenced for the most part within contemporary European discourses. Iceland became a Danish dependency as early as 1380 when the Danish and the Norwegian crowns were unified, Iceland having been colonized by Norway more than a decade earlier following the Commonwealth period in the ninth century. Iceland's 'struggle for independence' is usually seen as starting in 1851, when nationalistic ideas swept through Europe. Icelanders have long emphasized their geographical isolation and the 'purity' of their ethnic origin, combined with grand narratives of how they gained independence and became one of the richest nations in the world. Accompanying Icelandic financial investments overseas, and thus increased participation in global markets, are growing numbers of immigrants. The expansion of the Icelandic economy called for added immigration to supply the increased demand for labor, increased immigration thus being the response to a demand from Icelandic industries and businesses. The issues of multiculturalism have become increasingly debated and discussed with the visual destabilization of this idea of a homogenous, 'white' Iceland. When the three largest banks in Iceland collapsed in October 2008, the economic situation of the country became almost so bad overnight that the Icelandic government saw itself forced to seek financial assistance from the International Monetary Fund (IMF). The high unemployment and insecurity that has followed could increase the likelihood of a growing prejudice against these new Icelanders. Iceland's past entanglement as a dependency, and the current jump from its status as one of the richest countries in the world to a recipient of IMF loans, clearly demonstrates the importance of looking at Europe as a contested and problematic term.

In this article, I explore the construction of 'white' identity in Iceland within colonial and post-colonial contexts, attempting to contribute to a dynamic and historical view of racism within colonial and post-colonial Europe, its maintenance, gendered implications, and how it had to be constantly remanufactured through various discourses and praxis.[2] I show how the formulation of Icelandic identity included, as in the rest of Europe, a racialized visualization of whiteness as both a distinctive and normative category, which today still continues to inform Icelandic identity. The interwoven racial, gendered and nationalistic ideologies associated with Europe's colonial project were very much a part of Icelandic identity, even though Iceland was also considered a dependency at the time. Simultaneously, this construction of Icelandic identity has to be seen as meaningful in particular local contexts and deriving from local politics and events, although a part of more global currents of nationalism and racism.

My theoretical orientation is based upon the work of authors who have criticized how ideas of modernity, civilization and nationalism have often been seen as arising within European contexts as isolated from imperialistic and nationalistic situations. Post-colonial scholars have emphasized the need for more extensive explorations into the ways in which colonial contact shaped the colonizers themselves. Paul Gilroy (1993) uses the term 'Atlantic world' to capture the transnational and intercultural perspectives which have formed the world and the nationalistic identities of today, thus criticizing what he calls 'cultural insiderism', which focuses on national entities as fully formed within their own spaces rather than as products of transverse dynamics (p. 3). The celebrated meta-narrative of the Enlightenment as the age of discoveries leading to the advancement of science has, as observed by Nicholas Dirks (1992), to a great extent ignored the colonial project as stimulating and facilitating the scientific imagination. Meta-narratives of civilization have thus focused on how Europeans brought civilization to 'others', rather than seeing the idea of 'civilization' itself as taking shape within various transnational and geographical encounters. Furthermore, European gendered identities were shaped by racial policies in the overseas colonies (Stoler, 1992).

I start the discussion by contextualizing it theoretically within feminist and post-colonial theories of gender and whiteness, stressing the importance of seeing identity as relational and contextual; individuals occupy different subject positions that are situationally dependent. Contextualizing Icelandic identity within colonial ideologies by the use of nineteenth century texts, I show that even though the Icelanders identified strongly with the colonizer's discourse, their own subject position varied and is in some instances seen as part of the civilized world but in others as colonized subjects. I show how the gendered aspects of this identification, based on Mary Louise Pratt's ideas of 'brotherhood' (1990), and narratives of colonial explorations, served for Icelandic men as a way to visualize and situate themselves as part of the educated European elite. I use texts from the annual periodical *Skírnir* dating from the late nineteenth to the early twentieth century, as well as schoolbooks from the same period, in order to capture the insights that, as stressed by Pratt (1992), through textual means nineteenth century Europeans were able to imagine themselves in relation to people they had never seen.

Focusing on the current post-colonial reality of Iceland, I map out currently debated issues relating to race and difference in a contemporary Icelandic context utilizing blog pages. Blogging can maintain and create a cohesive, nationalistic identity outside geographical boundaries, especially for nations utilizing a language that is not widely spoken. Blogging has become increasingly important in Iceland partly due to how individuals can link their comments to news stories in one of the most popular media-based websites, *Morgunblaðið*, creating vivid forums of public discussions, as well as increased accessibility for people to have their viewpoints heard. My analysis limits itself to discussions on a few blogs published on *Morgunblaðið*'s blog hosting service that are often linked to particular stories in the newspaper, the link being clearly visual with the news itself. One discussion refers to Muslim women and the other comments on the republishing of the book *The Negro-boys*. The blogs in question are personal blog pages that have been linked with a particular news story in the net-based version of *Morgunblaðið*, making these viewpoints likely to be widely heard. These personal blogs have then been responded to by various individuals, posting their personal comments on the same blog-page. Placed together these 'texts' give important statements of difference and gender within the Icelandic context.

Theorizing gender, race, and whiteness

Whiteness as a scholarly subject has, however, become extremely important across various disciplines and is studied from different angles (Fine, Weis, Pruitt, & Burns, 2004, p. ix). This theoretical trend can be seen as connected to the scholarly emphasis on turning the gaze not only towards those who have less power and are marginalized within society but also at those holding more powerful positions or status. Scholarly studies have in general had a tendency to focus less on those in power, as reflected in Peter Rigby's critical comment that scholars need to pay attention to this discrepancy, and focused on the 'culture of the rulers, rather than that of the ruled' (1996, p. viii). Nirmal Puwar (2004), among others, has stressed how power rests with the normalization of certain bodies, their invisibility hiding how access to power within society is clustered along social variables. It is this invisibility, its deconstructing and decoding, which scholarly analysis must address. In my opinion, anthropology has been valuable in this regard in its classical tradition of what Vincent Crapanzano has called 'defamiliarization'; that is, the self-distancing required to recognize social constructions and to 'reevaluate our respective cultural presumptions' (2003, p. 4). Feminist scholars from various disciplines have highlighted and made visible the relationship of power embedded in different relationships, predating in various respects the post-modernism emphasis on representation and power (Mascia-Lees & Sharpe, 2000; Moore, 1994). Importantly, feminist scholars have also shown that power is not singular and that individuals have different subject positions and identities. It is important to stress the situational character of power and to situate people as creative beings, resisting and manipulating various conditions, and who can thus simultaneously be oppressors and oppressed within certain structures of power (see also Loftsdóttir, 2004). Feminist analysis importantly acknowledged the gendered bias that was predominant in academic studies (Moore, 1988), but for the last few decades the focus has extended to men *and* women, the gendered constructions of men just as women, as well as the relationship between men and women. The analysis of gender as evolving simply around women does not challenge men's normative position, stressing the importance of studying men and masculinities. Gender is both constructed socially and textually but also produced (Miescher & Lindsay, 2003, p. 7) through various encounters and interactions, locally and through multiplex translocal encounters. Nevertheless, there is still a tendency within masculinity studies to focus more on men who are perceived as marginal in some sense (Wright, 2005).

The emphasis placed by gender studies on identities as fluid and fractional also draws attention to the interrelationship between racism and sexism in society. Race is constituted as an important and meaningful social category, and as a source of identity, exclusion and domination. Scholars have disputed when to date the appearance of racism, some seeing it as primarily arising in the nineteenth century while others see its roots as much older (Stoler, 1995, pp. 27–28, 91; Isaac, 2004). Underlying these disputes are questions about how 'racism' is defined.

Classifications based on skin color were certainly evident prior to the nineteenth century – but during that time the association of skin color with certain social variables was not as fixed as it became in the late nineteenth/early twentieth century. Also, going further back it is certain that even though we find negative references to dark skin color in mediæval times (but also positive ones), human diversity in general was conceptualized in rather different ways from those which became evident later on (Loftsdóttir, 2006).

As studies of masculinity challenge the normative categorization of maleness, studies of whiteness can similarly be defined as explorations of how whiteness has been treated as a normative category, as if race had nothing to do with socially defined categories of whiteness. Frankenberg's (1993) breakthrough study of white women's identity emphasized how these women did not 'see' race as a part of their identity formation. Placing the spotlight on whiteness can help to demonstrate how certain groups – those defined as white – can benefit from such an apparently socially neutral category that creates various institutional arrangements that to whites seem to have no racial basis (Hartigan Jr., 1997, p. 496). Whiteness can thus be seen as including certain privileges where individuals can 'afford' to forget their own skin color and position of power (Loftsdóttir, 2003).

In more recent times, the concept of 'multiculturalism' has been used to capture the fluid character of contemporary societies. In some sense, the term implies that multi-cultural society is a new phenomenon, thus hiding to some extent that societies have always been composed of different cultures (and the rearrangement of identities within certain nationalistic categories during the eighteenth and nineteenth centuries). There is also a tendency to use the term multiculturalism to refer only to the culture of 'other' people, i.e. those marginalized within the nation state and thus to some extent normalizing the culture of the dominant majority (see discussion in Skaptadóttir & Loftsdóttir, 2009, pp. 207–208). As Sandra Ponzanesi (2007) points out, multiculturalism has always had to do with the 'inclusion and exclusion of multiple cultural forms within the nation-states' (p. 92), thus involving a way of framing identities in particular localized contexts. Usage of the term multiculturalism can be seen as an acknowledgement of the nation-state being composed of people of different origins and a celebration of that difference. As scholars have increasingly emphasized, racism in contemporary societies often takes new forms, increasingly attaching itself to other features such as religion and culture, making them often difficult to untangle. Culture is used instead of race as an explanation for the marginalized positions of certain groups, in the process objectifying and homogenizing a large group of people similar to the way biological features were used before. Further, such cultural arguments are often embedded in the language of nationalism and ethnicity (Balibar, 1991). In this context, scholars have spoken out about the growing prejudice against Muslims, especially in the aftermath of the September 11, 2001 terrorist attacks on the USA. Matti Bunzl (2005) speaks of Islamophobia as a phenomenon which aims at safeguarding the 'future of European civilization' (p. 506), with Muslims being represented as a homogenous threat to its existence. As Faye V. Harrison (2002) claims, racism has simultaneously become more diverse in terms of visibility ranging from 'subtle, hidden subtexts to flagrant acts of hate speech' (p. 150).

Icelandic men – European civilized men

In 1850, the population of Iceland was only 60,000 and in 1900 the population had increased to 78,000 people (Statistics Iceland, 2008a). Within a European context, Icelanders had an ambiguous status.[3] Even though Icelanders were generally not represented as complete 'savages', neither were they seen as fully belonging to 'civilized' peoples. Travelers who visited Iceland often remarked upon the drinking, ignorance and general filthiness of Icelanders, but also observed that Icelanders were happy in their simple lives, hospitable and childlike. Similar views can be seen represented in some narratives of Icelandic immigrants to North America in the late nineteenth century (see for example discussion in Þorsteinsson, 1940, p. 201). More positive images of Icelanders also existed, particularly in connection with rising nationalism in Europe, but within such ideas peasants became increasingly viewed as uncorrupted and as the pure essence of the nation. Under such influences, intellectuals had a growing interest in Germanic and Celtic history (Ísleifsson, 1996, pp. 84–85; see also discussion in Loftsdóttir, 2008). The growing importance of racial classifications at this time must have given Icelandic people a new status, with the opportunities of becoming a part of a 'white and civilized race'. The ambiguous position of Icelanders can be seen to be reflected in a protest made by Icelandic students about the Danish colonial exhibition in 1905, where Icelanders or Icelandic subjects were supposed to be represented as other Danish colonial subjects. The Icelandic students' comments show that they felt that by participating, Icelanders were being reduced to the same status as other colonized people, such as those from Greenland and Africa (Loftsdóttir, 2008).

The journal *Skírnir*'s discussion on colonialism is particularly informative in order to understand the Icelandic authors' engagement and conceptualization of colonialism. *Skírnir* was initiated in 1827 to publish annual overviews of major events in the world and in fact, became one of the most importance sources of foreign news in Iceland during that time (Sigurðsson, 1986, pp. 22, 34).[4] The journal was published by the *Icelandic Literature Association*, founded in 1816, which celebrated the importance of the Icelandic language and cultural traditions (Pálsson, 1978, p. 71), and fostered feelings of nationalism. The opening words of the author of *Skírnir* in 1853 provide a positive assessment of colonialism stating that 'the year 1852 has been very prosperous for the world', adding that some nations do not yet participate in the world's progress. There are, the text adds, still many nations, especially in the north, that have lost or not yet gained their freedom which is so important to them. The text then states that whole continents are now being built by educated men, bringing their experience and knowledge with them (p. 5). The text thus draws a rather sharp distinction between northern nations that need and deserve freedom and nations that need educated men from far away (read Europe) to direct them towards the path to progress. Certain high ranking Icelandic individuals, such as Magnus Stephensen, show sympathy with Latin America and Greece's fight for independence (Sigurðsson, 1996, pp. 44–45) – a sympathy that can be seen echoed in *Skírnir*'s discussion of the United States of America and Latin America from 1852 (p. 154). The edition of *Skírnir* published almost 20 years later in 1874 gives a similar viewpoint by stating: 'Many of those who are familiar with the black nations in Africa agree that they will never become anything unless the civilized states in our continent help them and rule over them' (p. 57). In 1874, Iceland was of course trying to lay claim to its own independence from Denmark, seeing independence as the natural right of Icelanders due to their long history and unique language (Hálfdánarson, 2000, p. 91). These remarks clearly show how, for the author, there is no common ground or similarity between colonial rule in different parts of the world, seeing it as natural that African nations are ruled by others.

Discussions of Africa in the nineteenth century Icelandic journal *Skírnir* revolve to great extent around white, European explorers – male explorers – that were seen as populating the different countries, subjugating and 'civilizing' them (Loftsdóttir, 2009). One example is the edition of *Skírnir* published in 1890. This issue details a 20-page review of Henry Morton Stanley's trip to Africa during 1887–1889,[5] focusing on Stanley's heroism and durability. This particular trip has been seen as Stanley's most ambiguous trip to Africa and was even criticized in Britain at that time (see Driver, 2001, p. 126), but this criticism is never clearly visible or dealt with seriously in the Icelandic discussion. A general lack of interest about the non-European populations can be seen in much of the news that focuses not only on Africa but on other parts of the world. *Skírnir*'s discussion about Australia and Asia from 1827–1832 rarely mentions native populations at all – evoking an image of Europeans as colonizing empty spaces. The analysis was more centered on the progress of the colonists, the future prospects for colonization and possible profit making. The discussions of Australia from 1888 (pp. 81–82) and 1889 (pp. 81–83), for example, hardly mention the colonized people of the continent. The aboriginal inhabitants are briefly mentioned in *Skírnir* 1827, but then as 'very ignorant savages' (p. 42).

In *Skírnir*'s discussion about Africa, women are usually invisible, especially European women. Radhika Mohanram's suggestion could be appropriate here, as she claims that when whiteness is linked to the body, women become a liability for establishing the supremacy of the whiteness. She states that if whiteness was 'reincoded within militaristic masculinity, then white women were not white in themselves but could be linked to whiteness only as a supplement' (2007, p. 25). *Skírnir*'s discussion about the Boer in 1900 refers to Boer women in two places: one speaks of a battle between the British and the Boer. The text emphasises the heroism and durability of the Boer fighters against the overwhelming number of British soldiers. It tells the readers that the Boer had sought shelter and there the women sat and sang psalms with the teenagers, while the men were fighting (p. 29). The text later on also notes the 'disgraceful' (*svívirðilegt*) British behavior toward Boer women (the phrasing implies sexual assaults) when the British burnt down Boer homes, even though there were only women and children at home, and claiming that in this the British behaved like 'true savages' (*örgustu villimenn*), of which there were no examples in the last century among 'civilized nations' (p. 88). In both of these texts the women have rather passive roles, being a liability in a sense in the later example, and even bringing out the savage in 'civilized' men.

Educational material published in Iceland during the nineteenth and early twentieth centuries supported such ideas of race and masculinity as expressed in journals and public discourses. The interconnectedness of these texts with the images expressed in journals must have helped to legitimize them, making them natural and unquestionable. What I find particularly interesting when analyzing schoolbooks from this period is both the visibility and invisibility of whiteness as a legitimate social category. Mohanram (2007) states that in the nineteenth century whiteness became invisible and universalized. In the Icelandic schoolbooks during the period from the late nineteenth century to the early twentieth century, this is dependent on what kind of schoolbooks we are speaking of. In history books that discuss historical events, whiteness is naturalized as 'the' history of the world. Within the social space of history, whiteness or maleness do not have to be mentioned even though the wheels of history are seen as driven by individuals having these 'qualities'. In geography books, whiteness is, however, spoken about openly within the context of racial classifications which are obviously seen as a 'geographical' subject, with races geographically determined. Within this textual space, whiteness can be openly spoken about, even though masculinity is, as before, naturalized and hidden. A geography book published in 1882 gives elaborate racial classifications using physical and linguistic indicators, referring to studies by other European scholars, probably to legitimize the classifications of people into different races as scientific (Gröndal, 1882). The style of Gröndal's writing indicates in fact how well established racist typologies had become in the European context at the time, as being natural and undisputed.[6] This emphasis continues in Icelandic geography books up to the beginning of the twentieth century. The 'white race', as it is called, is characterized in one geography book as having tall foreheads and soft curly hair (*liðast í lokkum*) (Sæmundsson, 1937, p. 9). At the same time, the Icelanders themselves are portrayed in history books for children as the best breed of the 'Nordic stock', an idea which was proclaimed in two such books that were used for several generations of children, in addition to being celebrated in other Icelandic texts (see discussion in Loftsdóttir, 2010). The historian Unnur B. Karlsdóttir's (1998) analysis of the eugenics movement in Iceland in the late nineteenth and early twentieth centuries reveals Icelandic self-conceptions as deriving from the 'noblest' part of the Nordic and Irish populations. This fitted well with the general ideology of the eugenics movement where some populations were seen as better breeds than others (p. 151). Guðmundur Finnbogason, a professor and rector at the University of Iceland,[7] vividly reflects such ideas in an article published in *Skírnir*, where he claims that Icelandic nature has weeded out the weakest of the Icelandic population, and the presumed 'quality' of the population is thus higher today than earlier (Finnbogason, 1925).

Contextualizing these texts within Icelandic political history and identity politics, they can be seen as evident of anxieties pertaining to the position of Icelanders within the world and concerns about Icelandic identity. In my view, they involve the positioning of Icelanders within the category of 'white' 'masculine' and 'civilized', but their positioning within that category can in no way been seen as secure, as is manifested by the treatment of Icelanders in the USA where they were occasionally seen as an inferior type of Europeans. The status of Icelanders as subjects of Denmark also categorized them – at least in a nineteenth century context – with people with whom they did not want to be associated. These texts can thus in some ways be seen as self-representations assuring the writer and the readers about where 'the' Icelanders belonged.

Engaging with multiculturalism

Foreign nationals have constituted a small proportion of the population in Iceland in comparison with most other European countries. During the period from the Second World War to the mid 1970s, out-migration often surpassed the levels of immigration

(Statistics Iceland, 2007, p. 2). In January 2008, foreign nationals constituted 6.8% of the population compared with 3.5% in 2004 and below 2% in 1996 (Statistics Iceland, 2008b). There is a sharp gender difference in these numbers: 7.4% of all men in Iceland were foreign nationals in 2006, compared with 4.7% of all women (Statistics Iceland, 2007, pp. 7–8). Despite the country's geographical isolation, there has always been mobility to and from Iceland. The Icelandic elite, for example, sought education in the nineteenth century in Denmark and other European countries; Iceland was occupied by British and American soldiers during the Second World War (Ingimundarson, 2004, p. 65). The majority of current-day immigrants come in search of work or are sought after by the Icelanders themselves, usually accepting the low skilled jobs that are rejected by native Icelanders. Iceland's new landscape of people also includes increased numbers of second generation immigrants, adopted children, and refugees, meaning that many of the new Icelanders with non-Icelandic backgrounds are born and raised in Iceland.

Not surprisingly, the concepts of 'multiculturalism' and multicultural society are increasingly heard in the Icelandic media and in popular discussions. These concepts are generally used by the government to address this change in a positive way, and to underline the plural nature of the nation-state. The term 'multicultural' has been used by others who want to celebrate the cultural plurality of Iceland but has also been used by those who claim that 'Icelanders' should in some sense reject multiculturalism (Skaptadóttir & Loftsdóttir, 2009). Following the current economic crisis, the belief is often heard that 'now' the immigrants will go back home as there is no more work for them. However, recent studies of Icelandic immigrants show that many immigrants have invested a great deal in their personal livelihood in Iceland (Skaptadóttir & Wojtynska, 2008), making it likely that many will choose to stay. What I find interesting is to read the debates about multiculturalism against this above-discussed history of whiteness, seeing Icelandic representations of non-European people in the nineteenth and early twentieth centuries as racist, masculine and embedded in notions that these 'others' were intrinsically different people.

Many of the blog posts commenting on news stories in *Morgunblaðið* have to do with multicultural Iceland or issues relating to multicultural society, in relation both to news about immigrants or multiculturalism in Iceland and in relation to news from the outside world. Some ideas reflected in these texts are quite similar to stereotypical views existing elsewhere, such as web pages proclaiming to tell the 'truth' about the horrors of the Koran, homogenizing Muslims everywhere as a unified body of terrorists who seek to destroy Western civilization. There is at least one case where a blog-site hosted by *Morgunblaðið* was closed as the domain owners considered its comments too hateful to Islam. Blog posts critical of or commenting on Islam tend to be highly gendered, focusing on dangerous male terrorists or oppressed Islamic women, with the veil seen as a primary symbol in regard to the latter. As Lila Abu-Lughod (2002) reminds us, there is a long history in the West of constructing Muslim women or women in the developing world as needing to be saved, justifying various interventions on such basis (see also Mazurana, 2005). In Iceland such hateful comments against Muslims are perhaps particularly striking due to the relatively slight visibility of Muslims in Icelandic society – only 0.12% of the population belong to the Muslims Association of Iceland in 2007 (Statistics Iceland, 2008c), which is the only officially recognized Islamic religious association in Iceland. One blog posted in April 2008 stated that: 'The Koran promotes violence, terror regimes, complete lack of rights for women, and child molesting. If a society should be established here that is based on Islam, then we Icelanders should know what is behind it'. After an elaborate discussion of Mohammad as a child molester, the blog mentions the spokesperson for the Muslim Association of Iceland by name, proclaiming that this is the man who finds Mohammad better than any other. On the same page there were also elaborate discussions about women's rights: 'If a woman in Afghanistan would all of sudden take the burka down and says to her husband and his people: Now, I am not going to be in this cave anymore, now I am going to dress in pants and a sweater. What do you think would happen?' ('Halla', 2008). The text on the same blog post continues, underlining the oppression of Muslim women and the portrayal of Muslim men as child molesters and oppressors. Even though this blog and others with similar messages are not specifically addressing Icelandic Muslims, it is hard not to read them against that background, especially when many of those commenting on this blog post ask in despair how people cannot see that Muslims are trying to take over European civilization. Such comments reproduce and position themselves within rhetorical Western models that have constructed the category 'Western' as opposed to the 'Muslim', implying that these are inherently different constructions.[8] With religion used as marker of inferiority or difference (see Abu-Lughood, 2002), such discourses aim at separating certain people from the semiotic fields of civilized and Western. Not only does that imply that being Western is to be non-Muslim, but that Muslims are seen as threat to Icelandic identity; thus, being Muslim is to be inherently different from being Icelandic.

The republishing of the book *The Negro-boys* mentioned earlier caused public debates in every corner of society, which was not the case with these earlier-quoted comments against Muslims, but there was no uniformed consensus that the book was racist. The book was originally published in Iceland in 1922, and was republished at least four times, the last publication prior to 2007 being in 1975.[9] Browsing through newspaper clips in relation to these earlier republications, I have not found any protest or concern with racist imaginary. This is reflected in that the rhymes from this book were, until recently, still sung at social gatherings in primary schools.[10] Many of the contemporary blog comments express surprise that the book has raised controversy, stating in particular that the book has nothing to do with racism. One comment says: 'In the world of blogs simple cases can be made complex. Parents and kindergarten teachers should prepare children originating from Africa by telling them that there is nothing degrading with being a negro' ('Benedikt', 2007). What is interesting here is not only the acceptance of the racial categorization of 'others' and that they should accept these labels, but also the notion that problems are being 'imported'. The 'multiculturalists' are, according to these views, making simple things complex. Such texts hegemonically claim that Icelanders are not racist and have not been racist, and that these are rather just 'trivial' imported problems – 'foreign' in a sense like the people involved. Another comment on another blog site reflects this:

> I think my fellow country men have lost themselves in political correctness. The world has become really complex and people can hardly turn around because they are so concerned to step down in the right way. This reminds me of Germany in the Nazi period where everything which was not acceptable to the state was either burnt or the

communist Soviets where the same was going on... People can choose to buy this book or not buy it, what ever they like. Most people here seem to have read it or sung the rhymes as children and have not become hurt by it.

A similar response by another person to the same blog: 'Sorry, I think this is rather funny..., I remember I had this book, and I also had Little Black Sambo, even the doll... I have never felt any prejudice against people with another skin color, no more than those with differently colored hair' ('Ragnhildur', 2007) A comment to another blog which also addressed the republication of the book states: 'In my opinion, the reality is that prejudice against all various things are mostly in one's own head... I can just smile about this general discussion and am certain that those children who read the Ten Little Negroes won't be more prejudiced or worse individuals than the children who don't do it' (Ásthildur, 2007). What is striking here is of course how the authors seem to feel that race and racism are just other people's problems, as long as they know themselves that their views are not racist, then that should be good enough. Whiteness is thus not only an invisible social category, but those speaking from the position of whiteness can dismiss racism as a thing of the past, having no relevance or connection to the present.

Final remarks

In my discussion, I have attempted to stress the importance of recognizing the Nordic countries in relation to colonialism, and how current debates on multi-culturalism in countries like Iceland have to be contextualized within post-colonial theories that critically engage with links between the past and the present. Icelandic national identity was formulated in close dialogue with European colonial identity based on whiteness as a distinctive and normative category, embedding it with masculine characteristics. One can claim that discursive strategies, such as those found within *Skírnir* and schoolbooks from this time, aimed at locating Iceland as a European country, allowing Icelandic readers to follow and identify with male explorers in other parts of the world, as well as celebrating Iceland's emergence under modernization. These historical racist ideas can be seen to some extent to materialize in contemporary racial views against immigrants – informing and giving them meaning. Reading the current debates about multicultural Iceland against this historical background, it becomes particularly striking how individuals secure their position of whiteness by separating themselves from racism, constructing it as an individual choice. These discourses seek to reinforce the notion of Icelanders as white and European, in contrast to the dark skinned 'others' and, in a more recent context, Muslims in particular. Further, the targeting of Muslims reflects the widespread rise of racism against Muslims in Europe and its gendered implications, having very clear linkages to past colonial discourses where historically 'saving women' has frequently been used to justify various prejudices and interventions. This is especially striking as Muslims are very few in numbers in Iceland and have historically not been singled out as a particular group. Comparing the two discourses, one about Muslims and the other about racist images, shows the selective use of the past. The fact that images such as those seen in the book *The Negro-boys* was part of comprehensive system of racism is judged non-relevant in contemporary contexts, while the discourses about Muslims constantly evoke a very old historical memory of Muslims as a dangerous threat to Europe. Focusing on race, gender and whiteness in Iceland reflects the importance of mapping out the differences and similarities of discourses within postcolonial Europe (see Gullestad, 2002, p. 45), but also to outline the different social meanings and context within which these similarities operate.

Many of the voices presented here, furthermore, do not question their own position and where they are speaking from. Instead, they perceive the issues of discrimination and race as having nothing to do with them. With scholars recognizing other forms of discrimination as entangled with racism, race has become an even more complex issue. Racism has, of course, historically never been solely about genetics and has always involved entanglements of gender, religion and other poles of identity. Race has become a more complex issue because even though there seems to be general agreement that racism is a bad thing there is no consensus on what racism is, what it has been and what it is becoming.

Notes

1. The text of the book is composed by a counting rhyme where you subtract one first from ten, then from nine etc.
2. The discussion is partly based on my research project *Images of Africa in Iceland* which was funded by the Icelandic Centre for Research and the Research Fund of the University of Iceland, and on research supported by the Development Fund for Immigrant Matters, run by the Ministry of Social Affairs in Iceland.
3. Iceland gained independence in the final years of the Second World War.
4. I have in particular analyzed textual representations in the journal *Skírnir* in relation to Africa. The Literature Association was based in Copenhagen until 1880, as transportation was better between Copenhagen and Reykjavík than between Reykjavík and other parts of Iceland for the most of the nineteenth century. *Skírnir*'s authors were obviously educated men, some writing one annual issue of the journal, others directing several issues and many became leading politicians, writers, and poets.
5. This particular journey is often called the Emin Pasha Relief Exhibition.
6. In Loftsdóttir (2007), I have discussed the current representation of Africa in schoolbooks.
7. He was also an important advisor to the Icelandic parliament with regard to reforms on the Icelandic educational system, giving various suggestions with regard to its improvement.
8. Samuel P. Huntington's (1993) highly influential writing on 'The Clash of Civilizations' can be mentioned as one such example.
9. The pictures in the book are made by Muggur, who is one of Iceland's most beloved artists.
10. This is according to correspondence with two primary school teachers.

References

Abu-Lughod, L. (2002). Do Muslim women really need saving? Anthropological reflections on cultural relativism and its others. *American Anthropologist, 104*, 783–790.
Balibar, E. (1991). Is there a 'neo-racism'? In E. Balibar & I.M. Wallerstein (Eds.), *Race, nation, class: Ambiguous identities* (pp. 17–28). London and New York, NY: Verso.
Bunzl, M. (2005). Between anti-Semitism and Islamophobia: Some thoughts on the new Europe. *American Ethnologist, 32*(4), 499–508.
Crapanzano, V. (2003). Reflections on hope as a category of social and psychological analysis. *Cultural Anthropology, 18*(1), 3–32.
Dirks, N.B. (1992). Introduction: Colonialism and culture. In N.B. Dirks (Ed.), *Colonialism and culture* (pp. 1–26). Ann Arbor, MI: University of Michigan Press.

Driver, F. (2001). *Geography militant: Cultures of exploration and empire.* Oxford: Blackwell Publishing.
Finnbogason, G. (1925). Eðlisfar Íslendinga [The nature of Icelanders]. *Skírnir, 99,* 150–160.
Fine, M., Weis, L., Pruitt, L.P., & Burns, A. (2004). Preface. In M. Fine, L. Weis, L.P. Pruitt & A. Burns (Eds.), *Off white: Readings on power, privilege and resistance* (pp. vii–x). New York, NY: Routledge.
Frankenberg, R. (1993). *White women, race matters: The social construction of whiteness.* Minneapolis, MN: University of Minnesota Press.
Freiesleben, B. (1998). *Fra St. Croix til Tivoli: En historisk beretning om to vestindisk børns lange rejse* [From St. Croix to Tivoli: Historical account of the long travel by two West-Indian children]. Ballerup: Acer.
Gilroy, P. (1993). *The black Atlantic: Modernity and double consciousness.* London and New York, NY: Verso.
Gröndal, B. (1882). *Landafræði löguð eptir landafræði Erslevs og samin eptir ýmsum öðrum bókum* [Geography adapted from Erslevs geography and by other books]. Akureyri: Björn Jónsson.
Gullestad, M. (2002). Invisible fences: Egalitarianism, nationalism and racism. *Journal of the Royal Anthropological Institute, 8*(1), 45–63.
Hálfdánarson, G. (2000). Iceland: A peaceful secession. *Scandinavian Journal of History, 25,* 87–100.
Harrison, F.V. (2002). Unraveling 'race' for the twenty-first century. In J. MacClancy (Ed.), *Exotic no more: Anthropology on the front lines* (pp. 145–166). Chicago, IL and London: University of Chicago Press.
Hartigan, J., Jr. (1997). Establishing the fact of whiteness. *American Anthropologist, 99,* 495–505.
Huntington, S.P. (1993). The clash of civilizations. *Foreign Affairs, 72*(3), 20–31.
Ingimundarson, V. (2004). Immunizing against the American other: Racism, nationalism, and gender in U.S.-Icelandic military relations during the Cold War. *Journal of Cold War Studies, 6*(4), 65–88.
Isaac, B. (2004). *The invention of racism in classical antiquity.* New Jersey, NJ: Princeton University Press.
Ísleifsson, S.R. (1996). *Ísland: Framandi land* [Iceland: A strange country]. Reykjavík: Mál og menning.
Jensen, L. (2005). De danske tropekolonier og den nationale forankring [Danish Colonies and Nationalism]. In L.B. Christiansen, L. Jensen, P.K. Johansen, S. Kok & K.H. Petersen (Eds.), *På sporet af imperiet: Danske tropefantasier* [Tracking down the imperior: Danish fantasies] (pp. 65–77). Roskilde: Institute for Sprog og Kultur.
Keskinen, S., Irni, S., Mulinari, D., & Tuori, S. (Eds.) (2009). *Complying with colonialism.* Burlington: Ashgate.
Karlsdóttir, U.B.(1998). *Mannkynsbætur: Hugmyndir um bætta kynstofna hérlendis og erlendis á 19. og 20. Öld* [Eugenics: Ideas of eugenics in Iceland and elsewhere in nineteenth and twentieth century]. Sagnfræðistofnun: Háskólaútgáfan.
Loftsdóttir, K. (2003). Never forgetting? Gender and racial-ethnic identity during fieldwork. *Social Anthropology, 10,* 303–317.
Loftsdóttir, K. (2004). Tómið og myrkrið: Afríka í Skírni á 19. öld. *Skírnir, 178,* 119–151.
Loftsdóttir, K. (2006). Þriðji sonur Nóa: Íslenskar ímyndir Afríku á miðöldum [Noah's third son: Medival images of Africa in Iceland]. *Saga: tímarit sögufélags, XLIV,* 123–151.
Loftsdóttir, K. (2007). Learning differences? Nationalism, identity and Africa in Icelandic school textbooks. *International Textbook Research. The Journal of the George-Eckert Institute, 29,* 5–22.
Loftsdóttir, K. (2008). Shades of otherness: Representations of Africa in nineteenth-century Iceland. *Social Anthropology, 16,* 172–186.
Loftsdóttir, K. (2009). Pure manliness: The colonial project and Africa's image in nineteenth century Iceland. *Identities: Global studies in culture and power, 16,* 271–293.
Loftsdóttir, K. (2010). Encountering others in Icelandic schoolbooks: Images of imperialism and racial diversity in the nineteenth century. In Þ. Helgason& S. Lässig (Eds.), *Opening the*

mind or drawing boundaries? History texts in Nordic schools (pp. 81–105). Göttingen: Vandenhoeck & Ruprecht UniPress.
Mascia-Lees, F.E., & Sharpe, P. (2000). *Taking a stand in a postfeminist world: Toward engaged cultural criticism*. New York, NY: State University of New York Press.
Mazurana, D. (2005). Gender and the causes and consequences of armed conflict. In D. Mazurana, A. Raven-Roberts & J. Parpart (Eds.), *Gender conflict, and peacekeeping* (pp. 29–43). Lanham, MD: Rowman & Littlefield Publisher.
Miescher, S.F., & Lindsay, L.A. (2003). Introduction: Men and masculinities in modern African history. In L.A. Lindsay & S.F. Miescher (Eds.), *Men and masculinities in modern Africa* (pp. 1–29). Portsmouth, NH: Heineman.
Mohanram, R. (2007). *Imperial white: Race, diaspora, and the British empire*. Minneapolis, MN: University of Minnesota Press.
Moore, H.L. (1988). *Feminism and anthropology*. Minneapolis, MN: University of Minnesota Press.
Moore, H.L. (1994). *A passion for difference: Essays in anthropology and gender*. Bloomington, IN: Indiana University Press.
Pálsson, H. (1978). *Straumur og Stefnur í Íslenskum Bókmenntum frá 1550* [Icelandic literature since 1550]. Reykjavík: Iðunn.
Ponzanesi, S. (2007). Feminist theory and multiculturalism. *Feminist Theory, 9*(1), 91–103.
Pratt, M.L. (1990). Women, literature and national brotherhood. In E. Bergmann, J. Greenberg, G. Kirkpatrick, F. Masiello, F. Miller, M. Morello-Frosch, K. Newman & M.L. Pratt (Eds.), *Women, culture, and politics in Latin America: Seminar on feminism and culture in Latin America* (pp. 48–73). Berkeley, CA: University of California Press.
Pratt, M.L. (1992). *Imperial eyes: Travel writing and transculturation*. London and New York, NY: Routledge.
Puwar, N. (2004). Thinking about making a difference. *The British Journal of Politics and International Relations, 6*, 65–80.
Rigby, P. (1996). *African images: Racism and the end of anthropology*. Oxford and Washington, DC: Berg.
Sigurðsson, I. (1986). *Íslensk Sagnafræði frá miðri 19. öld til miðrar 20. aldar* [Icelandic studies of history from mid nineteenth century until mid twentieth century]. Reykjavík: Sagnfræðistofnun Háskóla Íslands.
Sigurðsson, G. (1996). Icelandic national identity: From romanticism to tourism. In P.J. Anttonen (Ed.), *Making Europe in Nordic contexts* (pp. 41–75). Turku: Nordic Institute of Folklore, University of Turku.
Skaptadóttir, U.D. & Loftsdóttir, K. (2009). Cultivating culture? Images of Iceland, globalization and multicultural society. In S. Jakobsson (Ed.), *Images of the North* (pp. 201–212). Reykjavík: Reykjavíkur Akademía.
Skaptadóttir, U.D., & Wojtynska, A. (2008). Labour migrants negotiating places and engagements. In J.O. Bærenholdt & B. Granås (Eds.), *Mobility and place. Enacting Northern European periphery*. Aldershot: Ashgate.
Skírnir. (1827). Chopenhagen/Reykavík: Íslenska bókmenntafélagið.
Skírnir. (1852). Chopenhagen/Reykavík: Íslenska bókmenntafélagið.
Skírnir. (1853). Chopenhagen/Reykavík: Íslenska bókmenntafélagið.
Skírnir. (1874). Chopenhagen/Reykavík: Íslenska bókmenntafélagið.
Skírnir. (1888). Chopenhagen/Reykavík: Íslenska bókmenntafélagið.
Skírnir. (1889). Chopenhagen/Reykavík: Íslenska bókmenntafélagið.
Skírnir. (1890). Chopenhagen/Reykavík: Íslenska bókmenntafélagið.
Skírnir. (1900). Chopenhagen/Reykavík: Íslenska bókmenntafélagið.
Statistics Iceland. (2007). Population 1996–2006 with a focus on foreign nationals. *Hagtíðindi/ Statistical Series, 2*(18, April), 1–22.
Statistics Iceland. (2008a). Lykiltölur mannfjöldans 1703–2008 [Population Statistics 1703–2008]. Retrieved November 23, 2008, from http://hagstofa.is/Hagtolur/Mannfjoldi/Yfirlit
Statistics Iceland. (2008b). Hlutfall erlendra ríkisborgara af mannfjölda 1950–2008 [Foreigners as percentage of the Icelandic Population 1950–2008]. Retrieved November 23, 2008, from http://hagstofa.is/Hagtolur/Mannfjoldi/ Rikisfang-Faedingarland

Statistics Iceland. (2008c). Mannfjöldi eftir trúfélögum 1990–2007 [Population according to religion 1990–2007]. Retrieved November 23, 2008, from http://hagstofa.is/Hagtolur/Mannfjoldi/Trufelog

Stoler, A.L. (1992). Rethinking colonial categories: European communities and the boundaries of rule. In N.B. Dirks & A. Arbor (Eds.), *Colonialism and culture* (pp. 319–352). Michigan, MI: University of Michigan Press.

Stoler, A.L. (1995). *Race and the education of desire: Foucault's history of sexuality and the colonial order of things.* Durham, NC and London: Duke University Press.

Sæmundsson, B. (1937). *Landafræði handa gagnfræðaskólum* [Geography for high schools]. Reykjavík: Bókaverzlun Sigfúsar Eymundssonar.

Wright, L. (2005). Introduction to 'queer' masculinities. *Men and masculinities, 7,* 243–247.

Þorsteinsson, Þ.J. (1940). *Saga Íslendinga í Vesturheimi* [The history of Icelanders in the New World] (Volume 1). Reykjavík: Þjóðræknisfélag Íslendinga í Vesturheimi.

Blogs cited

'Ásthildur' (2007, October 31). Mér liggur þetta mál í léttu rúmi...[Comment on the blog entry 'Ævintýri og æsingur' posted 30 October 2007]. Retrieved November 11, 2007, from http://asthildurcesil.blog.is/blog/asthildurcesil/entry/351787/

'Benedikt' (2007, October 28). í bloggheimum er hægt... [Comment on the blog entry 'Tíu stórir rasistar' posted 28 October, 2007]. Retrieved November 11, 2007, from http://baldurkr.blog.is/blog/baldurkr/entry/349627/

'Halla' (2008, April 22). Kóraninn þolir ekki dagsljósið [Blog entry]. Retrieved May 15, 2008, from http://hallarut.blog.is/blog/hallarut/entry/515429/

'Ragnhildur' (2007, October 23). Sorry, mér finnst þetta eiginlega bara fyndið...[Comment on the blog entry 'Tíu litlir negrastrákar' posted 23 October 2007]. Retrieved November 13, 2007, from http://fridaeyland.blog.is/blog/fridaeyland/entry/345575/

Asylum seekers as Austria's other: the re-emergence of Austria's colonial past in a state-of-exception

Brigitte Hipfl[a] and Daniela Gronold[b]

[a]Department of Media and Communication Studies, University of Klagenfurt, Klagenfurt, Austria; [b]Center for Peace Studies and Peace Education, University of Klagenfurt, Klagenfurt, Austria

> Analyzing a racist statement of former Carinthian governor Jörg Haider this paper argues that this is a form of racism that only can be understood when it is contextualized in a historical examination of the ways in which Austria – and Carinthia in particular – has been dealing with the other and with difference. Following Paul Gilroy's claim that an engagement with racism involves moving simultaneously onto historical and political grounds the authors juxtapose Austria's imperial history with its more recent policies regarding immigration and asylum seekers. This enables the authors to demonstrate how the positions that had been given to the colonized re-emerge in contemporary discourses on asylum seekers in Austria and are articulated with a re-definition of refugees as guests to legitimize the 'state of exception' the governor defines. With the critical examination of the re-emergence of colonial thought in the narratives and political practices in one of Europe's 'worksites' (Balibar, 2004, p. x), this paper makes an intervention towards dismantling the permanence of the colonial heritage.

On 19 August 2006, a fight between a group of young Chechen men and a group of local male adolescents in Klagenfurt, the capital of Austria's most southern province, Carinthia, was reported in two regional newspapers. Initially, the fight was presented as another example of violence taking place in a district of the city that already has a history of violent events between local groups, raising again questions of violent youth and security that have become of relevance in recent years. The fact that Chechen adolescents were involved in this particular brawl is reported as a rather marginal point. However, in the days following, the incident was re-framed into an attack by aggressive Chechen asylum seekers, positioning them as the ones who started the fight with 'local children'. The Chechens are presented as being more aggressive and using a different means of attack, arming themselves with sticks. One explanation given is related to the fact that asylum seekers come from countries that undergo severe unrest. Similar to a virus, the construction goes, asylum seekers bring along tensions and conflicts from their home country and infect their new environment. Another explanation stresses cultural differences that result in different forms of dealing with conflict. The fact that the Chechen youth involved in the fight asked their family members for help is represented as the Chechen 'mob' that assaults local children. This is then constructed as a culturally unacceptable way of dealing with conflict, and as a social practice that is related to vendetta, itself being considered a pre-modern way to reinstall family honor, signaling backwardness.[1]

Jörg Haider, the province's governor at that time, reacted to the emerging image of threatening Chechens with the promise to make Carinthia 'Chechen-free' soon. Five days after the incident, the governor addressed the Carinthian people directly through a full-page advertisement in the two local newspapers *Kleine Zeitung* (23 August 2006, p. 17) and *Neue Kärntner Tageszeitung* (24 August 2006, p. 14). His statement is presented as a personal letter to each Carinthian, including his signature, a picture and the logo of the province's government. The bold type was used in the original text (translation B. Hipfl and D. Gronold)[2]:

Violent asylum seekers cannot stay with us!

Dear Carinthians!

Recently **violent asylum seekers** from Chechnya have caused outrage and anxiety in the Carinthian population of the Fischl district of Klagenfurt. As governor **I reacted** immediately and authorized the **deportation of the Chechen aggressors**.

One thing has to be clear: we have no room for violent asylum seekers who attack domestic families with children. Those who come to us as guests also have to behave as guests. Those who do not act accordingly and who endanger the social peace in Carinthia and abuse our help have forfeited the right to our hospitality and will be expelled.

As governor of Carinthia, I have to **protect and secure social peace in the province**. Hence I will make sure also in the future that only those refugees who adhere to **law and order** and are willing to **adjust to our culture and way of life** will be allowed to stay in Carinthia.

Furthermore, in order to guarantee the security of the population, **no more Chechens** will be accommodated **in Carinthia**. All violent and delinquent asylum seekers will be investigated and expelled. **Carinthia is one of the safest provinces of Austria and will remain so!** That is my promise!

Best regards and yours,
Jörg Haider

Shocked by the severe political reaction to what seems to be a rather insignificant incident and by the public discussions in which the governor's letter was criticized but also strongly supported, we became interested in exploring the specific conditions that make it possible for a political statement like this to be made and accepted by a part of Carinthia's population. In this paper we will argue that this is a form of racism that only can be understood when it is contextualized in a historical examination of the ways in which Austria – and Carinthia in particular – has been dealing with the other and with difference. Following Paul Gilroy's (2004, p. 33) claim 'that to engage racism seriously involves moving simultaneously onto historical and political ground', we will juxtapose Austria's imperial history with its more recent policies regarding immigration and asylum seekers. This enables us to demonstrate how the positions that had been given to the colonized re-emerge in contemporary discourses on asylum seekers in Austria and are articulated with a re-definition of refugees as guests to legitimize the 'state of exception' the governor defines. The intervention that this paper intends to make is twofold. Firstly, it wants to draw attention to what Balibar (2004, pp. 5–6) calls 'local projections' of the forms of confrontation characteristic for all of Europe, which instead of just local pathologies should rather be understood as images and effects of Europe's own history. Secondly, this paper wants to contribute to an understanding of the ways in which Europe's colonial heritage is still shaping contemporary Europe.

Traces of Austria's imperial past

We will make the claim that the homogenizing and exclusionary statements in Haider's letter bear traces of Austria's colonial past. This might sound irritating at first since the Austro-Hungarian Empire that came to an end with World War One was characterized by its diversity of people with different ethnic backgrounds and languages – the so called 'Vielvölkerstaat' (Feichtinger, 2003, pp. 16, 18). So, one would expect that this legacy would continue in contemporary Austria where a new kind of diversity is emerging through new groups of immigrants. And, one would assume, Austria could dwell on its past experiences of dealing with diversity according to the official principle of the Austro-Hungarian Empire 'unity in diversity' (Feichtinger, 2003, p. 21). However, a closer look at the ways in which the imperial past has become part of Austrian collective memory and how this past has been appropriated shows that this is a nostalgic, transfigured view of the Empire. What is not taken into account is the hegemonic dominance of the Austrian part of the Empire and the ways in which it worked towards homogenizing and colonializing the other. We will make the argument that it is exactly this imperial past of Austria that has not been worked through and has not become part of public consciousness that prevents Austria from defining itself as a multicultural state in the present. It is the new immigrants and asylum seekers who are – unconsciously and subtly – confronting Austria with its past. They are not only challenging the comfortable, convenient view of the Habsburgian exemplary case of 'multiculturalism', they also bring back the loss of the once glorious past of the Austro-Hungarian Empire in which the Austrian part was the privileged one that held the power to govern the other.

The Austro-Hungarian Empire, the so-called 'K&K' monarchy[3] still plays a key role in Austria's collective memory. The continuous reproductions of nostalgic images of the Empire are the foundation of contemporary Austrian identity. The 'Habsburgian myth', first named by Italian literary critics Claudio Magris (1966) to characterize the transfigured and bemoaning way the Empire was referred to in the literary writings of Austrian authors from the second half of the nineteenth to the first half of the twentieth century, is still present in everyday life in Austria. For example, in Vienna, the former center of the Empire, now Austria's capital with a population of about 1.6 million, the imperial past is being sold as a tourist attraction. Schönbrunn Palace, the traces of Empress Sissy, the Spanish Horse Riding School, to name just a few, are examples of the historical elements that are being appropriated to let contemporary Austria still shine in its imperial resplendence. No references are ever made to the other side of the Empire, its colonial practices, such as the enslavement of people, expropriation of land and economic exploitation (Suppanz, 2003, pp. 304–305).

Austrians themselves in general also have positive connotations of the past monarchy, as it is shown in the study by Ruth Wodak and her research team on the discursive construction of Austrian national identity (Wodak et al., 1998). Following the dominant public discourse that presents the Habsburg monarchy as the ideal formation which allows for the cohabitation of different cultures, ethnicities, and religious traditions, the concept of multiculturalism is only positively referred to in the context of the Habsburg Empire, not in the contemporary context, in the same study. However, the other side of the Habsburg monarchy, its imperial power relations that acted out the official policy of 'unity in diversity' in such a way that the German-speaking parts dominated, is not part of the public discourse of Austrian history and Austrian identity. Politically, the Habsburgian past was instrumentalized in the 1980s and the early 1990s by the conservative party with its spokesperson Erhard Busek, who pushed the idea of 'Central Europe' as a cultural space defined by its common cultural and political history (see also Reisenleitner, 2002; Ruthner, 1999). When Austria became a member of the European Union in 1995, the idea of a separate spatial unit within Europe lost its persuasive power.

Academically, the critical exploration of Austria's glorification of its past has been an important issue addressed by historians and scholars in German studies and political science. At the end of the 1990s and the beginning of the new millennium, the possibilities to further the analyses by using analytical tools from postcolonial theories started to be explored.[4] What all of them seem to share is an understanding that although Austria did not have any colonies, and therefore cannot be equated with colonial powers like Great Britain, Spain, France, Portugal or the Netherlands, it nevertheless should be approached as a hegemonic formation that in many respects is on a par with a colonial situation. By that, the discourse of the monarchy's practiced multiculturalism gets deconstructed, although some praise its utopian potential (see, for example, Gauß, 1998). It is especially the processes of homogenization that were pushed by the monarchy that are comparable to the dominance of the colonizers in their relationship with the colonized. Often, the term 'inner colonization' has been used to characterize the processes of domination inherent in the Austro-Hungarian monarchy. These processes were fueled by the mission to 'civilize' the non-German speaking parts of the Empire (with the exemption of Hungary). This is clearly expressed by Moritz von Engel, an expert for external trade, who in 1902 commented on the fact that the Austro-Hungarian monarchy was not part of the ongoing competition of European powers to colonize the world by calling this a 'very good fortune' since it would allow the monarchy to concentrate on its foremost task, which was to colonize South-Eastern Europe (von Engel, cited in Prutsch, 2003, p. 36).

As a matter of fact, Austro-Hungary clearly acted as a colonizing power with the occupation of parts of Bosnia-Herzegovina in 1878. Previously Bosnia had been ruled by the Ottoman Empire that controlled large parts of the Middle East and southeast Europe from the sixteenth to the nineteenth century. One of the legacies of the Ottomans is the name 'Balkan' that they used for the southeast European peninsula (see Todorova, 1997, p. 27). As Todorova so poignantly demonstrates in her book *Imagining the Balkans* (1997), the term 'Balkan' has received increasingly negative connotations from its early use in travel writings in the nineteenth century – where the

Slavs living in these areas were described as oppressed and backwards, but also were exoticized – to the pejorative use of the term that emerged after World War One, and made it to a '*Schimpfwort*' (swear-word in English, originally used in German by Todorova). Because of its geographical location as a contact zone between western European imperial powers and the Ottomans, who were associated with the East and the Orient, 'the Balkans have been compared to a bridge between East and West' (Todorova, 1997, p. 16). However, the Ottoman reign in the Balkans was structured in such a way that it did not allow for a local nobility in the Balkan societies because the Ottomans pushed small peasant holdings (Todorova, 1997, p. 172). In some examples of travel literature, the people are described as living in similar to medieval standards; in comparison with modern western Europe they were depicted as backwards and underdeveloped (Todorova, 1997, pp. 18–19). Additionally, the Ottoman reign was perceived as an invasion of Islam in Europe, representing an alien element, which makes that part of Europe not quite Europe. It is in this context that the actions of the Habsburg Empire have to be understood as measures towards (re-)Christianization and stabilizing western culture.

As Prutsch (2003, p. 36) points out, the Habsburg Empire presented itself in opposition to the 'masculine' 'Prussian' imperialism as a 'soft' and 'motherly' power that was taking care of its 'children' through its cultural politics. Within the double monarchy, especially the Slavic groups – and here again those who were summarized under the label 'the Balkans' – were considered the less civilized parts of Austro-Hungary. As is exemplified by nineteenth-century literature, the population often was compared with children or even animals, and in general the people were presented through a high proximity to nature. It is in such practices that the colonial strategy of de-humanizing the subjects that are being colonized takes place and, at the same time, this strategy legitimizes the process of colonization. The mission of bringing civilization to these 'uncivilized' members of the Empire was supported by the idea that Austro-Hungary perceived itself as a 'nation of culture' (see Szabo-Knotik, 2006). This materialized itself through an administrative order where German was the customary language in all parts of the Empire despite the fact that the Austro-Hungarian constitution stated: 'All races of the empire have equal rights, and every race has an inviolable right to the preservation and use of its own nationality and language. The equality of all customary languages in school, office and public life is recognized by the state'.[5] This was fostered by a policy that all the administrative positions regarding civil society, the military, jurisdiction, schools, and universities were given to representatives of the governing power. This had wide-ranging effects on the status of local languages, especially for the Slavic languages that had never been granted the same status as German, as opposed to Italian which had been accepted as the language of a highly appreciated culture. The domination of German in the administration of everyday life, which also led to the re-naming of houses and streets, reduced the range, importance and dignity of the local languages. These colonizing practices resulted in a devaluation of the local cultures as inferior in comparison to the Austro-Hungarian, German-speaking culture that stood for Europe, the West, modernity and progress. These processes successively and strongly affected the identity of the people living in the peripheral areas of the Empire commonly named the Balkans (see Wagner, 2002).

This is the context in which the contemporary struggles of east and southeast European nations have to be placed. Todorova's observation 10 years ago that all

'Balkan nations are competing to be more "European" than the rest' (Todorova, 1997, p. 58) and that for all of them the Turks represent Easternness and Orientalness still holds today. For example, a positive image of German speaking rulers in the Habsburg empire is even used by former Yugoslavian republics who are trying to integrate the Habsburg heritage as part of their imagined cultural belonging in order to establish a link to 'European culture'. And it also works the other way around, in the sense that Austrian politics regarding the EU enlargement is still defined by its colonial past: Austria acts like the advocate of countries such as Slovenia and Croatia and offers them help on their road to 'European standards', yet at the same time, it strongly resists the admission of Turkey into the EU.

The special case of Carinthia

In Carinthia, because of its geopolitical location as the southern-most province bordering Slovenia and Italy, the differentiation drawn between Western Europe and 'the Balkans' has been experienced very closely through the ways the border towards Slovenia/former Yugoslavia has been administered both politically and mentally (see Hipfl, Bister, Strohmaier, & Busch 2002). In addition, Carinthia comprises an ethnic minority of Slovenes, which has become an issue of constant tension because of a politics that reiterates the cultural dominance of the German culture in the Austro-Hungarian Empire. The devaluation of the Slovenian culture reached its atrocious height during National Socialism when Slovene speaking inhabitants were either forced to avow themselves to the German speaking culture or they were expelled (Malle, Entner, Stuhlpfarrer, & Wilscher, 2002). After the end of World War Two the Slovenes who had been deported were able to come back to Carinthia, still suffering from their traumatic experiences.

In Austria's national treaty of 1955, the ethnic minority had been adjudicated the protection of their ethnic culture through bi-lingual topographical signs, amongst others (Austrian National Treaty 1955, Article 7). The fact that this has not been fully executed by Carinthia's governors and that official Carinthia does not embrace, let alone celebrate, its bi-cultural specificity, has been positioning the Slovenian minority as the unwanted other. Haider, especially, was officially reprimanded by the Austrian president, the federal chancellor and a group of experts of the European Commission for defying the legal rights of the Slovene minority.

Over and above the violation of constitutional law, Haider constantly re-activated historical tensions between German speaking and Slovene speaking inhabitants of Carinthia by accusing the Slovenes of putting in unjustified claims and ungratefully exploiting their special status, thus constructing them as a threat to Carinthian (meaning German speaking) culture. This particular way of Haider to exercise power is exemplary for practices that are typical for the 'state of exception' where the powers of government are extended in times of crisis (Agamben, 2005). Agamben conceives such a prolonged state of exception as 'a legal civil war that allows for the physical elimination not only of political adversaries but of entire categories of citizens who for some reason cannot be integrated into the political system' (Agamben, 2005, p. 2). As has been argued recently (see Agamben, 2005; Hardt & Negri, 2004), the 'state of exception' has become permanent under contemporary postmodern conditions, which are defined by the constant rhetorical appeal to fight for social order. The letter regarding Chechen asylum seekers is another example of Haider presenting himself as the all-powerful governor who is operating outside the law.

Tracing Chechens past and their current situation in Austria

In 2003, a fight between Chechens and Moldavians in Austria's central refugee camp prompted the Austrian minister for interior affairs to expel the Chechens from this camp, and divide them up among all Austrian provinces. His argument was that in this way Chechens would be prevented from creating consolidating communities (see http://www.inforos.com/?id=21685). Here we can see the persistence of the discourses that positioned Chechens in a particular way in Russia. As Ferguson (2000, pp. 9, 13) points out, the connotations regarding Chechens that dominate in the West are either reiterating the nineteenth century tropes used in travel writings, which presented them as less-civilized mountain people with a warrior tradition, or they follow the official Russian constructions of Chechens as 'bandit formations' and, more recently, as fundamentalist terrorists linked to Osama bin Laden. Without being explicitly articulated, the argument of the Austrian minister refers to both subject positions that have been historically given to Chechens by Russia. This opens up a space of fantasies of backward, uncivilized and violent people whose culture is incompatible with ours and whose presence is a threat to our communities. They are best kept at a distance and rigorously controlled.

What is left out of the discourse provoked by the Austrian minister are all those elements that, from the perspective of the Chechen refugees, are responsible for the particular situation they find themselves in. On the one hand is the fact that Chechens throughout their history have been fighting for their independence. Chechnya's geopolitical location in the North Caucasus region between the Black and the Caspian Seas has always attracted the interest of different political power formations. Throughout its history, Chechnya continuously had to face different conquering empires and their colonizing practices – from the Mongols to the Persian, Ottoman, and Russian empires, the Soviet Union and contemporary Russia. There is a certain pride that comes with Chechen cultural narratives that describe numerous occasions where the military forces of oppressive powers seemed to be overwhelming, but because of their community orientation, bravery and perseverance Chechens were able to change the situation to their advantage. Chechens also fought courageously in World War One on the side of Russia, but never received official recognition for that in the light of the damaging and devaluating discourses of being wild and uncivilized in the perception of the Russian public. On the other hand, the traumatic experiences Chechens had to undergo in their recent history because of Soviet and Russian actions are not referred to at all: the deportation of the entire Chechen population to Kazakhstan at the end of World War Two by Stalin; their treatment as second-class citizens by their Russian colonizers when they returned; the First Chechen War (1994–1996), after Chechnya became independent, started by Russia to prevent its losing control over Grozny, which in the meantime had become an important oil refining center and a key junction for oil pipelines and natural gas in the 1990s; the Second Chechen War (starting in 1999) when, after blaming Chechen terrorists for the bombings of Russian cities, Russia invaded Chechnya and faced strong resistance by Chechen rebel fighters; the official Russian rule of Chechnya accompanied by an increase of Russian atrocities and the radicalization of the Chechen rebel movement in 2000 (see Ferguson, 2000; Souleimanov, 2004; Kondakov, n.d.; Bisayev, 2007; Ebel, n.d.). As a result, of the 90,000 appeals to the European Court for Human Rights regarding human rights violations in 2007, 20,000 dealt with the Russian Federation (*Neue Zürcher Zeitung*, 26 February 2007, p. 2).

About 300,000 Chechens left the country as refugees during the First Chechen War[6] and a second wave of refugees was caused by the Second Chechen War. Most of the refugees now live in European Union countries. Chechnya is still a very insecure and unstable country, defined by corruption, poverty and the so-called 'Chechenization' of the conflict between Russia and Chechnya (see Sokirianskaia, 2007, p. 10), which started in 2002 when key political, administrative and military positions were given to those ethnic Chechens loyal to Russia. Now the conflict has turned into a fratricidal war where Chechen representatives of the Russian government and the guerilla warfare of Chechen separatists are fighting each other. To a large extent this fight, however, is fought on the body of the civil population when, for example, in the course of the so-called anti-terror-operations of secret Chechen government units, family members of separatists have been kidnapped, tortured and displaced or killed, creating an atmosphere of fear in Chechnya's population. Russian censorship of media coverage of the situation in Chechnya resulted in the murder of the critical Russian journalist Anna Politkowskaja in 2006.

This would strongly speak in favor of the obligation of countries like Austria to help victims of violence, persecution and fear according to the Geneva Refugee Convention. But the dimension of Chechens being the victims of the violent actions of the Russian government, which is the main reason why they fled from their country, is not part of Austrian public knowledge and is hardly mentioned in media reports and political statements concerning the situation of Chechen asylum seekers. Only some of the NGOs that are involved in human rights and refugee issues make an effort to inform the Austrian public of the extremely difficult situation Chechens face and to address the Austrian government to ease the procedures for asylum seekers. In this context, the fact that Haider in his public statement blatantly equates Chechen asylum seekers with violent aggressors can be seen as a particularly powerful act of re-producing the very discourse of the threatening unwanted other.

Austrian newspaper reports in general either focus on political events in Chechnya or on the difficulties and problems related to Chechen refugees and asylum seekers living in Austria. This is also the case for the way Carinthian newspapers have been reporting these issues. More thorough attempts to work out the connections between the two sides that would give the reader a better understanding of how unsafe life is in Chechnya, and what made Chechens take refuge, are rare (see Gronold, 2008, pp. 39–40). The voice that has constantly been presenting a nuanced and critical view in the Austrian media context is Susanne Scholl, the correspondent for the Austrian public broadcasting (ORF) in Moscow and author of a book on survival strategies in Chechnya (Scholl, 2007).

The discursive change from 'Gastarbeiter' to 'foreigner' and asylum seeker

In Austria, there are three historic-specific contexts in which larger groups of people, other than visitors and tourists, came into the country. These particular contexts are also related to specific ways of positioning the newcomers legally and culturally. The first has to do with Austria's geographical location, notably with the fact that it bordered countries that were communist from the end of World War Two up to the 1990s, or were involved in the Balkan war and the conflicts in former Yugoslavia. Refugees from Hungary (1956/1957), Czechoslovakia (1968), Poland (1981/1982) and from Croatia, Bosnia and Kosovo (in the 1990s) were all seeking protection in Austria (see UNHCR Austria, http://www.unhcr.at). Austria followed a liberal asylum politics at that time (see Nationaler Kontaktpunkt Österreich im Europäischen Migrationsnetzwerk, 2004, p. 13) and both the Austrian government and the Austrian population were very supportive of these refugees. This certainly has to do with the fact that most of the countries (or at least parts of them) formerly belonged to the Austro-Hungarian Empire. But it is also due to the public discourse that regarded communist regimes as oppressive and restrictive and the Austrians were keen to support their disadvantaged neighbors.

The second context has to do with Austria's way of resolving the shortages in the labor force in the 1960s. In a similar way to Germany, Austria was recruiting workers from Spain, Turkey and former Yugoslavia, so-called 'Gastarbeiter', who, according to the idea that workers should rotate, were supposed to work for a few years in Austria and then to return to their countries of origin. The use of the term 'Gastarbeiter' and not migrants had far reaching consequences for the new workers. They were seen as guests who were expected to adjust to the rules of their hosts and leave after a while. Austrian legislation did not offer the 'Gastarbeiter' any legal position other than being foreigners who are temporarily working in Austria. Hence foreigners in Austria were and still are defined as non-citizens (see Bratic, 2003). The principle of 'sans-sanguinis', according to which the citizenship of children conforms to the citizenship of their parents, also applies to the children of foreigners/'Gastarbeiter' who are born in Austria.

The public discourse put 'Gastarbeiter' in a position where they had to render themselves useful and were supposed to be unassuming and cheap workers. Additionally, the image of 'Gastarbeiter' was associated with being dirty, simple minded and subordinate, thus representing the opposite image to Austrian self-perception. These ascriptions made the character of the 'Gastarbeiter' appear less loyal to the Austrian state, thus demanding more control and regulation (see Bratic, 2003). Here we can find a racist pattern of differentiation that had been in place already under the Habsburgian rule. In the dual monarchy, it was the Slavic members at the south-eastern periphery that were labeled this way; now it was the foreign workers, many of them coming from this very region. In both cases they were positioned in a way that affirms the structural role they were given, namely to support the wealth of the Empire, or the nation, with cheap labor. With the international economic crisis in the 1970s, when many Austrians were afraid of losing their jobs in the course of the so-called 'oil-shock', the 'Gastarbeiter' who would not return to their 'home countries' came to be perceived as a burden and as competitors in a shrinking labor market. One of the effects was that the term 'Gastarbeiter' was replaced by the term 'foreigner' which no longer has any allusion to 'work' (see Bratic, 2003). Instead, it carries the semantics of strangers that do not belong to this place.

The third context, relating to another discursive change regarding people coming to Austria, started in the late 1990s with an increasing number of refugees applying for asylum in Austria. The number of asylum applications reached its height with about 30,000 in 2001 and 39,000 in 2002 (see UNHCR Austria, and Oezsan, 2002). This prompted the People's Party/Freedom Party government in 2003 to pass a new asylum law in 2003 which had the effect that the number of new asylum applications dropped to about 13,300 in 2006, 12,000 in 2007 and 13,000 in 2008 (www.bmi.gv.at/asylwesen/). The United Nations High Commissioner for Refugees heavily criticized the new law because of variances with the Geneva Refugee Convention.[7] Asylum seekers inhabit the lowest rank in the hierarchy of the law that defines the rights of non-Austrians. During the asylum procedure – which can take up to two years – asylum seekers are not allowed to work. They have to follow strict rules to be granted federal care, which comprises a small monthly allowance and accommodation either in federal run camps or in isolated private boarding houses. Each provincial government is obliged to take responsibility for a certain number of asylum seekers, a regulation that was not conformed with by former Carinthian governor Haider. He referred to the discourse of the 'criminal asylum seekers' who are a threat to the locals – as, for example, in his letter regarding Chechens – to legitimize his non-compliance and to seek consent from the Carinthian population.

Actions like these, but also statements from other members of the political right and the conservatives in Austria, have been strengthening a discourse where asylum seekers are seen as the bad foreigners that are threatening Austrian society. The slogans of the 2008 campaigns of the political parties represented in Austria's parliament make this very clear.[8] The political right that as a result of Haider's splitting from the FPÖ and launching an 'alliance for Austria's future' in 2005 is represented by two parties (FPÖ and BZÖ), explicitly tried to interpellate the voters through nationalist and xenophobic messages. 'Austria for Austrians' ('Österreich den Österreichern') and 'because of you. Austria' ('deinetwegen. Österreich') were the slogans of the BZÖ, whereas the FPÖ trumpeted similarly 'First of all Austria' ('Österreich zuerst'), 'Now, we, the Austrians, are at stake' ('Jetzt geht's um uns Österreicher') and 'Our country for our children' ('Unser Land für unsere Kinder'). The conservatives, represented by the Austrian People's Party, promised to secure the 'safe homeland' ('sichere Heimat') through forceful legislation of asylum rights, privileging integration before immigration and securing the borders as a means to warrant a reduced criminality rate. The front-runner of the Green Party curtly stated that he would not take part in agitating whereas the Socialist Party did not explicitly refer to these issues in their election posters. The exclusionary, nationalistic approach and a politics of law and order, on the one hand, and silence on the other are represented as answers to the – albeit not directly addressed – threat that unwanted newcomers represent to Austria and Austrianness. Public discourse has been dominated by measures of defense, control and exclusion that are discussed as the ways to manage the 'problem' of incoming immigrants and asylum seekers. The opposite position has been marginalized, a position mainly taken by non-governmental organizations and grassroots activities like Caritas, Aspis, Integrationshaus, Bündnis für eine Welt, Eine Welt, Kulturinitiative kärnöl, or the Aktionskommitte für Toleranz und Menschlichkeit in Kärnten fostering a multi-cultural view of Austrian society and embracing immigrants, while also arguing that it is the very newcomers that will ensure Austria's economic future.

The differentiation between good and bad foreigners or asylum seekers is undertaken on cultural grounds by referring to their 'cultural origin', which then is compared with Austrian culture. The larger the cultural difference, the more dangerous and threatening the members of the 'other culture' become. In accordance with the idea that cultural differences have to be accounted for – an idea, that informs the new kind of racism that Balibar and Wallerstein (1991) called 'cultural racism' – a regulation of these differences is called for. The Austrian government supports this approach by prioritizing the discourse of security, which allows for the rigid regimentation, surveillance and control of those who inhabit the lowest rank in the hierarchy of cultures (see Bratic, 2003). In the case of Haider's letter, it is the Chechen asylum seekers' 'violent, aggressive, criminal behavior' that marks their cultural difference.

The re-emergence of the colonial other and the re-activation of the 'guest' – enabling the 'state of exception'

The 'structure of feeling' (Williams, 1978) that is part of Austria's dominant discourse regarding asylum seekers is based on the re-emergence of the colonial other and the connotations of the threatening foreigner. All the connotations of the colonial other re-emerge with the presence of 'Gastarbeiter' or asylum seekers. However, there is a difference in the way Chechen asylum seekers are being perceived compared with asylum seekers and 'Gastarbeiter' from the Balkans. In the case of people from the Balkans, there still is a tacit imperial understanding in place according to which Austrians perceive themselves as superior and – in a patronizing sense – feel responsible for supporting them (see Hipfl, Hipfl, & Jagodzinski, 1996). This is a comfortable position from the Austrian point of view since it reiterates the imperial and powerful past that still is part of Austrian identity. Chechen asylum seekers, on the contrary, do not fit into the same pattern. They represent the people who are not willing to take on the position given to them by colonizing powers. They resist and fight against it. In this way they embody the very challenge of dominant powers and, at the same time, they confront Austria with the loss of its imperial power – something that still has not been worked through in the contemporary Austrian psyche and can be seen as a threat to Austrian identity.

This is the Austrian context that helps explain why the actions of Carinthia's governor that we described at the beginning of the paper were broadly acclaimed. Additionally, Haider's reference to asylum seekers as 'guests' re-activates another field of connotations that is now connected with asylum seekers. Guests do not have any rights, they are expected to adjust to the customs of their hosts and to leave sooner or later. By stressing the 'inappropriate' behavior of asylum seekers as exemplary for the way guests are not supposed to act, Haider totally rejects the Geneva Refugee Convention that does not impose a certain behavior on refugees as a precondition for asylum, but stresses the protection responsibilities towards refugees. Stepping over the Geneva Refugee Convention with its commitment towards human rights and the protection of refugees, and instead re-defining asylum seekers as 'guests' is Haider's way of legitimizing the 'state of exception' that also strengthens his position to demonstrate power and control.

What is striking in both Haider's and the common-sense discursive constructions of the aggressive, threatening asylum seeker is the fact that it is exclusively based upon notions of deviant masculinity. In contrast, female asylum seekers are publicly discussed as exemplary for well-integrated refugees or – in the case of Chechens – as mothers seeking protection for their families (Gronold, 2008, pp. 37–38). The strict gender differentiation that characterizes current discourses on asylum seekers reproduces the stereotypical way in which men and women are imagined differently in their function in society (Yuval-Davies, 1997, p. 9): men are linked with warfare, women with the reproduction of a social community.

We hope that the critical examination of the re-emergence of colonial thought in the narratives and political practices in one of Europe's 'worksites' (Balibar, 2004, p. x) is a first step towards dismantling the permanence of the colonial heritage. Additionally, we hope that this contributes to the manifestation of Balibar's idea of Europe as a 'democratic laboratory' where the diagrams of possible worlds can be redrawn (Venn, 2006, p. 3).

Notes

1. Study conducted in the two regional newspapers *Kleine Zeitung* & *Neue Kärntner Tageszeitung*, August 2006, by Daniela Gronold.
2. The authors regret that permission to print the original letter was refused.
3. The terms are used synonymously.
4. The discussions are documented for example in the website 'kakanien revisited', www.kakanien.ac.at and in the online journal 'spaces of identity', www.spacesofidentity. net/, and in the book *Habsburg postcolonial* (Feichtinger, Prutsch, & Csáky, 2003).
5. See http://historicaltextarchive.com/books.php?op = viewbook&bookid = 2&cid = 11
6. See http://www.pbs.org/wnet/wideangle/uncategorized/media-by-milosevic-timeline-explore-chechnyas-turbulent-past/1110/
7. One major concern refers to the fact that asylum seekers are made to tell the history of their flight at one go without being allowed to add new details later. People who have undergone violence, torture and traumatizing experiences are often unable to talk about what had happened to them in such a way that this is being considered reasonable for granting them asylum. In addition, the new law enables the deportation of some groups of asylum seekers, even though their asylum procedures have not yet been completed.
8. See http://www.wien-konkret.at/politik/nationalratswahl2008/wahlwerbung/

References

Agamben, G. (2005). *State of exception*. Chicago, IL: University of Chicago Press.
Balibar, E. (2004). *We, the people of Europe? Reflections on transnational citizenship*. Princeton, NJ: Princeton University Press.
Balibar, E., & Wallerstein, I. (1991). *Race, nation, class: Ambiguous identities*. London: Verso.
Bisayev, K. (2007). A game of Russian roulette? Chechen refugees and the Dublin regulation. *European Parliament*, 21 March. Retrieved September 6, 2008, from http://www.ecre.org/projects/eastern_europe/russian_documents/814
Bratic, L. (2003). Diskurs und Ideologie des Rassismus im österreichischen Staat [Discourse and ideology of racism in the Austrian nation state]. *Kurswechsel*, 2. Retrieved August 18, 2008, from http://no racism.net/antirassismus/texte/diskurs_ideologie.htm
Ebel, R.E. (n.d.). *The history and politics of Chechen oil*. Retrieved August 25, 2008, from http://amina.com/article/oil_op.html
Feichtinger, J. (2003). Habsburg (post-)colonial: Anmerkungen zur Inneren Kolonialisierung in Zentraleuropa [Habsburg (post-)colonial. Notes on the inner colonization in Central Europe]. In J. Feichtinger, U. Prutsch & M. Csáky (Eds.), *Habsburg postcolonial: Machtstrukturen und kollektives Gedächtnis* [Habsburg postcolonial. Structures of power and collective memory] (pp. 13–32). Wien/Innsbruck/Linz: Studienverlag.
Feichtinger, J., Prutsch, U., & Csáky, M. (Eds.) (2003). *Habsburg postcolonial: Machtstrukturen und kollektives Gedächtnis* [Habsburg postcolonial: Structures of power and collective memory]. Wien/Innsbruck/Linz: Studienverlag.

Ferguson, R. (2000). Chechnya: The empire strikes back. *International Socialism Journal*, *86*. Retrieved September 12, 2008, from http://www.isj1text.ble.org.uk/pubs/isj86/ferguson.htm

Gauß, K.-M. (1998). *Ins unentdeckte Österreich: Nachrufe und Attacken* [Exploring undiscovered Austria. Obituaries and attacks]. Wien: Zsolnay.

Gilroy, P. (2004). *After empire: Melancholia or convivial culture?*. Abingdon: Routledge.

Gronold, D. (2008). Wer denkt an die Opfer?' Repräsentationen tschetschenischer EinwanderInnen in den österreichischen Medien ['Who remembers the victims?' Representations of Chechen immigrants in Austrian media]. *MedienJournal*, *32*(3), 31–40.

Hardt, M., & Negri, A. (2004). *Multitude: War and democracy in the age of empire*. New York, NY: Penguin Press.

Hipfl, B., Bister, A., Strohmaier, P., & Busch, B. (2002). Shifting borders: Spatial constructions of identity in an Austrian/Slovenian border region. In U.H. Meinhof (Ed.), *Living (with) borders* (pp. 53–74). Ashgate: Aldershot/Burlington.

Hipfl, B., Hipfl, K., & Jagodzinski, J. (1996). Documentary films and the Bosnia-Hercegovina conflict: From production to reception. In J. Gow, R. Paterson & A. Preston (Eds.), *Bosnia by TV. British Film Institute* (pp. 34–54). London: British Film Institute.

Kondakov, T. (n.d.). Transport and energy communications in Caucasus and Black Sea. Retrieved August 20, 2008, from http://www.globalpolitician.com/print.asp? id = 1317

Magris, C. (1966). *Der habsburgische Mythos in der österreichischen Literatur* [The Habsburgian myth in Austrian literature]. Salzburg: Müller.

Malle, A., Entner, B., Stuhlpfarrer, K., & Wilscher, H. (Eds.) (2002). *Die Vertreibung der Kärntner Slowenen/Pregon koroskih Slovencev* [The expulsion of Carinthian Slovenes]. Celovec: Drava.

Nationaler Kontaktpunkt Österreich im Europäischen Migrationsnetzwerk. (2004). *Der Einfluss von Immigration auf die österreichische Gesellschaft. Eine Bestandsaufnahme der jüngsten österreichischen Forschungsliteratur. Österreichischer Beitrag im Rahmen der europaweiten Pilotstudie 'The Impact of Immigration on Europe's Societies'* [The impact of immigration on Austria's society. A review of recent Austrian research. Austria's contribution for the European pilot-study 'The Impact of Immigration on Europe's Societies']. Wissenschaftliche Koordination: Wien.

Neue Zürcher Zeitung. (2007, February 26). p. 2

Oezsan, V. (2002). *Government directive on asylum sparks row in Austria*. Migration Policy Institute. Retrieved September 3, 2008, from www.migrationinformation.org/Feature/

Prutsch, U. (2003). Habsburg postcolonial. In J. Feichtinger U. Prutsch & M.Czaky (Eds.) *Habsburg postcolonial: Machtstrukturen und kollektives Gedächtnis* [Habsburg postcolonial. Structures of power and collective memory] (pp. 33–44). Wien/Innsbruck/Linz: Studienverlag.

Reisenleitner, M. (2002). Central European culture in search of a theory, or: The lure of 'Post/colonial Studies'. *Spaces of Identity*, *2*. Retrieved August 26, 2008, from http://www.spacesofidentity.net/

Ruthner, C. (1999). Habsburgischer Mythos versus K.(u.)K. (Post-)Kolonialismus. Neuere Publikationen zum österreichischen Heimat-Bild [Habsburgian myth versus k(u.)k (post-)colonialism. Recent publications on the Austrian self-image of home]. *Germanistische Mitteilungen*, *49*, 95–103.

Scholl, S. (2007). *Töchter des Krieges: Überleben in Tschetschenien* [Daughters of the war: Surviving in Chechnya]. Wien: Molden Verlag.

Sokirianskaia, E. (2007). *Human rights in Russia: The case of Chechnya. Resümee der Veranstaltung vom 2.3.2007* [Human rights in Russia: The case of Chechnya. A summary of a presentation on 2 March 2007]. Renner Institut Wien. Retrieved August 27, 2008, from http://www.rennerinstitut.at/download/down_eeuropa0409.htm

Souleimanov, E. (2004). *History of Russian-Chechen relations: Attempt at a polemic view*. Prague Watchdog. Retrieved January 4, 2004, from http://www.watchdog.cz/?show = 000000-000015

Suppanz, W. (2003). Die Bürde des 'österreichischen Menschen': Der (post-)koloniale Blick des autoritären 'Ständestaates' auf die zentraleuropäische Geschichte [The burden of the 'Austrian people': The (post-)colonial view of the corporate state regarding central European history]. In J. Feichtinger, U. Prutsch & M. Czaky (Eds.), *Habsburg postcolonial:*

Machtstrukturen und kollektives Gedächtnis [Habsburg postcolonial. Structures of power and collective memory] (pp. 303–314). Wien/Innsbruck/Linz: Studienverlag.

Szabo-Knotik, C. (2006). Sustaining studies of Central European cultural diversity. 'Liegst dem Erdteil Du inmitten, einem starken Herzen gleich': How central and/or European is Austria's cultural identity? *Spaces of Identity, 6*, 75–93. Retrieved August 28, 2008, from https://pi.library.yorku.ca/ojs/index.php/soi/article/view/7996/7141

Todorova, M. (1997). *Imagining the Balkans.* New York, NY/Oxford: Oxford University Press.

Venn, C. (2006). *The postcolonial challenge: Towards alternative worlds.* London/Thousand Oaks, CA/New Delhi: Sage.

Wagner, B. (2002). Postcolonial Studies für den europäischen Raum [Postcolonial studies for Europe]. In C. Lutter & L. Mussner (Eds.), *Kulturstudien in Österreich.* Wien: Löcker.

Williams, R. (1978). *Marxism and Literature.* Oxford: Oxford University Press.

Wodak, R., de Cillia, R., Reisigl, M., Liebhart, K., Hofstätter, K., & Kargl, M. (1998). *Zur diskursiven Konstruktion von nationaler Identität.* Frankfurt am Main: Suhrkamp Taschenbuch Verlag.

Yuval-Davis, N. (1997). *Gender & nation.* London: Sage.

Spelling out exclusion in Southern Italy

Claudia Buonaiuto and Marie-Hélène Laforest

American, Cultural, Linguistic Studies Department, University of Naples 'L'Orientale', Italy

This article offers a reading of the city of Naples in Southern Italy as a European borderland, a space where the North/South configuration wavers and mutates in the wake of immigration flows. Historically a place of contrasts, symbol of the Southern Question, Naples seems to be adding to its age-long ills a problematic racial question. The article reports and analyzes some interviews with migrant women living in the city and its surroundings. The life stories of Sri Lankan, Nigerian, and Ukrainian women provide a vivid picture of how they are building their lives in an inhospitable environment, in search of a place of their own. Their experiences testify to forms of social and cultural practices among the local population which are blatantly segregationist. It is an alarming portrayal of the forms of racism against and exclusion of women immigrants in Naples which weakens the prospect of the peaceful construction of a multicultural society in the southern Italian context.

My Sister, she said, you've come for a year, maybe two, but you'll stay longer. (Merle Collins)

A large number of studies have analyzed the impact of migration on Western metropolises, pointing out how the displacement of peoples from poorer to overdeveloped parts of the planet has made modern cities more cosmopolitan and thus more uniform (Chambers, 1994; Sassen, 2001, 2006; Young, 2003; Rigo, 2007). In this sense Naples, in Southern Italy, is beginning to look like the global cities of the rest of Europe as the presence of a wide range of ethnic groups has changed its humanscape. But the comparison ends there, for Naples has more often than not been compared to Third World cities with its share of poverty, degradation, and unruliness.

The aim of this article is to take a close look at the 'porous city', as Walter Benjamin called Naples in 1925, in its relation with the new inhabitants which have settled in the Campania Region (Benjamin, 2007, p. 6). The paper is based on accounts provided by women immigrants who, despite social hostility, ethnic and racial prejudices at a local level, and criminalization by the media at a national level, have had to find spaces of negotiation in this part of Italy.

If traditional migration patterns have seen Southern Italy principally as a port of entry into Europe, since the 1980s a very diverse group of immigrants has made the city of Naples and the larger metropolitan area their home.[1] With the highest population density in Europe, 2,600 inhabitants per square kilometers, and one of the lowest *per capita* incomes in the country, Naples has been the symbol of the Southern Italian question. Known for its scenic beauty, its music, and its happy-go-lucky inhabitants, in recent decades it has become the emblem of inefficient government and mismanagement of public funds. This became evident in the garbage crisis which reached dramatic proportions in the spring of 2007 and the municipal corruption cases which exploded in December 2008.

The city and its surroundings have been described as peripheral and pre-modern, but also resourceful and adaptable (Dickie, 1997; Moe, 2002; Macry, 2003). It is a liminal area of the country where work and play are not kept distinct, where singular interests multiply, and laws are seen as pliable. In this context the sale and purchase of stolen goods take place in open-air markets, a sign of the permeable borders between legal and illegal activities. What is more, Naples and its conurbation are also plagued by control of the '*camorra*' over large portions of its territory.[2] The *camorra* represents a parallel form of power which has its grip on both the natives and the immigrants: shop owners, street vendors, and sex workers in particular are subjected to its illegal law. It was recently discovered that a group of Roma from a disheveled encampment in Ponticelli, seven kilometers from Naples, paid the *camorra* a tribute which granted them the right to beg and rob in the area (Zagaria, 2008). The influence of organized crime coupled with the fear of civil unrest from the hordes of unemployed has led to a *laissez-faire* policy in the management of public life. This, in turn, has brought about a corresponding laxness on the parts of its citizens to such an extent that the exchange of favors seems to be the rule of the land.

It is precisely the porosity of its borders in addition to sporadic police control which has attracted a high number of *sans-papiers* to this large southern city. With the tightening of immigration laws (Bossi-Fini legislation in 2002), Naples seemed to have offered a haven to undocumented workers. According to 2008 official police records, the province counts 63,447 legal foreigners, the city, 30,074 but there might be almost as many undocumented workers as those with regular sojourn permits. In the inner city, while Sri Lankans constituted the largest group in the early days of migration, they have been supplanted by Ukrainians who are the most numerous today. Closer to the rural areas a large number of Africans have settled, especially in the Litorale Domitio north of Naples.[3]

Whereas the majority of immigrants in the city are employed in domestic service, those outside the urban centers are exploited as field hands. Immigrants also engage in trade as peddlers of fake brands on the city streets in winter, on the nearby beaches in summer. No area of the Campania Region, but especially the larger Naples metropolitan area, seems to have been untouched by the immigrants' arrival.[4] As is to be expected, the domestic schemes, which allowed immigrants into the country in the mid 1970s attracted mostly women. It is of some significance to note that although Italy has one of the lowest percentages of women in the workforce among European Union member states, in the 10-year period between 1993–2003, the number of women who entered the marketplace increased by 1.2 million (Mezzana, 2008). As Italian women went out to work, non-Italians found jobs substituting them in the home, in child rearing and in caring for the elderly. Today a number of them have moved into other lines of work, but women immigrants, especially dark-skinned ones, are still represented in the media as solely employed in domestic service. Eastern European women, who are mostly *badanti*, that is, caretakers for the elderly, are depicted in addition as husband stealers.[5] The 'collective European unconscious', which Frantz Fanon (1967) denounced, is being maintained through the media as they create social knowledge through the selective representation of the marginalized, relying on what Edward Said called 'the known at the expense of the knowable' (Said, 1991, p. 23).

In the last 10 years we have conducted a series of interviews among women from different parts of the world living in Naples: Albania, Côte d'Ivoire, Nigeria, Russia, Sri Lanka, Senegal, and the Ukraine. They are representative of the ethnic communities in the city and its surroundings. Most of these women are our friends; sometimes they have asked us to report their experiences, using us as a means to express themselves, as in the case of Chandima Fernando from Sri Lanka, whose story was in the *Corriere del Mezzogiorno*, the local section of the Italian newspaper, Il *Corriere della Sera* (Laforest, 1999). Others, like Mari E. from Nigeria, we have met and interviewed through a monitoring project on migration in Castelvolturno, to the north of Naples, conducted in coordination with the human rights association *Jolibà*.

We have chosen to report the stories of two groups of women, Sri Lankans and Ukrainians as they constitute the majority of the foreign presence in the inner city. At the same time we have quoted a Nigerian voice, which testifies to the increasing presence of sub-Saharan Africans outside the city proper. Their experiences of migration should reveal not only how the 'us' against 'them' difference is constructed and maintained, but they should also point to the way women migrants negotiate their space in the context of a foreign country and the role they play in the practice of citizenship in Southern Europe. Saskia Sassen's conceptualization of the practice of 'informal citizenship' produced by the 'excluded' in a given nation-state (2006, p. 290), is particularly useful to analyze the Neapolitan context. The migrant women we have met all live on the margins of local communities, struggling for participation in public life, hoping for full recognition of their human rights.

Our analysis has been conducted through the lens of postcoloniality which provides, as Simon Gikandi has put it, 'the language that enables conjuncture or disjuncture' (2005, p. 609), the two poles around which the immigration battle is being fought. On the one hand, Europeans are in need of a fresh workforce to maintain their high standard of living, but want to keep the immigrants in a subordinate position. On the other, the immigrants are eager to obtain citizenship rights, but in some cases their values might be at odds with European traditions. Similar tensions experienced during colonization have been explored by postcolonial thinkers, whose standpoints have drawn 'on the discursive formations with which it has been in solidarity, such as feminism, race studies, cultural and development studies' (Venn, 2006, p. 1). These approaches, along with the view of scholars like Achille Mbembe and Paul Gilroy, have inspired our research – especially their insight that the legacy of colonialism has determined current relations between natives and immigrants, in particular those coming from formerly colonized countries (Mbembe, 2001; Gilroy, 2004; Venn, 2006).

The myth of temporary abode

There are many myths circulating around current immigration to Italy, both on the part of Italians and on that of the new residents. Italians have defined themselves '*brava gente*' (a good people), a vision of themselves which had already been disclaimed when Southern Italians, in the wake of the industrialization of the north in the early 1960s, migrated to cities like Turin and Milan and were subject to abject forms of discrimination.[6] But the myth has endured even if it was disproved again when Italian troops, as part of a United States-led mission, were deployed in Somalia in 1993 and were accused of gross violation of human rights.[7] It was obviously also evoked with the arrival of the first immigrants in the 1970s despite early proof of xenophobic behavior.

Among immigrants, the most persistent myth is that their presence in the country is temporary – their Italian hosts, too, are still not totally convinced that they are here to stay. Ukrainian women certainly see Italy as a temporary dwelling place. Until 2006 they used to spend three to four years working and then went home for as long as a year. But when inflation in the Ukraine began to eat up their savings faster, they were forced to return after a few months. Sri Lankans, too, buy homes in their country of origin with the intention of settling there. But because of their Italian-reared children and unfavorable economic and political conditions in Sri Lanka, some, like Chandima Fernando, have been forced to sell. The persistence of 'the myth of return', however, has kept the first generation of Sri Lankans in a netherland and discouraged them from investing emotionally in Italy. The sense of being transient has made the burden of racism less harsh to bear, but has, at the same time, made them accept colonial forms of subjection:

> I insist on my name, which is not that difficult anyway, but some of my compatriots let Italians change their names. My brother-in-law let people call him Giulio and let them call his daughter by an Italian name. (C. Fernando, personal communication, 2 May 2002)

In changing the immigrants' names, Neapolitans seem to be oblivious to the violence they are enacting on them. Even if it has been widely recognized that the colonial practice of un-naming and re-naming has left deep scars on the colonized, Neapolitans joke about it and expect the immigrants to laugh along.[8] They want to show them a good time. This is a telling symptom of the hegemony of vision of Western thinking which postcolonial studies has denounced. A unilateral and provincial gaze which, in establishing itself as universal, is reproducing the worst effects of colonialism as it is not expected that the gaze will be turned on them (Chakrabarty, 2000; Chambers, 2001).

When in 1999 we first interviewed Chandima Fernando, who had been in Naples for 17 years, she told us in fluent Italian: 'I'm happy to talk about us. We are in this city. We exist'. Since she had arrived at 14, she knew the ins and outs of the city, but her first complaint was that of being seen as a 'non-person' by the Neapolitan population at large. 'When I'm at a bus stop, I smile and try to start a conversation with a woman or a girl. I force them to speak to me' (Laforest, 1999). Chandima can be seen as one of the many 'overlooked subjects' in the double sense Homi Bhabha uses the term, surveilled and ignored, controlled and excluded, invited and unwelcome (1994, p. 236). Her other grievance was harassment by young males in the streets. Other Sri Lankans, male and female, have reported frequent acts of aggressiveness: young Neapolitan males spit at them or kick them from their fast moving scooters. These assaults seem to be dictated by both racism and frustrated sexual desire since older Sri Lankan women are generally ignored when they walk the streets.[9] One of these women's cruxes, instead, is their inability to protect their children from racism. Some send them 'back home' in care of relatives or try to safeguard them through other means:

> Those who have not sent their children to the International School are sorry. The Italian school is not good for us while in the American one everybody is equal. Americans are used to behave like this. Our children come home crying everyday from the Italian school. They call them, 'black', 'negroes' and they cry. They get home and are very sad. It's a terrible thing. So now they all take their children to the International School. It's very expensive. But they learn English at a young age and they also laugh. (Laforest, 1999)

Sri Lankans tend to form small communities and do not practice exogamy like some other ethnic groups living in Naples, Capeverdians, Brazilians or Dominicans. This is also brought about by the higher number of male residents from Sri Lanka. They seem to have carried over from the former British occupation of their territory the habit of working in a household. Thus the men as well as the women are employed in domestic labor. This creates the most paradoxical of situations as traditional gender roles are nonetheless replicated in the family setting:

> When I get home I have to start cooking. He likes his rice cooked every day. He does not like leftovers. I'm just as tired as he is, but I have to cook and clean our house. He sits down and puts his legs up or he lies in bed. (Susima F., personal communication, 19 September 2004)

A large majority of Sri Lankans live independently in the inner city of Naples, but rarely are jobs beyond the unskilled, manual ones offered them. They often live in substandard street-level apartments (often there is a plaque outside which reads 'unfit for human habitation') or in dilapidated buildings concentrated in three low-income neighborhoods known as Montesanto, Spanish Quarters, and Piazza Cavour. The Neapolitan class structure, which has traditionally been reproduced in the edifices' vertical housing arrangements, speaks volumes (see Gribaudi, 1993); the refusal on the part of Neapolitans to rent apartments – other than street level ones – to the immigrants is a clear sign of their placement on the lowest rung of the social hierarchy (Figure 1).

Theoretically this housing arrangement should exclude them from the possibility of bringing their children over. According to current regulations, they must first obtain an 'entry permit through relatives' which implies submitting an application in which they certify that their domicile meets established norms: a separate bedroom for the child and a bathroom with a window. It is obvious that most Neapolitans in their neighborhood do not have apartments which conform to these regulations and that this is demanded only of them. This law has sent many foreign nationals to look for housing at the outer edges of the city where rents are also lower, but not the Sri Lankans.

Figure 1. 'City Council of Naples. Street-level house not fit for housing'. Courtesy of Aniello Barone.

As the first group to arrive in large numbers in Naples, they have grown savvy about the application of laws and tend to find their way around the system. They do not gather in large numbers in public spaces, respecting the unmarked spatial boundaries of the city; instead they organize concerts in enclosed spaces and cricket tournaments in areas assigned by the municipal authorities. They are also well aware of their rights as workers and usually earn more than their Eastern European counterparts. Sri Lankans began to arrive in Italy when border control was less strict and have continued to enter the country by making use of the 'entry permits through relatives' provision, but also through false passports or through the re-utilization of passports with valid entry visas:

> See how short her hair is... in the front. It has just started to grow. She had shaved her hair to broaden her forehead to fit the passport picture which is of someone else. (Maria C., personal communication, 19 September 2004)

Their status as legal immigrants with work contracts has led to resentment on the part of Neapolitans. Documented workers with contracts benefit from social security and severance pay, which is more than a large number of Neapolitans have obtained.[10] Many prefer to enter the black labor market in order to enjoy benefits provided for the unemployed, like free drugs and health care, free books and free access to university for their children. Their perception however is that immigrants are obtaining more than what they themselves have received from the state. Often they extract money from them, as if to make them pay for what they have not had:

> One day a friend of mine found his apartment open, the front door had been taken off. All his video equipment had been stolen. He was furious and said he would go to the police. The thieves found out, so one of them came and gave him some money and told him where to go to buy a VCR and a TV set in an apartment. It was stolen stuff. So

these thieves steal from a store, then steal from us, then they resell the stuff to us. This is Naples. (C. Fernando, personal communication, 2 May 2002)

But while apparently accepting this state of things, Sri Lankans find different forms of resistance. As cultural mediator Julia Lagaskaia has affirmed, 'the workers' response to the obedience required is a refusal of cultural assimilation' (Coppola, Curti, Fantone, Laforest, & Poole, 2007, p. 98). Among middle-class Neapolitan families, many who have 'foreign' house help want to recreate within their homes a lifestyle more consonant with nineteenth century aristocracy, but as Chandima Fernando testifies, there is resistance:

> She said: 'You wear grey gloves during the week and white ones when I have company'. This she said to my husband who was to serve at table. Then there were jackets with ordinary buttons and those with gold buttons to wear when she had company. 'Tonight I have company', she would say almost everyday. And to me she had said right away you have to call me, '*Signora Marchesa*' when you address me and when you speak to me use '*Lei*'. Instead, I just called her '*Signora*' and used '*Voi*'. At the end of the two weeks [trial period] she called us and said: 'For me it's fine, you can stay'. S. did not want to say anything, so I said to the Marchesa, 'For us it's not fine. We're leaving'. She stood open-mouthed. She paid us half a month not one cent more, even if one night S. had stayed up till six a.m. to clean the kitchen. (Laforest, 1999)

'*Lei*' is the polite form of address and used for superiors in Italian. '*Voi*' is a lower class form of deference in the Neapolitan vernacular, but it is commonly used by people of the upper classes towards those considered of lower social standing. Here the form of resistance deployed by Chandima made use of extremely sophisticated language skills which immigrants are commonly seen as lacking. Just as they are seen as not knowing the intricacies of the law regarding their condition and are therefore taken advantage of. But many have taken their employers to court to obtain severance pay: this is one way of gaining recognition:

> Very often they refuse to pay us. I took this one woman to court, but most often they'd rather pay than go to court. There was this woman, from Posillipo, mind you, she cheated her house servant. She took the doorman of the building with her to testify in her favor. I don't know how she convinced him, but she had him tell the judge that he had given the Sri Lankan an envelope containing 1600 Lire [about 800 Euros]. And it wasn't true at all. But the judge believed her. How can a Signora lower herself to that level, to the level of her doorman. That I just can't understand. Asking him to lie like that. Where is her dignity? Doesn't she have any dignity? (Laforest, 1999)

The collapse of social boundaries, well evident in this case of collusion between the *Signora* and her doorman, is not surprising in the Neapolitan context. What is unusual is recourse to the law on the part of immigrants – including some undocumented workers. They have increasingly had to resort to the judicial or municipal institutions to defend themselves from the Neapolitans (Figure 2).

Unlike the 'citizen', the immigrant or the 'alien' is constructed as a partial subject as much by the law as by policies and cultural practices. In Naples, on the border of Europe, new practices and forms of citizenship are taking place among the immigrants, like the recourse to justice as granted them by labor legislation, although they are never entirely bearers of rights. They are today's 'demizens' or 'semi-citizens' (Rigo, 2007, p. 124): permanent residents, integrated in the social life

Figure 2. Posters in Naples Spanish Quarters. Courtesy of Aniello Barone.

of the Region, but without recognition of their presence and obviously without political rights, like the right to vote.

The M1 bus line: segregation on wheels

The most visible 'demizens' in Naples and its surroundings are the Africans. As the largest undocumented community in Castelvolturno in the province of Caserta, 35 km from the city of Naples, they staged a street protest against the *camorra* on 19 September 2008. It took place in the wake of the killing of six innocent Ghanaians in what the police had erroneously attributed to a drug war between Nigerian pushers and the *camorra*. The Africans marched to ask the police to protect them against the local criminal organization. Since then the government has decided to station army troops in the area.[11] Even in this case the locals argued that the police were never there for them and were giving preferential treatment to the immigrants. A common but obviously false view. As of 12 December, the bodies of the six Ghanaians had still not been sent to their relatives in Africa, as the municipal authorities had pledged (Sardo, 2008). This broken promise was, to say the least, not propitious to trust in the authorities, but that same month, the African residents organized a second protest to demand that the municipality act on its words, once again leaving the locals baffled. From their point of view, the immigrants, indistinctly called 'clandestine' should not be negotiating with the public powers.

Castelvolturno is made up of small, semi-detached houses which mushroomed without building permits in the 1980s as holiday homes. In the mid-1980s, the local authorities expropriated most of the houses to give them to the 1980 earthquake victims, without providing the area with infrastructure and services. Since then, it has become an extended, blighted neighborhood where crime has flourished. It holds a high concentration of immigrants from Nigeria, Ghana, Senegal, and Côte d'Ivoire and, more recently, in lesser numbers, from Romania, Albania, the Ukraine, Moldavia, China, Bangladesh, and Pakistan. It is a degraded tower of Babel, a border zone where drugs and arms trafficking thrive thanks to the local mafia, and where women prostitutes line the streets at all hours. The Catholic church is trying to rescue the women from their street life and has also opened the 'Centro Fernandes', a community center for refugees.

In 2006 we met some women in Castelvolturno, through a Senegalese cultural mediator who had previously lived in the area.[12] One of these women is Mari E. who lives in the vicinity of the Church center and is one of the few 'lucky' women who has a sojourn permit and a decent job. She is striving to raise her children in a 'comfortable and safe place':

> I am a lucky woman. I live by the church and the catholic community center, I therefore feel safe. I also have my sister with me; that is a great help. My children grow up here and thanks to the Catholic association I can send them to kindergarten and to school, organized by volunteers for immigrants. I like to live here. All my friends are here and I feel part of a community that supports and helps me. I've been in Italy for about eight years. I think people back home should be more informed about the situation here. (Mari E., personal communication, 10 January 2006)

The road linking Castelvolturno to the Central Station in Naples is served by the M1 bus line, on which a pilot project of traveling cultural mediators was experimented. The bus is one of the few enclosed spaces in which Italians and a large number of 'foreigners' are contiguously present. In this confined space, during the one-hour ride, episodes of racism and discrimination are frequent. So much so that cultural mediators on the bus route became necessary to prevent aggression. Immigrants constitute 70% of the passengers on the M1 bus and their presence is apparently a source of great anxiety for the Italians who travel this route. They are angry, resentful citizens who turn the bus journey into an open confrontation between 'us' and 'them'. Neapolitans, whose propensity to litter is no myth – as the garbage-strewn streets attest – all at once associate filthiness, bad smells, and diseases with others. Unabashed, they tell the immigrants to their faces that they ought to be kept separate. It is common to hear someone say out loud, 'These people stink' or 'They carry all this bulky luggage', or 'I cannot share a seat with these intrusive people'. The immigrants are insulted throughout the entire journey and when they answer back the situation becomes explosive.

In 2004 the Caritas regional immigration office, the most active association working with immigrants, launched a campaign called 'Contact' to improve communications between the public transport companies in the Neapolitan district and the 'foreigners', as poor knowledge of Italian and of transport regulations often led to 'misunderstandings and conflicts'. The project aimed at forming cultural mediators who would travel on board of buses with a high concentration of 'foreign' passengers. The cultural mediators were chosen from one of the immigrant groups and were to work as social operators to create better relations between the 'foreign' passengers, the locals, and the drivers (Pentelescu, 2006). Mari was one of them:

> At the beginning it was very hard, but now I have a job and my permanent permit is not giving me nightmares anymore. I work on buses every afternoon. I've become a worker who helps immigrants. The problem with immigration here is first of all the absence of communication and information. We don't really know how things work in Italy. We don't understand the laws and yet we have to produce lots of documents and papers to

do everything, like going to a hospital. The only social aid we get from the state is in the information offices, which just help us with the bureaucracy; these offices are very few and far, hard to reach since we live in areas with very few infrastructures and services. Besides, we are afraid to move from here, because without documents we don't know what can happen to us. I wished I knew before coming to this country what I was going to go through. I didn't know anything, I only knew I was going to Europe, and that it was a good place, wealthy and rich. I didn't even know that in Europe you had different languages. (Mari E., personal communication, 10 January 2006)

Mari, from Nigeria, has been working as a cultural mediator on the bus over the last three years. Since the area she lives in is segregated, she is well aware of the reluctance of Italians to share the same space with immigrants. Still, her job consists in trying to bridge the gap between 'natives' and 'foreigners':

When I meet the people on the bus I have to tell them about many things, like addresses of immigration offices, those of workers' unions, or tell them about hospitals and health services. Sometimes they also bring me some papers they want to get translated, and I do that on the bus. I also give them advice on how to get jobs, because you know, the most important thing is to get a job that will give you a permit. Everybody needs documents and the laws are not helping us at all. I understand that there's a political problem with jobs for immigrants and what we all wish for is another amnesty for our brothers and sisters. (Mari E., personal communication, 10 January 2006)

Her effort is geared to explaining to the immigrants how they can improve their lot. There are no signs that she has managed to start a dialogue with the locals and much less between locals and immigrants.

Castelvolturno has been renamed the Italian Soweto by one of Naples' most outspoken and indignant voices, Roberto Saviano (2008).[13] This urban conglomeration can be seen as the ultimate frontier of Europe where the illegal trafficking in drugs, weapons, and human beings in the global market regularly takes place (Saviano, 2006). Castelvolturno is one of those places within the European borders where some individuals, namely those without legal permits, are in a jail without walls, and where most basic human rights are suspended. Paraphrasing Étienne Balibar, it represents the enactment of 'European apartheid', where the discourse of the 'inclusion and exclusion of citizens and citizens' social practices' is played out on the edge of the European sense of community and welfare (Balibar, 2007, p. 9). Once more, Mari's case, like the Sri Lankan residents' conduct, questions full citizenship in contemporary Europe. Her regular sojourn permit and her practice of what Sassen calls 'informal citizenship' did not however protect her from the effects the vicious killing of the six young Ghanaians has had on the Castelvolturno community.

In the inner city, efforts to bridge the gap of segregation are no better. On 19 December 2008, in the city's central artery, via Roma, the municipality of Naples organized an event called 'Naples in color. Music as the art of ethnic cohabitation'. The Senegalese men involved in the project set their bongos on the sidewalk, but no sooner had they begun to beat their drums than the shopkeepers jeered at them. Under the pretext that the music was too loud, they started to hurls insults, 'Go back to Africa', someone shouted. Newspaper reports of the racist incident did not mention whether the police intervened, they only declared that ethnic rapprochement through music had failed (Immigrati contestati, 2008).

Kiev-Piazza Garibaldi: the route to care taking

There is another bus route which is instead off-limits to Italians; that is, the Kiev-Piazza Garibaldi line, which has brought thousands of Ukrainian women to the Naples Central train station. The facility of entry by ground transportation and the possibility of returning home, despite the risks involved, has made of the Ukrainians the largest 'foreign' group in the city. They are mostly women with a high percentage of middle-aged ones, all supporting their families in the Ukraine. The age group of these women may explain their propensity for care work:[14]

> In the case of Eastern Europe, it is the women who migrate. Men accept women's generosity and end up becoming economic parasites. This leads to many marriage break-ups. Men do not realize the sacrifices women are making. As for children, separation is really traumatic, even where there is the opportunity to join the mother later on. (Coppola et al., 2007, p. 96)

Italians have become totally dependent on the presence of foreign *badanti* for their well-being. This is not surprising since 'care work has come to be pivotal to the functioning of local as well as global economy' (Yuval-Davis, 2008, p. 282). The women *badanti* usually live with one elderly person, but sometimes they have to take care of two people who are not self-sufficient and need to be helped or watched over day and night. Under the laws passed by the center-left governments in the pre-Berlusconi era, employers need to sign a contract with workers – specifying wages, holidays, and severance pay – provide them with their own bedroom and bathroom. However controls are scarce and getting around the law is seen as normal in Naples, a sign of shrewdness, therefore a virtue. As state subventions became available for live-in caretakers all socio-economic groups have had recourse to this benefit:

> I went to see that woman, because someone had told me she was looking for a caretaker. I didn't like the neighborhood to start with, but after showing me around her apartment, when I asked her where I would sleep, she said, pointing to her double bed: 'Why? Here, we can share the same bed'. (Aleksia C., personal communication, 12 June 2005)

Despite the responsibility placed on immigrants to whom the care of children and the elderly is entrusted, the language of the media never fails to confine their identity in absolutes and ethnicize them. As Valerie Bryson has pointed out, when 'employment involves the caring work traditionally done by women, it is still economically penalized' (Bryson, 2007, p. 44). Widely used today, the term *badante* itself has degraded caretakers to a lesser humanity (De Rienzo, 2008). Half of the *badante* population is constituted of undocumented workers, even if they are among those who can obtain entry visas to Italy. As demagogue politicians are haranguing the citizens against the presence of 'illegal foreigners' because of the danger they represent for the community, these people are taken into Italian homes as live-in workers. They live in close contact with Italians, a set up which allows them to acquire greater familiarity with Italian life-styles. As they share with the locals the intimacy of the house, they also learn Italian faster and better. Today, a few have managed to become cultural mediators and negotiators.

Unlike Sri Lankans, the Ukrainian women meet in the city's open spaces, using city parks as picnic areas, or under the central train station canopy. The habit of eating on park benches immediately associates Ukrainians with foreignness, alien as this use of parks is to Neapolitans who prefer to stroll along the lanes and flower beds. At the central station, where the bus from Kiev arrives once a week, the women gather in hundreds to welcome newcomers or send off packages to the Ukraine. This is where ironically blond, blue-eyed native women, who have represented the epitome of beauty in Southern Italy, are taken for Eastern Europeans and treated with disparagement.

Ill-treated on the one hand, as this seems to reinforce the status of struggling Neapolitans, the Ukrainian women are also coveted by middle-aged to elderly men. Seen as sexual objects to be possessed, they are followed in the streets, approached on park benches when they meet there on their afternoon off. Younger women instead are even more openly harassed:

> I used to run into this man, until I realized he was following me. This young man looks mentally handicapped to me. The fact is that he'd been following me for the past week. I have to go through a fairly deserted area to get to the train station. One day when he was close enough to me, he said: 'sooner or later I'll f— you.' I was terrified. Next time I had my cell phone ready, so I took his picture. He shouted that he would kill me. I went straight to the police. The police said that he wasn't well and that they would speak to his family, so there was no need for a formal accusation, which means they won't do anything. But now I have to leave the neighborhood. I have to move. I'm looking for a place. (Natalya U., personal communication, 23 October 2007)

At the same time, Italian men see Ukrainians as potential wives and lovers because 'they are pretty, they settle for less than the Italian women and they do the housework' (Meletti, 2008). Meletti also reports that there are roughly 3000 weddings celebrated each year between Italians who are over 70 and Eastern European women. According to one source, married men in Naples are renting apartments for Ukrainian women. This new set up goes back to the times when 'kept women' were a commonplace in society, before the feminist revolution of the 1960s brought women towards economic independence. In Olga's case she has stopped working and has her own space, a luxury being paid by a married man who visits her twice a week (Olga V., personal communication, 14 December 2007).

From the Italian women's viewpoint, the Ukrainians are 'husband stealers'. Through this definition they are obviously excusing 'their men' from any wrong-doing. In a typical fashion, 'it's generally the other woman, not the husband, who will bear the brunt of the scorned wife's wrath' (Hart, 2002). While the Ukrainian women themselves point out in their defense that they do not get first choice men:

> They say that we do this in order to enter the homes of those with money. But what we, young women from Eastern Europe, receive are almost always second-hand husbands: widowers, old men, the sick. I know the story of so many of my friends who have arrived from Russia, the Ukraine, Romania. I can tell you that they are divided into two categories: *badante*-wives like me and wives who will soon become *badanti* since they have married men who are at least twenty years older. (Meletti, 2008)

The number of liaisons between Italian men and Eastern European women points to difficult male-female relations in Italy, but most importantly seems to indicate a choice to 'marry white'. This raises the racial question and with it the submerged Italian colonial history. During colonialism, fascist laws on mixed-race marriages, particularly in Ethiopia, denied citizenship to the offspring of white and black. In 1937 all mixed relationships between Africans and whites were forbidden by law (Adarabioyo, 2003, p. 90). Avoidance of miscegenation and constructions of ontological differences have reappeared under a more subtle form today. In 2006 the Immigration Office in Milan published two guidelines for mixed-race couples on the different laws passed in Italy and in other countries, like Morocco, Egypt, and Tunisia, on marriage, childbirth, and separation. The idea was to overcome 'misunderstandings and troubles' for those who marry foreigners, as 'love is not enough to overcome [a couple's] problems' (Dazzi, 2006). No such text has circulated in Naples, but the configuration of the city and the contempt for 'foreigners' is obviously not conducive to closer contact between natives and immigrants. Non-Italian-born women are designated under a collective 'foreign' identity and are discussed in terms of numbers; few take the time to get to know them as individuals. Relations between native women and 'foreign' women, which would have been a sign of integration, are practically non-existent. Thus only sexual relations between native males and immigrant women appear to be the path currently breaking down xenophobic barriers.

The southern question, the racial question

The military language of war and invasion recurrent in discussions of immigration by the Italian media does not seem to differ much from that of other European countries:

> Once the idea of immigration has been constructed as a problem with national dimensions, history goes out of the window and we get transported into the frozen realm of mythic time. That domain is ruled by the timeless, iconic constructions of Europe's post-colonial melancholia. Criminals, spongers, and their numberless alien offspring. (Gilroy, 2005, p. 82)

For xenophobic and racist Italians, as for their European counterparts, it is patriotically fitting to continue the fight against the newcomers in order to preserve their 'Italianness'. Based on blood and soil, Italian identity, in their view, has remained unchanged in the course of time. *Jus sanguinis*, indeed, remains the law of the country. Provisions for refugees are for all practical purposes non-existent, those to acquire Italian citizenship are complex and restrictive. But many second-generation children are growing up in Italy – officially 700,000 – and are coming of age. A new generation of 'semi-citizens' is therefore appearing on the Italian scene as these youngsters turn 18 and have to be taken off their parents' sojourn permit, without the possibility of becoming citizens (Porqueddu, 2008).

No model of immigration – melting pot, mosaic or multiculturalism – has been officially decreed in Italy as in the United States, Canada or England, but public debates oscillate between a vague form of multiculturalism and cultural assimilation as the path to accepting the new residents. Questionable as this is, it is assimilation which is evoked most often and is apparently being enacted through even more problematical choices like the institution of separate classes for the children of immigrants as a 'policy of integration'.[15] According to official discourses 'episodes of intolerance' are to be expected when a people's turf is being invaded. However in the case of Naples, if the southern question is pounded over concurrently with the racial question, a new outlook on the virulent reaction of the usually accommodating and easy going Neapolitan emerges.

In the wake of Italian unification in 1860, differences between northerners and southerners were racialized (Schneider, 1998; Moe, 2002). The latter were considered culturally and morally polluted by their vicinity to the Mediterranean Arab world; they were also seen as representing the backward part of the country which depended on government aid for its 'lazy' and 'unruly' citizens. Thus, closer to Africans than to Europeans, depicted as blacks, Southerners were seen as genetically predisposed to crime. The new language of social theory and engineering, enriched by Lombrosian criminology, helped construct Southern Italy as the 'other'. Naples has always stood as the symbol of the pathological South. The liminal and peripheral space it occupies both at a European and national level has made its citizens unsure of their identity, always on the verge of being otherized by their 'advanced' northern Italian compatriots or by their 'developed' northern European neighbors. In many parts of the Campania Region the memory of migration is still alive and Italian immigrants – the majority from the South – were equated with blacks in the United States in the nineteenth and early twentieth century (Stella, 2003; Gundle, 2005).

Struggling Neapolitans are hostile to immigrants as their economic circumstances are forcing them to associate with newcomers whom they have defined as the lowest of the low. It is a sign of their decline as individuals and the most tangible example of the way in which the state has abandoned them to their fate. They find themselves vying for social services in crowded hospitals, post offices, and packed public transports; even teeming inner-city streets can become contested ground. Thus immigrants often become the scapegoats for all the ills of the Region: from political corruption to its lack of economic clout and political prestige. Disillusioned and unhappy, afraid of becoming like the immigrants they despise, struggling Neapolitans can be compared to the petit-bourgeois class in Europe after the Second World War. The fear of becoming like the proletariat led the European petit-bourgeois to turn to Nazism and Fascism (Fromm, 1968). In the case of Naples, the immigrants mirror what many Neapolitans have been and could become in uncertain times. The poor, the unemployed, the former Neapolitan street vendors and street walkers, because of the economic hardship in the provinces of Naples and Caserta, have not been able to move up the economic ladder. Their fear and anger is expressed through old, constructed racist discourses, once dormant and now revived with the arrival of the immigrants.

Today immigrants are still commonly labeled '*extracomunitari*' in Italy – non-European Union citizens – clearly referring to a population which is excluded from the rights and benefits granted Italian citizens.[16] It is the only European member state in which such a segregating term is used and it consciously or unconsciously reiterates that the immigrants are out of place in the country. The currency of the term '*extracomunitari*' even in legal language is indicative of the way in which even the State normalizes exclusion. Italy's borders are thus not solely and principally the traditional geographical ones which marked off the interior from the exterior space of the nation, they are now domestic frontiers, within single localities. These new frontiers run between an imaginary 'us' and a constructed 'them' along lines which, even if mutable and repeatedly crossed, are policed to keep the 'foreigners' in subjugation to Italian nationals.

The perception of immigration as one of the most serious national problems is certainly putting at stake Italy's future as a multicultural state. The Northern League, a vociferous member of the current government coalition, has no qualms about constructing a three-tiered society consisting of Northerners, Southerners, and foreigners. Caught in between, Neapolitans can at last claim greater proximity to the North, distancing themselves from the 'foreigners' and accepting a curtailment of the rights of those who, they believe, are enjoying the privileges they have never had. Significant as they are, these issues have not been at the center of the Neapolitan political debate – even if the Region was ruled for the past 10 years (2000–2010) by a center-left coalition. At the national level instead, it is a paradox that one of the two political leaders who have been most outspoken regarding the extension of voting rights to immigrants has been Gianfranco Fini, head of the former Fascist party. Fini's declarations have alienated a large part of his constituency. Paolo Ferrero, too, former Minister of Social Solidarity and member of the Italian communist party, *Rifondazione Comunista*, has also denounced the treatment of immigrants in his volume *Immigrazione: Fa più rumore l'albero che cade che la foresta che cresce/ Immigration* [The tree falling down makes more noise than the forest growing] (2007); there he explains the flow of migrants not as an oceanic wave, but as strictly related to the logic of demographics and economics. On the other hand, the largest leftist party, *Partito Democratico*, has been more timid: not so much in denouncing abuses, but in implementing measures deemed necessary to help the newcomers integrate into the social fabric of Naples and the Campania Region when the party was in power.

The fear of losing consensus traverses many political forces. The average Italian and those unconvinced by the Vatican's paternalistic but steadfast defense of immigrants perceive these latter as a threat to their personal security. The media indeed never fails to identify offenders as immigrants and foreigners. Concurrently the obsessive reiteration of the 'immigrant problem' has led to a series of laws which have dramatized the situation. So perverse are the laws that they tend to transform immigrants who lose their jobs, whose work contracts or sojourn permits expire, into undocumented workers. To have their permits renewed in the Campania Region some have had to wait as long as eight months. The majority of migrants, then, live under the uncertainty of becoming undocumented and therefore invisible, with neither identity, rights or security. This condition illustrates a nasty exercise of state biopolitics in Foucauldian terms: the state acquires full control over the body of the individual through a system of inclusion and exclusion, granting citizenship thus subjectivity on the basis of documented work. In 1995, 'to better control the incoming populations', members of the Northern League had suggested to take the immigrants' fingerprints and footprints. They also proposed to get the '*extracomunitari*'s DNA, for sometimes 'these people burn their hands to hide their identity' (Adarabioyo, 2003, pp. 86–87). Not taken into account at the time, fingerprinting was voted by a large bipartisan majority in July 2008. By naturalizing ethnic coding, humiliation and harassment of foreigners by xenophobes and racists has been legitimized.

In a well-known 1980 talk, Audre Lorde pointed out how 'institutionalized rejection of difference is an absolute necessity in a profit economy which needs outsiders as surplus people' (1984, p. 115). Women, who constitute the majority of immigrants, will bear the brunt of these new measures which have further enforced their alienness to the national fabric. In northern as in southern Italy negotiating spaces of resistance and survival will become ever more complex.

The cases we have reported spell out the segregation women migrants experience in their jobs and explain how violence is woven through the daily tissues of their lives. Chandima, Mari, Aleksia and Natalya struggle every day in search of recognition in a society which is generally blind to their basic demands of human solidarity and respect. Since illegal immigration has been decreed a criminal offense, it has worsened the status of those who are already settled in the country and provoked a series of inhuman actions towards the hopeful and the desperate who cross the Mediterranean to reach Italy's southern coasts. At present, we record that in the local and national discourse the logic of exclusion is miserably ordinary and that the collective past and present conjoin to presage a glum future. It is all the more imperative that migrant women's voices rise above the clamor to empty it of substance.

Notes
1. Undocumented workers have traditionally come south, even when they used to arrive illegally through Trieste or Venice. For many years Philippine women were the largest ethnic minority in the city, but they have since moved north, where better-paid jobs are available, and are hardly present in Naples today.
2. In particular the two provinces of Naples and Caserta, objects of this study, are incontestably ruled by this criminal organization.
3. It is very difficult to establish the total numbers of immigrants in Naples, what is certain is that they are on the rise. The 2008 Caritas/Migrantes *Statistical dossier* reports 5,811,390 residents in the Campania Region of which 114,792 are estimated to be foreigners. Ukrainians constitute 27.5 %, while the number of Romanians has considerably increased. It is believed that they will become the largest presence in the Region since Romania is now a state of the European Union. As for Africans, in the absence of data on their actual presence, it has been reported that 10,923 workers from Africa had regular work insurance coverage in 2007 and 1928 African children were registered in the schools of the Campania Region (Caritas/Migrantes, 2008, p. 459).
4. The larger metropolitan area refers to the Naples-Caserta conurbation. They are also the two provinces with the lowest *per capita* income in the country: €16,066.99 in the province of Naples and €15,768.05 in Caserta. These data can be compared with those of the province of Milan where the *per capita* income is €39,442.08 (La qualità della vita [Quality of life], 2008).
5. The new word '*badanteli*' was coined in the 1980s to refer to the mostly women immigrants who provide assistance to the aging Italian population. The state has not built homes for the aged and has preferred to subsidize families in need of caretakers with a monthly allowance.
6. Luchino Visconti's 1960 film *Rocco and His Brothers* is a poignant representation of that internal migration.
7. Troops of Italy's Lightning division went into Somalia together with soldiers from other nations in a mission led by the United States to safeguard the delivery of food to starving civilians. A series of pictures in which Italian soldiers are seen applying electrodes to a naked Somali on the ground and sexually abusing young girls were published in the Italian press (Photos of Troops Abusing Somalis in '93 Shock Italians, 1993).
8. The link between re-naming, the erasure of previous identities, and the silencing of entire peoples has been explored in postcolonial studies (see for instance, Todorov, 1982; Benston, 1982).
9. Robert Young (1995, p. 150) has insightfully described the repulsion and attraction between dominant and subaltern in colonial settings.
10. The Sri Lankans have been able to take advantage of the 1990, 1995, 1998, 2002 amnesties which allowed the so-called clandestines to obtain a sojourn permit.

11. Castelvolturno was recently the theatre of a concert held against organized crime and in defense of human rights where 'Mama Africa', South African artist Miriam Makeba dramatically died on stage.
12. It is not uncommon for African migrants to spend some time in Castelvolturno before moving elsewhere in the region or in the country. The 2005 movie *Lettere dal Sahara/ Letters from the Sahara* by Vittorio De Seta testifies to this.
13. Roberto Saviano is the author of the 2006 best-seller *Gomorra*, an analysis of the pervasive role the *camorra* plays in the industrial and commercial development of the Campania Region. He has received serious threats to his life and is forced to live in hiding.
14. Even if they are present on the supply side, there might also be a request for white caretakers, which also explains why so many are engaged in this occupation.
15. This measure was discussed and voted in one of the two Houses of Parliament on 15 October 2008, but has not been made into law.
16. The recently emanated 'social card' – Law 133/2008 – is a case in point. It is a €40.00 per month credit card for low-income families which can be granted to Italian citizens only. Other discriminatory measures are currently under examination.

References

Adarabioyo, I. (2003). *Il Coraggio di Grace. Donne nigeriane dalla prostituzione alla libertà* [Grace's bravery. Nigerian women from prostitution to freedom]. Roma: Prospettive edizioni.
Balibar, É. (2007). Il diritto al territorio [The right to territory]. In E. Rigo (Ed.), *Europa di confine* [Borderland Europe] (pp. 7–31). Roma: Meltemi.
Benjamin, W. (2007). *Immagini di città [City portraits]* (2nd Ed.). Torino, Einaudi.
Benston, K.W. (1982). 'I Yam what I Am': Naming and unnaming in Afro-American literature. *Black American Literature Forum, 16*, 3–11.
Bhabha, H.K. (1994). *The location of culture*. London: Routledge.
Bryson, V. (2007). Perspectives on gender equality. Challenging the terms of debate. In J. Browne (Ed.), *The future of gender* (pp. 35–53). Cambridge: Cambridge University Press.
Caritas/Migrantes. (2008). *Immigrazione dossier statistico 2008 XVIII Rapporto* [Immigration statistical dossier 2008 18th Report]. Roma: Edizioni Idos.
Chakrabarty, D. (2000). *Deprovincializing Europe*. Princeton, NJ: Princeton University Press.
Chambers, I. (1994). *Migrancy, culture, identity*. London: Routledge.
Chambers, I. (2001). *Culture after humanism*. London and New York, NY: Routledge.
Coppola, M., Curti, L., Fantone, L., Laforest, M.H., & Poole, S. (2007). Women, migration and precarity. *Feminist Review, 87*, 94–103.
Dazzi, Z. (2006, March 19). Il manuale delle coppie miste [The manual for mixed race couples]. *Metropoli*, p. 5.
De Rienzo, G. (2008). *La parola in gioco 'badante'* [A word at stake 'badante']. Retrieved May 13, 2008, from http://www.corriere.it/Rubriche/Scioglilingua/scioglilingua030502.shtml
Dickie, J. (1997). Stereotypes of the Italians. In R. Lumley & J. Morris (Eds.), *The new history of the Italian south. Mezzogiorno revisited* (pp. 114–147). Exeter: University of Exeter Press.
Fanon, F. (1967). *Peau noire, masques blancs* [Black skin white masks]. Paris: Editions du Seuil.
Ferrero, P. (2007). *Immigrazione: Fa più rumore l'albero che cade che la foresta che cresce* [Immigration: The tree falling down makes more noise than the forest growing]. Roma: Claudiana.
Fromm, E. (1968). *Escape from freedom* [Fuga dal nazismo] (2nd ed.). (C. Manucci, Trans.). Cremona: Edizione di Comunità.
Gikandi, S. (2005). Globalizaton and the claims of postcoloniality. In D. Gauri & S. Nair (Eds.), *Postcolonialism: An anthology of cultural theory and criticism* (pp. 608–634). New Brunswick, NJ: Rutgers University Press.
Gilroy, P. (2004). *Between camps: Nations, cultures and the allure of race*. London/New York, NY: Routledge.

Gilroy, P. (2005). A cat in a kitten box or the confessions of a 'second generation immigrant'. In S. Ponzanesi & D. Merolla (Eds.), *Migrant cartographies. New cultural and literary spaces in post-colonial Europe* (pp. 79–92). Lanham, MD: Lexington Books.

Gribaudi, G. (1993, May 30). Familismo e famiglia a Napoli e nel Mezzogiorno [Familism and family in Naples and Southern Italy]. *Meridiana*, vol. 17, p. 30.

Gundle, S. (2005). Miss Italia in black and white: Feminine beauty and ethnic identity in modern Italy. In S. Ponzanesi & D. Merolla (Eds.), *Migrant cartographies. New cultural and literary spaces in post-colonial Europe* (pp. 253–266). Lanham, MD: Lexington Books.

Hart, B. (2002). Mean like me: A feminist author discovers that women aren't always nice. Betsy Hart says this isn't news to anyone who survived seventh grade – Woman's inhumanity to woman – book review. *Women's Quarterly*. FindArticles.com. Retrieved January 5, 2009, from http://findarticles.com/p/articles/mi_m0IUK/is_2002_Summer/ai_90305258.

Immigrati contestati. (2008, December 20). *Corriere del Mezzogiorno*, p. 9.

La qualità della vita. (2008). Dossier del lunedì [Quality of life. Monday dossier]. Retrieved December 29, 2008, from http://www.ilsole24ore.com/speciali/qv_2008/qv_2008_province_settori_classifica_finale.shtml

Laforest, M.H. (1999, May 18). La città straniera [The foreign city]. *Corriere del Mezzogiorno*, p. 11.

Lorde, A. (1984). Age, race, class, and sex: Women redefining difference. In M.-H. Laforest (Ed.), *Sister outsider. Essays and speeches by Audre Lorde* (pp. 114–123). Trumansburg, NY: The Crossing Press.

Macry, P. (2003). Se l'unità crea divisione. Immagini del Mezzogiorno nel discorso politico nazionale [If unity creates division. Images of the Mezzogiorno in the national political discourse]. In L. Di Nucci & E. Galli Della Loggia (Eds.), *Due nazioni. Legittimazione e delegittimazione nella storia dell'Italia contemporanea* [Two nations. Legitimacy and illegitimacy in contemporary Italian history] (pp. 63–92). Bologna: Mulino.

Mbembe, A. (2001). *On the postcolony*. Berkeley, CA: University of California Press.

Meletti, J. (2008, May 1). La moglie badante [*Badante* wives]. *La Repubblica*, pp. 40–41.

Mezzana, M. (2008). Il mercato del lavoro di Mario Draghi, il governatore descrive l'Italia che cambia [The labor market by Mario Draghi, the governor describes how Italy is changing]. Retrieved May 20, 2008, from www.politicadomani.it

Moe, N. (2002). *The view from Vesuvius. Italian culture and the southern question*. Berkeley, CA: University of California Press.

Pentelescu, G. (2006, March 19). In viaggio con i mediatori a bordo [Travelling with mediators on board]. *Metropoli*, p. 11.

Photos of Troops Abusing Somalis in '93 Shock Italians (1997). Retrieved May 5, 2008, from http://www.nytimes.com/1997/06/14/world/photos-of-troops-abusing-somalis-in-93-shock-italians.html

Porqueddu, M. (2008, May 9). Diciotto anni, il compleanno maledetto [Turning eighteen, the damned birthday]. *Il Corriere della Sera*, p. 11.

Rigo, E. (2007). *Europa di confine* [Borderland Europe]. Roma: Meltemi.

Said, E. (1991). *The world, the text, and the critic*. New York, NY: Vintage.

Sardo, R. (2008, December 12). Un intoppo burocratico blocca le salme dei ghanesi [A bureaucratic snag blocks Ghanaians' bodies]. *La Repubblica Napoli*, p. 11.

Sassen, S. (2001). *The global city*. Princeton, NJ: Princeton University Press.

Sassen, S. (2006). *Territory, authority, rights. From medieval to global assemblages*. Princeton, NJ: Princeton University Press.

Saviano, R. (2006). *Gomorra. Viaggio nell'impero economico e nel sogno di dominio della camorra* [Gomorrah. Journey into the *camorra*'s economic empire and its dream of dominion]. Roma: Mondadori.

Saviano, R. (2008, December 11). Ci ha insegnato la rabbia della fratellanza. È morta nella Soweto d'Italia [She taught us the anger of brotherhood. She died in Italy's Soweto]. *La Repubblica*, p. 51.

Schneider, J. (Ed.). (1998). *Italy's 'southern question'. Orientalism in one country*. Oxford: Berg.

Stella, G. (2003). *L'Orda. Quando gli albanesi eravamo noi* [The horde. When we were the Albanians]. Milano: Rizzoli.

Todorov, S. (1982). *La conquête de l'Amérique* [The conquest of America]. Paris: Editions du Seuil.
Venn, C. (2006). *The postcolonial challenge. Towards alternative worlds.* London: Thousand Oaks.
Young, R. (1995). *Colonial desire: Hybridity in theory, culture and race.* London: Routledge.
Young, R. (2003). *Postcolonialism.* Oxford: Oxford University Press.
Yuval-Davis, N. (2008). Nationalism, belonging, globalization, and the 'ethics of care'. In A.M. Gonzalez & V.J. Seidler (Eds.), *Gender identities in a globalized world.* Amherst, MA: Humanity Books.
Zagaria, C. (2008). Napoli, anche i Rom pagano il pizzo alla camorra [Naples, even the Roma pay protection money to the *camorra*]. Retrieved May 3, 2008, from http://www.repubblica.it/2008/02/sezioni/cronaca/camorra/pizzo-rom/pizzo-rom.html

Whose freedom? Whose memories? Commemorating Danish colonialism in St. Croix

Bolette B. Blaagaard

Centre for Law, Justice and Journalism, City University London, London, UK

The article addresses the issues of cultural and archival historical representations as they are presented in Danish journalism about historical events taking place in the former colonies of Denmark, the current United States' Virgin Islands (USVI). The (post)colonial relationship between Denmark and USVI has been overlooked by Danish and 'western'-based scholars for quite some time. The article presents the case of a journalistically represented reenactment in the USVI commemorating the emancipation of the Danish slaves on the three colonial islands St. John, St. Croix, and St. Thomas in 1848. The case shows that journalists often depend on documented historical accounts rather than cultural knowledge, myths and legends, that may tell a different (his)story. Engaging journalism with feminist theory and postcolonial theory, the article discusses how this bias determines who gets to speak and who is silenced, that is, journalistic objectivity. Finally the article seeks to develop another way of thinking about postcolonial memory constructions in journalistic representations.

Denmark colonized the three Caribbean islands St. Thomas, St. Croix and St. John for more than 200 years although the common cultural and political history and colonial relationship features prominently in neither Danish schoolbooks nor the media. Through an analysis and discussion of a reenactment of the emancipation of the slaves in the former Danish colonies, this article addresses the issues of cultural memory and the representations that are produced and presented in Danish journalism and in journalism practiced in the United States' Virgin Islands (USVI) on the issue of the (post)colonial relationship. The relationship between Denmark and USVI has been overlooked by Danish and 'western'-based scholars for quite some time. In contrast to Denmark however, in the USVI the historical relationship is part of the textbook curriculum. The difference between the two territories' historical representation and memory results in a skewed emphasis on the importance of the common history, which generates an extreme lack of acknowledgement, within the Danish general public, of Danish complicity in colonialism, slavery and the slave trade. This is exemplified by young Danes who are in their late teens but do not know that Denmark took part in slavery,[1] and the discourses and terminology of otherness often show traces of 'national self-conceptions of the

Nordic countries as not having the "burden of guilt"' (Marselis, 2008, p. 463). Although the Nordic colonies[2] are well-known in Denmark and are often linked to a common and heroic Nordic past as Vikings, the neglect of the history concerning the southern colonies[3] sets Denmark apart from other postcolonial and former slave trading nations. Throughout Europe and the US, emancipation commemorations and official apologies have taken place in recent years. In 2006, France's President Jacques Chirac made a public apology for slavery and announced 10 May to be a national day of remembrance for victims of slavery. In 2007, the British Prime Minister apologized for slavery and the Britons commemorated the bicentenary for abolition of the slave trade in the British colonies. In 2008, the United States passed a law offering a formal apology for slavery and the Jim Crow politics. Even Norway, which was a colony of Denmark during colonial times, has erected a monument in commemoration of the Danish-Norwegian slave trade. However, in Denmark there have been no attempts to offer apologies, laws have not been enacted that recognize Denmark's role in slavery and no monuments of remembrance have been erected, despite the fact that Denmark was the seventh largest slave-trading nation (Gøbel, 1996). The different ways former European colonial powers deal with their past reflect the diversity within postcolonial Europe and represent an argument for this issue needing further research and development.

Journalistic cultural memory

Among 'western' scholars, a handful of networks, conferences and exhibitions focusing on the issue of Danish (post)colonialism have emerged within the last 10 years.[4] In spite of a burgeoning interest in the topic, Danish media only show interest during controversies such as the reenactment of the 1998 commemoratory event, which is the focus here. In this article I understand these commemoratory events to constitute and construct a common cultural memory, which is strong in the USVI but less so in Denmark.

In the following I argue that both historical archives and culturally informed narratives are sustained by representations of the past and are embedded and embodied through journalistic cultural memory.[5] Journalistic narratives about cultural hybridization, homogeneity and heterogeneity throw into relief journalistic (co)production of 'identities' and belonging. As a former colony of Denmark, a present unincorporated territory of the US and a member of the Caribbean island chain, the question of cultural 'identity' and belonging are continuously debated in the USVI – most recently in connection to the Islands' fifth attempt at constructing a constitution. These circumstances foreground the multilayeredness and multiplicity in the USVI community and cultural 'identities'.

In this article the case of journalistic constructions of cultural memories, history and 'identities' will be informed by a range of theories; firstly a cultural studies approach; secondly, feminist and 'race' theories of accountability and identity; and lastly, a philosophical approach will attempt to illuminate the production of cultural memories in everyday journalistic narratives. Although I am not suggesting that journalists start reading philosophy in order to conduct a different journalism, I suggest that memory may be reformulated using the philosophers', Deleuze and Guattari, concepts of history and memory and teach us to look at journalism's construction of history and cultural memories differently, and thereby question journalism's claim to objectivity in a postcolonial setting.

The reenactment of 1998

The events that make up this case study unfolded in 1998. The commemoration of the emancipation of the Danish slaves on the Caribbean islands St. Croix, St. Thomas and St. John is an annual event and was celebrated on St. Croix in 1998 – the 150th anniversary of the emancipation. The celebrations included a reenactment of the moment when Governor Peter von Scholten (hard-pressed by a burgeoning revolt among the slaves) pronounced the words: 'You are now free – you have been emancipated!' Von Scholten has been ingrained in Danish history books for this (speech)act and during the commemoration his speech was re-enacted by Danish actor, Kurt Ravn. Present during the reenactment in Frederiksted, St. Croix, was the Danish journalist Alex Frank Larsen. He was on the Virgin Islands filming for a documentary that would be broadcast on Danish television under the title *Slavernes Slægt* (2005).[6] Larsen films the final rehearsal of the reenactment in Christiansted and follows Ravn to Frederiksted the succeeding day, where the actual speech was pronounced 150 years before. The commemoration event is filled with brass band music from Denmark, the playing of national anthems, theatrical scenes from slavery performed by visiting African actors and dancers. Suddenly turmoil breaks out at the stage where the invited guests are overlooking the festivities. The commemoration is disrupted because a man is trying to gain access to the stage, but is repelled by a security detail. Within a flash all the prominent guests, ambassadors and officials, are ushered into their bulletproof cars by their bodyguards. Ravn, the actor portraying von Scholten, is confused and startled. Both he and gospel singer Etta Cameron, who – it would seem – just happened to be there, express concern to Larsen's camera about the Danish role in the slave trade and slavery as well as the racial tensions between blacks and whites still evident in the post-colonial community. Cameron is shaken, she says, because there 'could have been a bomb or a pistol'; and Ravn reflects on being on the Islands as a white man knowing the atrocities his ancestors committed there. The scenario described above comprised three minutes of Larsen's TV documentary airing seven years after the event and situated completely out of context for the Danish viewers.

Watching the documentary it is difficult to know who the disrupting man is. Larsen's camera captures the man when he is already on the tribune, vacated when the VIP audience was whisked away. His appearance is subtitled with the name 'Adelbert Bryant' (which is a misspelling) and it is assumed that he is possibly a senator (which is correct). He is agitated and accompanied by supporting cheers while he asserts to the camera that 'the Danish people must understand that no one in Denmark is [his] friend ... until the head of state apologizes'. No other explanation is offered to understand Bryan's agitation and actions. Given this speech, in this context, one might expect Bryan to be a member of a reparation movement on the Islands. However, the TV-documentary never explains the situation further than Ravn's hearsay and Cameron's fears. Journalistically speaking this is, then, an amputated narrative of political, cultural and historical issues at stake in the USVI and in relation to Denmark's colonial past, which generates partial historical knowledge – a journalistic cultural memory.[7]

Re-membering the emancipation

Bryan's disruption of the reenactment event brings to light the dominant representation of the historical relation between Denmark and the USVI on two levels; firstly, it brings about a critique of the arrangement of the event, and secondly it questions the very historical assumptions on which the event was established. It is because of Bryan's actions that questions such as 'who in effect emancipated the slaves: Governor von Scholten or the revolting slaves?' and 'what are the political implications of the decision to perform the historical event: who gets to speak, who is heard and who is silenced?' Bryan's interruption made it clear that the event of reenactment of emancipation given to the Crucian slaves by Danish Governor von Scholten is a reenactment of the archival knowledge – a hegemonic and Euro-centric history-writing.

Librarian archivist and researcher Jeanette Bastian (2003) and sociologist Paul Gilroy (2004) argue that historical archives of written documents are pivotal to 'owning memory' and thereby owning the future (Bastian, 2003). The 'recovery of historical knowledge is felt to be particularly important for blacks because the nature of their oppression is such that they have been denied any historical being', argues Gilroy (2004, p. 280). The USVI is not in possession of its archived history which is shared with Denmark. When the Islands were sold to the US in 1917, Denmark was allowed to collect all official papers and documents pertaining to colonial administration and life in the colonies. These documents are publicly accessible in Copenhagen and written in Danish. It is therefore difficult for non-Danish speakers (such as most USVI citizens) to gain access to their recorded past. If a community does not have access to its historical records, Bastian argues, 'the community will replace them with something else – myth, legend, and oral tradition' (Bastian, 2003, p. 86). This type of cultural knowledge must be continuously defended against the archival and written knowledge figuring in Danish official documents, which only Danish speaking people – in effect the former colonizers – have access to, Bastian contends. This means that a hierarchal structure of power-knowledge is still operational and places the Danish (former) colonizers in an epistemological position of power over the cultural knowledge of the USVI citizens.

The reenactment dispute can be seen as a clash between archival history and cultural knowledge. In an article published in a Danish newspaper shortly after the reenactment in 1998, Larsen states that the disrupting Senator Bryan originally posed the idea of a reenactment of the events of emancipation on the third of July. However, Larsen asserts that Bryan did not intend for it to be a celebration of the Danish governor von Scholten. When the date of the commemoration event drew near Bryan was not included on the list of official speakers at the event, which made him 'storm the stage' (Bedminster, 1998a). Larsen quotes Bryan as saying: '[y]ou have nothing to celebrate. It was not von Scholten who emancipated the slaves. It was my ancestors – following general Buddhoe[8] –who took their freedom' (Larsen, 1998b, my translation). Bryan then demands Larsen make a formal apology on behalf of the Danish people in absence of the Danish queen and Danish politicians. Larsen declines.[9]

The alternative historical knowledge and cultural heritage that Bastian mentions and which Gilroy discusses in his work is based on oral, musical and performative cultural production. This culturally produced knowledge of legends and myths, such as the myth of Buddhoe etc. is prominent in the community of the USVI. The community (re)produces cultural historical knowledge through reenactments and commemorations. The cultural historical accounts can be named 'experienced' – not in the sense of 'being there when it happened' – but in the sense of experiencing the history through narratives, family history and reenactments. Whereas the archival historical accounts may conversely be termed 'documenting' because of their descriptive character – the descriptions of course tend to have a European bias as in the case of the von Scholten-led reenactment. In light of cultural memory productions in journalistic discourse and practice, in the following section, I draw out ways in which experienced and documenting historical narratives account for Bryan's challenge and intervention in the commemoration of the emancipation in 1998 through journalistic articles written in Denmark and the USVI.

Reporting journalistic reenactment

Not the emancipation, not the colonial connection nor the atrocities committed by Danish forefathers, but Senator Adelbert Bryan was the axis around which the journalistic narratives in 1998 spun – both in the USVI and in Denmark. Bryan allowed a cultural memory to be re-membered – drawing the past and the present together. In the two-day issue Sunday–Monday July 5–6 in 1998 of *The Avis*[10] journalist Jamie Bate writes about the turmoil surrounding the reenactment that 'the story of the day was again [like 150 years ago] establishment versus anti-establishment' (Bate, 1998, p.1). The establishment in the twentieth century, from which Bate writes, is represented by the Governor of the Islands, Roy Schneider, and the anti-establishment is represented by Senator Adelbert Bryan. Again, like so many years ago, 'anti-establishment' is depicted as African culture and virtues that are then correlated as disruptive and 'uncivilized' and the 'establishment' is left with a 'blank, stunned look on [its] face' (Bate, 1998, p. 2). Spectators are also left standing in 'unbelieving shock' (Bate, 1998, p. 2). Bate allows the parties of the fight to explain themselves, but nevertheless seems to keep an ironical –perhaps even sarcastic – distance from the subject matter when describing the sequence of events as follows:

> In the early afternoon, the pomp of colonialesque sounds from a brass band added a surreal soundtrack to a program-stopping melee in which Sen. Adelbert Bryan, in full African regalia, wrestled with burly members of Gov. Roy Schneider's security detail. (Bate, 1998, p. 1)

The way Bate insists on the surrealism of the historical adjectives to the events; the 'colonialesque' music and the 'full African regalia', is emphasized later in the story by the description of the audience's surprise and shock and Governor Schneider's 'blank, stunned' facial expression. This particular emphasis constructs Bryan as somewhat stereotypically outlandish. Simultaneously, Bate recognizes the situation as a replica of the past struggles in the sentence reproduced above: '... the story of the day was again establishment versus anti-establishment'. Bate seems to suggest that perhaps it is only the style in clothes (African regalia) and music (brass band) that is different – the issues are still the same. However, a mocking tone seems to find its way into the piece in the way the issues that remain relevant in the community are linked to a long-gone past and to African over-reaction versus white amazement (?). Whiteness is implicitly linked to the amazement over the disruptiveness of the explicitly Africa-centric man through long-established connotations of 'order', 'power' and 'establishment' (Dyer, 1997). Thus, the senator is portrayed as not fitting in when wearing his 'African regalia' and in the same way the surreal brass music from colonial times seems out of (contemporary) tune to *The Avis* reporter. In this article history belongs to and in the past and Bryan's intervention is described as forcing the past into the present where it does not belong. There is an implicit and fixed time-space continuum at work in the article in relation to which Bryan's intervention and Bryan himself stick out. Bate therefore describes it as 'surreal'.

In the *Daily News* Eunice Bedminster (1998) meticulously accounts for the moves and thoughts of the police, gives qualified guesses about Bryan's supposed speech topic had he been allowed to speak at the event,[11] Governor Schneider's plans to prosecute the senator for the disruption and the facial expressions of the USVI Delegate to Congress etc. When reading the *Daily News* article it becomes clear that the supporters of Senator Bryan are people convinced of the overshadowing importance of African roots. Bryan is quoted to say: 'I was born in Frederiksted and I will speak any time I want' (Bedminster, 1998, p. 2). The emphasis placed by Bryan on his place of birth goes hand in hand with a general debate in the community especially in St. Croix in which being 'ban'ya'[12] affords certain credibility to a person. Freedom of speech is in this particular context connected to the privileges that follow local heritage and direct the discussions towards an ideology of authenticity connected to a part of the population. Moreover, supporters express strong concerns that Senator Bryan was not allowed to speak, because 'He represents us all. The other colors up there don't mean anything to us' as one of the supporters expresses it (Bedminster, 1998, p. 2). The sense of urgency is replicated in Larsen's (1998a, 1998b)[13] description of the 'rustling' of the crowd when Bryan approached the stage, the 'shouting' and the 'pushing' of him and the bodyguards surrounding the invited guests and the violence, which occurred. Bryan, Larsen explains, is a politician who is working toward introducing 'original African values' to the USVI and to 'reserve the islands for people who can trace their roots to before the year 1927' (Larsen, 1998b, my translation).[14] The political persuasions of Bryan and his supporters are given space in these articles, but interestingly the issue of violence and criminal behavior is continuously linked to Bryan's politics. Thereby, these articles construct Bryan in an 'un-civilized' portrait focusing several times on his run-ins with the law. The portrait painted of Bryan is therefore stereotypical of colonial discourses focusing on foreignness, disorderly conduct and anti-establishment that are unbefitting and violent.

The USVI cultural memory differs markedly from the Danish in that it is part of a larger common social imaginary. The reenactment is presented as part of the regular daily news-flow and not a particular foreign news piece. This means that the journalists who are writing do not seem to focus so much on having to justify their interest in this issue. They can take the common cultural knowledge and memory for granted. This is evident for instance in that both papers focus on the future-present continuum. *The Avis*, keeping an ironic distance, identifies a dissonance in the representation of the cultural-historical issues on the contemporary political scene, whereas the core of the debate may be the same as underlined in the quote above: 'the story of the day was again establishment versus anti-establishment' (Bate, 1998, p. 1). Similarly, *The Daily News*, in the article 'Emancipation rolls on' (Bedmister, 1998b), accentuates the excitement and the feeling of coherence and contingency expressed by the audience to the event and the citizens of USVI in relation to the commemoration in general. *The Daily News* reporter seems to have perceived that politically the issues are torn and debated, but when it comes to the historical presence of a common past – i.e. the cultural memories – the USVIs are united. It follows that *The Daily News* split the story in two; one that reports on the events and one that focuses on the disruption by Senator Bryan. The disruption can be seen as not merely an interruption of that particular event in 1998 but an interruption of the USVI – and by extension the Danish non-memory – cultural memory. Journalistically, *The Avis* and *The Daily News* deal with this while Larsen, on the other hand, struggles to make the issue concern Denmark.

Journalism as well as academic investigations into colonial pasts and presents are always political (Downing & Husband, 2005). Larsen is political in his newspaper articles, but in a covert way – hiding behind (or perhaps bringing in the political through) a notion of journalistic 'objectivity'. Thus, Larsen represents a certain representational and political view from a Danish perspective to his Danish readers, although he declines to take a publically political stand. However, the USVI journalists draw on other paradigms, no less political than that of Larsen's, to deal with the disruption by building on the implicit commonsense of cultural coherence. Bate (*The Avis*) uses ironical distance to suggest an (at best) embarrassed attitude towards USVI petty politics whereas Bedminster (*The Daily News*) – having the benefit of two separate articles – focuses both on the personal meaning of the emancipation reenactment and the way it brings the community together, and on the political turmoil that divides the people. The two *Daily News* articles clearly show that the reenactment is a personal as well as a political event because of the implicit cultural memory connected to it.

Situated memories

What was emphasized in the journalistic articles from 1998, the experienced history or the documented? What can be learnt from Adelbert Bryan's intervention and contention that he has a right to speak – more so than the other 'colors' – because he is Crucian? It seems fair to say that Senator Bryan's view, as it is presented here, is both nationalistic and racially biased due to his own outbursts as well as those of his supporters. However, his position raises the question already mentioned above: what are the political implications of the decision to perform the historical event in the way it was done: who got to speak, who was heard and who was silenced? Whose version of history is remembered?

The articles portrayed and described Adelbert Bryan as aggressive, ridiculous and a criminal (and the quotes that were used underlined the irrationality of his account). Senator Bryan is depicted as 'the madman' in contrast to the 'civilized' people who stand in shock and awe over the wildness of his behavior. His portrait sets up an opposition between him and the reader in which this element of disorder needs to be suppressed in order to develop 'reason' (Foucault, 2006). Bryan disrupts order with the ambivalence he produces (Baumann, 1991). Bryan is black and he speaks out for the African descendants in St. Croix. The governor Roy Schneider is also black – as is more than 80% of the USVI population – however; within the journalistic narrative he is placed on the side of the 'establishment' and order – and thus on the side of Peter von Scholten, the white Danish governor who preceded him. In the community of the USVI it is not as much a question of hues as it is a question of belonging – on one hand it is a question of 'having been there twenty years and lived through at least one major hurricane'[15] – being 'ban'ya' – or on the other hand being part of the orderly, neo-imperial establishment.

If Bryan constitutes division *Daily News* reporter, Bedminster (1998b), writes about the future, present and past coinciding in the minds and hearts of the audience in a unifying – or perhaps post-racial – context and does not mention the particulars of race, gender, ethnic origin and class. In this way Bedminster may claim an 'objective' position and thus he can speak for all USVI citizens by allowing freedom of speech for all. However, in the feminist tradition this would be considered a mistake. Feminist theorists have argued for 'situated knowledges' (Haraway, 1986) and 'strong objectivity' (Harding, 1993) stemming from an acknowledgement of particularities. Both feminist and 'race' scholars have underscored the importance of embodied differences of experience. Feminist theorists argue that in order to understand and critique the foundations of a given knowledge claim one has to understand and be able to reflect on one's own particularities and situatedness. Reflexiveness is thus pivotal to engaging in a 'strong objectivity' which is rooted in the scientists' (and I argue the journalists') understanding of their own point of departure. This means that particularities such as gender, ethnic origin and 'race' become crucial to 'objectivity' – without an acknowledgement of difference and diversities there is no 'objectivity', feminist theorists argue. 'Race' scholars have in particular developed theories about the interpellating force of visual difference. The experience of looking different from the 'white' norm and the double consciousness (Du Bois) or third-person experiences (Fanon) enhances a certain position from where the world is viewed and known. Feminist ethnographer Gloria Wekker (2006) develops a radical relation against objectivity when she suggests that 'methodology provides information about the various ways in which one locates oneself – psychologically, socially, linguistically, geographically, epistemologically, and sexually – to be exposed to experience in a culture' (Wekker, 2006, p. 4). Wekker's 'inverted model' allows her to take upon herself an active and generative role in her research on female Afro-Surinamese sexuality. Wekker's implication in her research is total in the sense that she acknowledges her own methodological position – as 'an Afro-Surinamese anthropologist who loves women' (Wekker, 2006, p. 4) and who is romantically involved with the main informant of her research. This approach calls attention to the ever-present implicated and complicit position of the researcher. Journalists may find inspiration in Wekker's conceptualisation of positionality bearing in mind the embodiedness and embeddedness of anyone who tries to tell another subject's story. I would hold that merely striving for a journalistic representation emphasizing *unity* and ridiculing difference does not make journalism objective. Rather, the tension between the documented and the experienced 'facts' of the story remains and the journalist has to choose his or her 'truth' of the matter and the unity they choose to represent. All the journalistic products repeated above chose the established, historical and documented 'truth', though some lend space to a more culturally based manifestation of memory.

Becoming memories

I have rehearsed several journalistic accounts given about what happened during the scheduled reenactment of the 1848 emancipation in 1998, all of which displayed political or social bias – that is, they all said more than what was written. Using the reenactment as a case study I have tried to illustrate the implicit cultural and historical assumptions of the journalistic reproduction of cultural memories. Although there are different variations, journalistic practices seem to reproduce an account based on universal objectivity, which is understood to be an undifferentiated account. Feminist theorists have exposed this bias as a disembodied and disembedded 'god-trick'. The USVI constitute a postcolonial community of diasporic majority and are presently under the jurisdiction of the US; moreover they are culturally, historically, geographically and in terms of migration within the population a part of the Caribbean basin. These intrinsic diversities do not mean, however, that the journalistic representation of the culture there is beyond the reach of the paradigm of modernity. Feminist, 'race' and postcolonial theories – and theories of embodied and embedded journalistic practice and subjectivities – therefore offer new ways of analyzing the tensions and questions involved in USVI and Danish journalism about the historical and cultural representations in the USVI territories.

Bryan's interruption made it apparent that the event of reenactment of emancipation given to the Crucian slaves by Danish Governor von Scholten is not only a reenactment based on the archival, white and Euro-centric knowledge claim, but also a reenactment of the Deleuzian concept of 'History' (with a capital H). It follows the Danish official archives that are documents of an established European understanding of what happened. This History does not produce difference in repetition but reproduces a 'state of domination': a new fixed account of History rather than a flexible process of *becoming* memory. History and repetitive reenactment reterritorialize that which is deterritorialized and functions on a molar level – i.e. History is a discourse that is (re)constituted and (re)produced continually by for example journalism – that *unifies* under the heading of the God-trick, the claim of 'objectivity'. Objectivity constructs a 'factual' consensus, which we may all agree upon. However, instead of employing the fixating concept of History, Deleuze and Guattari suggest using memory as a tool of re-creating the past in lines of flight – deterritorialized – and singular. Although the reenactment and commemoration celebrated by Crucians are constructed by memories based on experience (Bastian, 2003) it is a reterritorializing representation built on Historical accounts. Even so, that is not a strong enough departure if we are to utilize the Deleuzian concept of singular memory.

Adrian Parr's (2006) reading of Deleuze and Guattari's concept of memory sees memory as a reterritorialization – a reenactment – a fixing of an event and secondly as a notion of 'singular memory' (Parr, 2006, p. 130). The importance of 'singular memory' is an a-historical force (minoritarian) and its concern with 'history of desire-production' (Parr, 2006, p. 135). To Deleuze and Guattari, memory plays an imaginative role in the reinvention of the self. It is not an imagining of the self as other (Scarry, 1996) because this notion merely resets the binary of self and other, but an imaginative and creatively productive reinvention of the self 'on the basis of what you hope you could become' (Braidotti, 2006, p. 168). It is about creating or experiencing the virtual possibilities that will have been. It is the future perfect tense, which dissolves the past and the future in the remembering of the non-unitary self. To paraphrase Bob Marley, it is a way of not forgetting history and of knowing destiny. Marley's term 'destiny' is important here because destiny can be seen as the future perfect tense: that which will have been. Knowledge produced through remembering history is a creative production and re-invention of the (future) self. Thus, cultural memory of legends and myths and songs is not enough. A *creative imagining* and productive will to allow change to occur, is necessary.

From the above analysis we see that rather than representing history as a majoritarian event the memory or repetition of history needs to question the underlying assumptions of representation – thereby becoming *minoritarian*. Thus the turmoil occurring in relation to the 150th anniversary of the emancipation of the Danish slaves can be seen as a disruption and a questioning of the reenactment and the History it was repeating. The scare caused by the disruptiveness of Bryan created the turmoil that threw into relief the consumerism of the reenactment and the celebrations. His perceived aggressiveness brought forth the complicity of the white colonizers (whose admirable (speech)act of emancipation was on display and in focus) and made apparent 'the comfort found in repressing its own complicity' (Parr, 2006, p. 134) as well as it exposed it to be neo-colonialist and imperialist. The turmoil or disruption, I think, may present a challenge to the representation in that it exposes it as a construction, which in turn is underlined by the Danish actor's remark that he will 'probably not be going on stage today ...'. The archival performance of the day was cancelled; however this does not mean that Bryan's political agenda 'wins' over the agenda set for the reenactment event rather the disruption brings about the possibility of creating a new historical beginning that signals new ways of remembering and writing history (Parr, 2006, p. 142).

Through encounters with others processes occur and, as mentioned above, the disruption created the potential for new spaces of interpretation of the event. But did it enable a creative process or did it reposition the binary of oppression and hegemony? The encounter of the event within the event (as it was abruptly presented in the TV documentary and to some extent in the newspaper articles) was depicted as an aggressive and fearful circumstance. In my analysis, I argue that the un-contextualized aggression blocked the possibility of an affirmative generated *becoming*. Instead the aggression forced a dialectic re-positioning of 'us' and 'them' which denied the viewer a chance for empathy or ethical response. The representation of Bryan was stereotypical of the aggressive African male and did not allow for empathy. Moreover, Bryan underscores the dichotomy of 'us' and 'them' and thus reconstitutes a structure which he holds in common with the Historical view. Bryan relies on an identity-based approach to historical accounts – an approach which re-stabilizes or fixates what his intervention into the reenactment event de-stabilized; and he exchanges History for another History – but a History nonetheless – when he insists on a closed experience of slavery generating a binary of two respectively reciprocal entities. Identity politics, such as this, limits the dialogues and relations between people because it denies access to the other in what might be termed singular relations. It also re-posits memory in the reterritorializing realm of History and common social imaginary. In contrast '[t]he nomadic subject ... engages with his or her external others in a constructive, 'symbiotic' block of becoming, which bypasses dialectical interaction' (Braidotti, 2002, p. 119).

In order for journalism to enable another form of memory production devoid of binaries and negative drives, both the genealogical archival accounts and the memory-driven and legend-based accounts of history need to be questioned. Instead, an affirmative knowledge production may give space for creative imaginings and productions of re-inventions within journalistic production. General and journalistic knowledge about Denmark's colonial past is desperately needed in Denmark, and the USVI journalistic practices may gain creativity by introducing challenges to post-colonial politics and practice. Journalistic practice has to stay aware of the constant repositioning of journalistic production and journalistic subjectivity and assume accountability for the constant re-making of journalistic cultural memories.

Notes

1. Alex Frank Larsen: *Slavernes Spor* [Traces of slaves]. Medialex TV & Film 2007.
2. Denmark colonized most of the Nordic region, such as Norway, Iceland and Greenland. See Loftsdottir for more information in this special issue of *Social Identities*.
3. Besides the Virgin Island possessions, Denmark's southern colonies consisted of forts on the Gold Coast in Ghana and Tranquebar in India.
4. See projects such as www.rethinking-nordic-colonialism.org and conferences like http://blackatlantic.engerom.ku.dk/. On the particularity of the Nordic colonialism see Charpentier, Keskinen, Tuori and Mulinari (2009).
5. The idea of 'journalistic cultural memories' is based on the work and concepts of José van Dijck (2007), who develops the concept of 'personal cultural memory' and defines it as: '*the acts and products of remembering in which individuals engage to make sense of their lives in relation to the lives of others and to their surroundings, situating themselves in time and place*' (van Dijck, 2007, p. 6, italics in original).
6. Frank Larsen, *Slavernes Slægt* [Descendants of slaves] (2005) Medialex TV & Film. For an analysis and discussion of this documentary see Marselis (2008). *Slavernes Slægt* is one of the few journalistic productions dealing with this issue of Danish colonialism.
7. It is not my intention to explore why Larsen kept these three minutes of turmoil in the documentary, although I believe his intentions to be politically engaged.
8. Buddhoe is a local hero and said to be the leader of the emancipation movement which eventually achieved its goal.
9. Larsen's positioning as an 'objective' journalist declining to take a political stand, though his work is obviously politically motivated, is interesting in itself and will be pursued in future work.
10. The USVI has two major newspapers covering the daily news on the islands, *The Virgin Islands' Daily News* (*The Daily News*) and *The St. Croix Avis* (*The Avis*). *The Daily News* is based in St. Thomas, but covers all three islands. It prides itself on its Pulitzer Prize winning articles and its history of investigative journalism. *The St. Croix Avis* or simply *The Avis* is a traditional newspaper still carrying its Danish given name, 'avis', meaning 'newspaper'. The main focus of *The Avis* is the Island of St. Croix where it is considered the local paper. *The Avis* covers many cultural stories and issues of education and health, though investigative journalism also finds its way to the printed pages.
11. Most likely the article states he would have emphasized the lack of General Buddhoe and the superfluous use of the character Gov. Peter von Scholten. – This concurs with Larsen's articles mentioned above.
12. 'Ban'ya' is a Crucian expression meaning 'born here'.
13. In this article I am unfortunately unable to elaborate in detail on the importance of journalistic practice, subjectivity and positioning. This will, however, not be neglected in future work.
14. This particular date corresponds to the time in history when the Afro-Caribbean population on the islands was granted US citizenship, but this is neither explained in the televised nor in the written journalistic narration.

15. Bill Kossler made this questionable remark during an interview about his journalistic work in the territories. Kossler is white, male and in his forties. He is born, raised and has been working for most of his life in the 'continental' US.

References

Bastian, J. (2003). *Owning memory: How a Caribbean community lost its archives and found its history.* Westport, CT and London: Libraries Unlimited.
Bate, J. (1998, June). Emotional high. *The St. Croix Avis*, 155, 1–2.
Baumann, Z. (1991). *Modernity and ambivalence.* Cambridge & Oxford: Blackwell.
Bedminster, E. (1998a, June 4). Bryan storms stage. *The USVI Daily News*, 1–2.
Bedminster, E. (1998b, June 4). Emancipation party rolls on. *The USVI Daily News*, 1–2.
Braidotti, R. (2002). *Metamorphoses.* Cambridge: Polity.
Braidotti, R. (2006). *Transpositions.* Cambridge: Polity.
Charpentier, S., Keskinen, S., Tuori, S., & Mulinari, D. (Eds.) (2009). *Complying with colonialism: Gender, race and ethnicity in the Nordic region.* London: Ashgate.
Dijck, J. van. (2007). *Mediated memories in the digital age.* Stanford, CA: University.
Downing, J., & Husband, C. (2005). *Representing 'race' Racisms ethnicities and media.* London, Thousand Oaks, CA and New Delhi: Sage.
Dyer, R. (1997). *White.* London and New York, NY: Routledge.
Foucault, M. (2006). *Madness and civilization.* New York, NY and London: Routledge.
Gilroy, P. (2004). *After empire: Melancholia or convivial culture?* London and New York, NY: Routledge.
Gøbel, E. (1996). Foreword. In L. Svalesen, *Slaveskibet Fredensborg og dansk-norsk slavehandel i 1700-tallet* [The slaveship Fredensborg and Danish-Norwegian slavetrade in the eighteenth centrury]. Copenhagen: Hovedland.
Haraway, D. (1986). *Simians, cyborgs and women.* London: Free Associated.
Harding, S. (1993). Rethinking standpoint epistemology. What is 'strong objectivity'? In L. Alcoff & E. Potter (Eds.), *Feminist epistemologies.* London and New York, NY: Routledge.
Larsen, A.F. (1998a, August 9). Dansk Vestindien: se, hvad I har gjort [Danish West Indies: Look what you have done]. *Politiken.* Retrieved November 1, 2008, from http://www.infomedia.dk/mediada/politiken.htm
Larsen, A.F. (1998b, June 5). Tumult på vestindiske øer [Turmoil on the West Indian islands]. *Politiken.* Retrieved November 1, 2008, from http://www.infomedia.dk/mediada/politiken.htm
Marselis, R. (2008). Descendants of slaves: The articulation of 'mixed racial ancestry' in a Danish television documentary series. *European Journal of Cultural studies*, 11, 447–469.
Parr, A. (2006). Deterritorializing the holocaust. In I. Buchanan & A. Parr (Eds.), *Deleuze and the contemporary world* (pp. 125–146). Edinburgh: Edinburgh University Press.
Scarry, E. (1996). The difficulty of imagining other people. In J. Cohen. (Ed.) *For love of country: Debating the limits of patriotism* (pp. 98–110). Boston, MA: Beacon.
Wekker, G. (2006). *The politics of passion.* New York, NY: Columbia University.

Europe in motion: migrant cinema and the politics of encounter

Sandra Ponzanesi

Media and Culture Studies/Graduate Gender Programme, Utrecht University, Utrecht, The Netherlands

The article focuses on the contested notion of the (new) Europe from the vantage point of migrant cinema. The aim is to explore how cinematic language offers alternative modalities of representation and subjectification in relation to migration, gender and identity. The emphasis of this analysis is on the politics of encounter: how the presumed strangers to Europe are figurations of Europe's othered self while also embodying the material practices of exclusion. The politics of encounter is explored in three films made by European filmmakers in which the main female character struggles to negotiate her identity in between colonial legacies and global terror, as in the British-Pakistani *Yasmin* (Kenneth Glenaan, UK, 2004), between transsexual and transnational politics, as in the case of the Iranian refugee in *Unveiled* (Angela Maccarone, Germany, 2005), or in between trafficked bodies and renewed citizenship as in the case of the Eastern European immigrant prostitute in *The unknown woman* (Giuseppe Tornatore, Italy, 2006). These visual and ideological commentaries participate in the redefinition or abolition of the notion of Europe by proposing the representations of the strangers within not from original and unexpected positions but by highlighting the transformation of the 'European subject' through the politics of encounter. The article furthermore raises questions about the agency of Muslim women who opt for religion in the midst of the self-professed secular Europe, explores debates on homophobia and the refugee's state of exceptionalism and offers a feminist reading of the phenomena of trafficking of women.

> We have been trying to theorize identity as constituted, not outside but within representation; and hence of cinema, not as the second-order mirror held out to reflect what already exists, but as that form of representation which is able to constitute us a new kind of subjects, and thereby enable us to discover places from which to speak. (Stuart Hall, 1993, p. 402)

Migrant cinema in Europe

This paper focuses on the contested notion of the (new) Europe from the vantage point of migrant cinema. It intends to explore how cinematic language offers alternative modalities of representation and subjectification in relation to post-colonial migrants, political refugees and 'trafficked' women. The emphasis is on the politics of encounter; on how the presumed strangers to Europe are figurations of

Europe's othered self but also embody material practices of exclusion. As Sara Ahmed (2000) poignantly writes:

> Through strange encounters, the figure of the 'stranger' is produced, not as that which we fail to recognise, but as that which we have already recognised as 'a stranger'. In the gesture of recognising the one that we do not know, the one that is different from 'us', we flesh out the beyond, and give it a face and form. (p. 3)

The politics of encounter highlights how strangers were never outsiders but a constitutive part of Europe's project of modernity and of its contemporary global dynamics. This article explores these dynamics in three films made by European filmmakers. Different forms of encounter are staged in the films by proposing alternative models of belonging, identification and affectivity. The main characters in all three films are females struggling to negotiate their identity in between colonial legacies and global terror (as in the case of British-Pakistani *Yasmin*), between transsexual and transnational politics (as in the case of the Iranian refugee in *Unveiled*), and in between trafficked bodies and renewed citizenship (as in the case of the Eastern European immigrant prostitute in *The unknown woman*).

These films are part of a new emerging strand of films generically referred to as migrant cinema. Migrant cinema in Europe is characterized by its primary focus, but not exclusively, on wider socio-political processes that address concepts of European identity and national belonging as a state of being that is contested and fluid. Migrant cinema looks at how colonial legacies and new forms of colonialism, some of which operate under the aegis of globalization, powerfully affect both individual nations and Europe as a whole, and are responsible for new forms of racism, violence and exclusionary practices. Migrant cinema attempts to locate and voice how those who have been kept invisible have become centre-stage multi-cultural and multi-ethnic presences which have revitalized contemporary Europe. This transition is reflected in a growing number of films made by migrant or European filmmakers who challenge traditional concepts of national identity and of 'Europeanness' by revisiting the notions of borders, language and identity from new vantage points. They proffer perspectives that were previously considered marginal and 'external' to the core of Europe. From an aesthetic point of view, migrant cinema introduces a complex and eclectic mix of styles, genres and forms often emanating from non-Western traditions (Naficy, 2001).

Despite agreement on these key elements, migrant cinema remains a rather controversial notion since cinema depends on an extensive collective effort, more so than other creative forms (i.e. literature, art, photography) and therefore complicates the limitations of the label of 'migrant' via a correlation to the director. 'Migrant cinema' stretches along more complex lines of modes of production, distribution channels and targeted audiences. The genesis of film making is therefore less clear when it comes to the question of origin and attribution. To simplify this, we can say that migrant cinema in Europe still hinges on two major definitions: (1) films made by non-European filmmakers; and (2) European films dealing with migrant themes, characters and issues. In this paper I focus on the second definition in order to analyze how European cinema sees itself through the encounter with the other.

The first movie, *Yasmin* (2004), directed by the British Kenneth Glenaan, deals with rising Islamophobia in a town in the north of England following the 9/11 attacks. The film is centered on the figure of Yasmin, a modernized Muslim woman who easily straddles cultural divides. *Yasmin* dramatizes the increasing polarization between the British and Asian immigrant communities, which will eventually lead to Yasmin's retreat into Muslim identity. This article raises questions about the agency of Muslim women who opt for religion amidst an increasingly globalized and homogenized vision of Muslim otherness.

The second film, *Fremde Haut* (*Unveiled*, 2005), directed by the German Angelina Maccarone, deals with the question of political refugees in contemporary Germany by comparing an urbane world (the cosmopolitan Teheran of the sophisticated Fariba and the transgression of sexual boundaries) with an obtuse rural Germany that is prey to bureaucratic totalitarianism, police repression and alienating refugee centers. In this film, unveiling becomes a metaphor for the disguise of identity, both sexual and political. The film can be read against the wider debates on refugee's exceptionalism and homophobia.

The third film, *La sconosciuta* (*The unknown woman*, 2006) was made by the Oscar-winning Italian director Giuseppe Tornatore and deals with the question of migration and the trafficking of women from Eastern Europe to Italy. Migrant women from Eastern Europe who almost 'pass as white', are often forced to deal with the stigma of prostitution before entering the 'legal' circuit of acceptance and social integration. *La sconosciuta* is read against wider debates on trafficking of women and the feminist reading of the phenomenon.

These 'European' filmmakers tackle the social and representational 'emergencies' around old and new flows of migration in their respective countries; and it is interesting to analyze how they give a visual and an aural rendition of the 'other' in European cinema. The other in these films is staged as the main character – the locus from which the echoes of many other possible stories of immigration are refracted. Through the kaleidoscope of personal narratives, the three films attempt to flesh out larger dynamics that are at stake in multicultural Europe by reproducing and contesting many of the stereotypes that the 'female' strangers occupy.

The choice of a female protagonist for these dramas is an interesting one, the more so because it highlights some of the prejudices and stereotypes, though benevolent and paternalistic, on immigrant women who are rebelling against tradition in an era of globalization. Religious fundamentalism, immigration laws and the trafficking of women are some of the recent emergencies created by the speed of globalization that increases the mobility of people, goods and knowledge. These socio-political currents affect the north and the south of the world in unequal ways and resurrect the problems of colonialism, gender discrimination and xenophobia in new and unprecedented ways. Questions of nationality, borders and identity become more intertwined with the market economy, redefining the patterns of global consumption on the material bodies of the newly demarcated outcasts (once the black colonized, and the now Muslim, refugee and trafficked other), the new guests awaiting Western citizenship and welfare.

Strangers in paradise: postcolonial encounters and global terror
Yasmin is a film about a British-Asian woman who easily alternates between her traditional Muslim background and modern Britishness. The film's subtitle is also fitting: 'one woman, two lives'. The film is set in Keighley, one of West Yorkshire's

Figure 4. Yasmin under custody in Muslim clothing. Courtesy of Film4 Library.

stand in an indeterminate state between culture as we see from Figure 4, where she has opted to dress in Muslim clothes while detained in a British police station under the accusation of witholding information about her 'suspected terrorist' husband. She undergoes an identity crisis and begins to find new strength and meaning in her previously transgressed Muslim identity. The film closes with Yasmin veiled and clothed in traditional Muslim garments in the city centre.

Yasmin depicts a failed politics of encounter. The assimilated 'other', in this case Yasmin, metamorphoses from a successful immigrant to a feared stranger. The 'stranger danger' illustrated by Sara Ahmed works differently here since it does not operate as a projection of the Western fear into the 'other', but as a voluntary estrangement embraced by Yasmin to pronounce her difference, making herself into a figure of the unassimilable. By choosing to defend her identity politics, Yasmin becomes the 'figured' other, in which the 'modeled' otherness is borrowed from the West's representations of what makes the 'other' other. Yasmin enacts Spivak's dictum that the subaltern woman cannot speak as she is erased in the act of epistemic violence. Confined between embracing a normative Western identity and a 're-fashioned' Muslim one, Yasmin is silenced in the clash of civilization. Though the film shows her embracing religion as an act of conscious, reasoned free choice, the question remains as to whether she would have turned to Islam had the Western community maintained its multicultural credo.

While men are seen as 'radicalizing' when they turn to Islam, and therefore entering the path of fundamentalism out of choice and free will, women tend to be seen as victims of a patriarchal society that manipulates their religious devotion for political goals. The age-old paradigm of women materializing as the site of conflict between tradition and modernization is re-enacted, replicating colonial times when Western rulers proposed to 'unveil' the Oriental woman in order to lead the backward colonies into modernity (Fanon, 1965; Lewis, 1996; Woodhull, 2003).

In feminist scholarship, the issue of women in fundamentalist movements is highly contentious because there is a tendency to equate religion, in the wider sense but Islam in particular, with women's oppression. A vast scholarship has addressed the issues of how to detect the agency of female converters and whether this would be a case of false consciousness (Saghal & Yuval-Davis, 1992; Bracke, 2004; Mahmood, 2005; Braidotti, 2008). False consciousness in the case of women and fundamentalism is often seen as the manipulation of female agency by religious orthodoxy, which creates the false assumption that women act and operate of their own free will (by choosing to be religious and by being active within society) without realizing that they are part of a larger ideological system that actually oppressed them and steers their choices as independent and autonomous.

This has been contested by several scholars such as Saba Mahmood (2005) who, in her influential work *The politics of piety*, investigates how the adherence of women to the patriarchal norms at the core of Islamic religious movements in Cairo parochialize key assumptions within feminist theory about freedom, agency, authority, and the human subject. Similarly, in her work on women in fundamentalist movements, Sarah Bracke (2008) attempts to unearth the paradox of women who embrace religious fundamentalism, and must therefore conform to strict codes of conduct and clearly defined gender roles, while simultaneously gaining a sense of empowerment within the spaces allocated by the fundamentalist movements. The paradox lies in the contrast between the submission to gender restrictions while at the same time gaining agency through the activism implied in the assertion of the act of devotion. The debate has been previously illustrated by Spivak in her groundbreaking analysis of the rite of sati in colonial India and whether women could be seen as agents in their religious choice of immolation and sacrifice or whether they are the victims of ancient patriarchal oppression that praises their self-annihilation under the banner of devotion (Spivak, 1988).

Though the film does not address the conversion of Yasmin as a path to fundamentalism *per se*, it does show how the foreclosure of a community by xenophobia can lead to 'choices' that can be seen as paradoxical from a feminist perspective. Yasmin's choice is portrayed as a 'cultural need' to find support and offer support to an endangered community. At the end of the film Yasmin embraces her frail and ageing father, who is shaken by the events and the disappearance of his beloved son: this simple and emotional scene shows that in a time of war, family ties and communal cohesion are more important than the independent gains of individual emancipation. Again, the message is complex because it both affirms and problematizes many of the discussions on the incompatibility of feminist agency with group rights.[2]

Yasmin resonates with the wider debates in contemporary Europe about whether or not immigrant women should practice their religion in the private sphere and submit to the enforced model of European secularization, however ambivalent that might be in the public one. The issue of the veil is paradigmatic of the uneasiness with which Europe deals with its internal multiplicity, which makes women, once more, the symbol of conflicting loyalties. This is well addressed by Joan Scott's (2007) book on the *Politics of the veil* which explores the hysteria around the foulard debate in France but whose analysis could also be extended to other European countries where the headscarf is seen as a symbol of Islam's resistance to modernity and as a challenge to values of secular liberalism.[3] The issue of the modern and the secular is more fully explored by Talal Asad (2003) in his *Formations of the secular* in which he argues that anthropologists have oriented themselves to the study of the 'strangeness of the non-European world' and to what are seen as non-rational dimensions of social life (things like myth, taboo, and religion), without adequately studying concepts, practices and formations of the secular which cannot be viewed as a successor to religion, or be seen as on the side of the rational.

The film clearly resonates with all these issues and debates that stirred Europe after 9/11 without falling into didascalic or historically precise references. Yet, as mentioned, it manages to capture the increasing anxiety and tension among radicalising communities, with a clearly emphatic view on the paradoxical position of women as carriers of conflicting cultural values and messages.

In the skin of the other: refugees and sexual politics

Fremde Haut (*Unveiled*, 2005) is a German film directed by Angelina Maccarone that deals with the arbitrary violence of sexual persecution in Iran and of asylum policies in Europe. It is a political film but also a compelling story about the potentiality of migration and the power of love across nations, color and sex. Literally translated, the title of the film is 'stranger's skin', which implies the wearing of another person's identity, as the movie's poster (Figure 5) so effectively visualises. However, the official English version is entitled *Unveiled* and encompasses both the material and symbolic practices of othering. As the director commented in an interview 'Fariba does not have to wear the veil anymore when she arrives in Germany but she has to hide her

Figure 5. Angelina Maccarone's Fremde Haut, *Unveiled*, (Germany, 2005) official German poster. Courtesy of Ventura Film.

true self behind a male disguise. She longs to get rid of this new veil and at the same time fears to be unveiled as a woman by others'.[4]

The film relates the story of the Iranian woman Fariba Tabrizi, played by Jasmin Tabatabai,[5] who flees to Germany to escape persecution for being a lesbian. In Iran homosexuality is a crime punishable by death under the country's theocratic Islamic government. In Europe, asylum is traditionally granted to political refugees who are viewed as victims of persecution by the state. Article 1, part 2, of the United Nations Convention relating to the status of refugees stipulated in 1951, and amended by the 1967 Protocol, provides the definition of a refugee as:

> A person who owing to a well-founded fear of being persecuted for reasons of race, religion, nationality, membership of a particular social group or political opinion, is outside the country of his nationality and is unable or, owing to such fear, is unwilling to avail himself of the protection of that country; or who, not having a nationality and being outside the country of his former habitual residence as a result of such events, is unable or, owing to such fear, is unwilling to return to it.[6]

The legislation is therefore unclear as to whether it supports other kinds of persecution. In the refugee detention centre at Frankfurt airport, Fariba does not dare to claim asylum because of sexual persecution, but she chooses to claim asylum for political reasons in order to comply with the most standardized procedure. Her application is rejected and in desperation she assumes the identity of a fellow asylum seeker from Iran who has committed suicide (Siamak Mustafai), and uses his temporary permit to remain in Germany by swapping her identity with that of a male refugee.

Fariba (on paper Siamak) is relocated in Sielmingen, a rural town near Stuttgart, as we can see from Figure 6, where she has to uphold her male disguise in cramped bedsits. She works illegally as a seasonal employee in a strenuous job at a sauerkraut factory in order to save money for newly forged documents. Fariba is educated, intellectual and well read. She worked in cosmopolitan Teheran as a professional

Figure 6. Fariba as Siamak in front of a German bakery. Courtesy of Ventura Film.

translator and knows German culture and people only from literature. The contrast with the German community is starkly rendered in the scene where she helps her prison guard finish his crossword puzzle by suggesting he adds the word Novalis, which the prison guard is not capable of spelling so he asks her if it is spelled with V or W.

The police interrogation scenes are remarkable and portray the complexity of refugee negotiations. In these scenes, in which an Iranian translator mediates her answers (while she hesitates to communicate her real motives for escape), Fariba becomes frustrated by the style of the interrogation and by the approximations and linguistic errors of her translator. Speaking in perfect and fluent German, she blurts something out, leaving the immigration officer and the translator flabbergasted. By doing so she claims her authority and agency by speaking the language of the reluctant hosts, but at the same time she weakens her status as a victim.

Fariba undermines her claim to asylum because, as Mirian Ticktin (2005) writes, the refugee has to rely on the politics of exceptionalism. Refugees are already discursively positioned as victims in order for provisions to be legitimated. This means that narratives of exceptionalism need to be spun and told. Language and testimony become an essential part of the legal definition of victimhood. These ideas of exceptionalism work as the subtext to the right of protection. Those memories and autobiographical accounts force the refugee subject to create a depiction of self-representation that is left to the vagaries of interpretation and translation. In that sense, testimony, representation and translation are forms of the instrumentalisation of refugees. Fariba's ability to speak fluent German and to overrule her translator undermines her position of victimhood, and her assertiveness contrasts with the narrative of helplessness that she needs to reflect.

Media discourses play a crucial role in the construction of the identity of refugees because they tend to articulate the fears and anxieties of the dominant culture rather than describe the status of the refugees. It is a story about us and not them. Refugees as subjects and as objects: refugees as victims and as individual and collective (faceless and nameless). We see in *Unveiled* how the personal story of Fariba is magnified and depicts the voiceless, faceless and nameless refugees, who in the film only have background roles.

In this respect, Sandro Mezzadra (2001) attempts to expand the model of war to the study of violent processes of control and oppression that target 'illegal immigrants' and also affect asylum seekers and refugees, who are kept at the threshold of the Schengen space. He discusses how the rapidly expanding exploitation of the 'nomadic' labor force goes hand in hand with endemic forms of violence and even overt wars. Mezzadra's analysis of the 'border war' of Europe refers not only to the statistics of the permanent increase in the number of deaths in areas at the periphery of Europe which are officially recorded as casualties or tragic accidents, but it refers to the analysis of the contradictory effects of the violent security policies waged in the 'name of Europe' now aggravated by the conjunctures on the war on terror (as cited in Balibar, 2004, p. 15).

Dal Lago and Mezzadra have also widely explored how the tightening of immigration policies and the strengthening of border controls do not reduce the legal channels of immigration to Europe but have actually resulted in increased illegality as structural characteristics of migration flow (Dal Lago & Mezzadra, 2002). This is also demonstrated by Fariba's story, who enters the path of criminality when

Figure 7. Anne and Fariba in love. Courtesy of Ventura Film.

Siamak's permit of sojourn runs out. To avoid deportation to Iran – where she will most likely be incarcerated and tortured and possibly raped by the prison guards – she resorts to the illegal circuit of passport forgers. In order to raise money to pay for the documents, she steals a car with the complicity of Anne, her German female co-worker. Fariba runs into trouble when she falls in love with Anne, as we can see from Figure 7, and comes dangerously close to unveiling her true identity. Soon after, Fariba reveals her disguise as a man to Ann, a police raid abruptly stalls Fariba's dream and she is deported back to Iran as a 'woman'.

The film builds to an unexpected climax and the final scene, which is the same as the opening one, shows Fariba traveling in a plane above Iranian soil. However, the two scenes differ dramatically: in the opening scene we see Fariba going to the toilet to remove her veil as the pilot announces that they have crossed the Iranian border. In the final scene, on the way back, she goes to the bathroom and we assume that she will re-veil herself and re-enter Iran as Fariba Tabrizi. But with an unexpected twist of the plot, she puts on the glasses and clothes belonging to Siamak and returns to Iran in a 'Fremde Haut', a stranger's skin – once more disguising her identity and gender.

Unveiled revolves around the unstable categories of identity which can be used as a skin to dress, shifting around notions of expectation, complacency and 'passing'. Fariba's attempt to pass as a man in Germany has completely different meanings and functions from those that are enacted when she disguises herself as a man in Iran. Her unveiling becomes a metaphor for the disguise of identity, both sexual and political. Fariba's sexual disguise effectively renders the ambivalence with which the European subject and the stranger encounter each other. Despite Anne's open attitude and interest in Fariba, she recoils when Fariba's true sexual identity is revealed, incapable of restoring the intimacy she has shared with him/her.

> Strange bodies are precisely those bodies that are temporarily assimilated *as* the unassailable within the encounter: they function as the border that defines both the space into which the familiar body – the body which is unmarked by strangeness as its mark of privilege – cannot cross, and the space in which such a body constitutes itself as (at) home. The strange body is constructed through a process of incorporation and expulsion – a movement between inside and outside, which renders that the stranger's

body has already touched the surface of the skin that appears to contain the body-at-home. (Ahmed, 2000, p. 54)

Unveiled offers a subtle view of the problems of identity and its intersection with race, sex and class, stretching the skin of Europe to encompass the infinite variations of othernesses that are already within. The film magnifies the theme of the immigrant having to penetrate Fortress Europe not only by crossing its borders but also by challenging its dominant discourses of heteronormativity. *Unveiled* contests the notion that homosexuality is a Western concept which stands for emancipation and liberation while attempting to reconcile the idea of immigrant, the stranger, with queerness. The model of Europeanness as accommodating sexual 'strangerness' is therefore deconstructed by placing heterosexism as one of Europe's dominant formations in relation to its racist ideology.

Disposable bodies: global mobility, labor and trafficking

La sconosciuta (*The unknown woman*, 2007), was made by the well-known Italian director Giuseppe Tornatore[7] and deals with urgent social issues such as migration, trafficking of women and forced adoption via an aesthetically sophisticated cinematic language. The film could easily be defined as a thriller with a migrant flavor and is in line with a series of Italian films that explore, in a fictionalized way, the encounter between Italian subjects, usually male, with Eastern European migrant women.[8]

Though the motivations behind the making of these films are honorable, as they deal with issues of illegal migration and violence against vulnerable women, the cinematic language used is somewhat ambivalent and often contradictory since the woman is subjected to the logic of the gaze and portrayed as young and naïve but also as a seductive erotic object. *La sconosciuta* is not different. It tells the story of Irina, (played by Xenia Rappaport) a young immigrant woman from Ukraine, who has arrived in Southern Italy through illegal networks. She finds herself entangled in prostitution, where she is exploited for orgies and other abuse by her pimp (played by the famous actor Michele Placido) who is sadistically obsessed with her. Irina eventually manages to escape to an opulent north Italian city (in reality Trieste), where the film is set.

Irina's past and her traumatic memories are conveyed through recurrent flashbacks, whose haunting character can be seen in Figure 8. In one of these scenes we see her being shown naked, in line with many other women, with her face covered by a mask. The location is an abandoned factory and the setting resembles a meat market. We see a pimp peeping through a hole in order to select the 'faceless' women for a prostitution circle. The mask stands for the sexualized representation of the female body, without a head and a name (they have to invent a new 'artistic' one), a body exposed for voyeuristic pleasure and sexual consumption. After her escape, Irina manages to find work as a cleaner in a luxurious apartment complex that is mostly inhabited by the jewellers who live in the northern city. After a while she manages to get herself a position as a nanny for the wealthy Adacher family. Step by step Irina succeeds in infiltrating the life of the Adachers and establishes a strong but increasingly morbid relationship with their daughter Tea, as Figure 9 suggests. Irina is portrayed as a silent and efficient worker but also as someone with a hidden

Figure 8. Xenia Rappaport as Irina in Giuseppe Tornatore, *La sconosciuta* (Italy, 2006). Courtesy of Outsider Pictures.

agenda. Throughout the film Irina repeatedly searches the Adacher's safe in what, we assume, is an attempt to steal the family's valuables. However, at the end of the movie, when Irina is arrested, having been accused of having killed her employer, Tea's mother, we discover that she was searching for Tea's adoption papers, which could prove that Irina is Tea's biological mother.

Through her statement to the police, which is the only moment the spectator is allowed to hear the story of the immigrant woman from her own perspective, we learn that Irina has not only been exploited for prostitution but also for illegal adoption practices. The nine children born of her 'monitored' pregnancies were all sold by her exploiter for a significant sum of money to wealthy Italian families through illegal practices that were legitimized into 'legal ones', her financial return in these transactions being minimal. In her confession Irina explains why she was

Figure 9. Tea carried by her mother after an attack. Courtesy of Outsider Pictures.

determined to claim Tea back, unlike her other progeny. Tea is her last born, and the only child born out of a love relationship with Gino, an Italian man. In the flashback we see Gino sharing with Irina the only happy moments she has had since her traumatic passage to Italy.

La sconosciuta's plot is complicated, full of ambiguities, suggestive metaphors (the dead plants on Irina's windowsill) and many unresolved crimes (Irina's lover, the Adacher's previous nanny, Tea's mother, Irina's pimp) some of which Irina is guilty of in the first degree. Irina will eventually be released from further charges, but is unable to claim her right to motherhood as the DNA test will show that Tea is not her biological daughter. The film leaves us with the idea of Irina as a woman who strikes back and avenges herself, but who remains somewhat empty handed since her future depends on the persuasiveness of her Italian lawyer to spin tales of victimhood in order to get her off the hook with the police. Irina is once again at the mercy of her Italian hosts, even though the terms of negotiation have changed from passive objectivity (the disposable body of the trafficked woman) to illicit subject (the Slavic immigrant as the criminal other).

La sconosciuta does not delve into the reasons behind the migration of many women such as Irina, instead it emphasizes the many forms of criminalization attached to it and the biased reception of Eastern European women in Italian society, stigmatized, despite their often high educational level, as 'oppressed' but also as 'dangerous'. Áine O'Healy comments that Italian films on female migration made in the 1990s offer representation strategies that serve both to eroticize and depict the abject suffering of the Eastern European female migrant. These strategies resonate with the inherent sadistic paradigm of Oedipal narratives as described by Teresa de Lauretis (1982) as these films:

> Offer striking images of injury and debasement enacted against the women immigrant, who is alternatively fetishized and positioned as an abject other by the signifying strategies of the filmic text. Yet, the violence perpetuated against her is carefully 'justified' by the patriarchal logic of narrative realism, ostensibly appealing to the spectator as compassionate witness to her abuse. (O'Healy, 2008, p. 41)

La sconosciuta proffers an example of the dominant representation and commentary (both stereotypical and otherwise) on issues of immigration and trafficking of women in Italy. Italy has an exceptional position on immigration as its colonial legacy was denied only until recently (Del Boca, 1976–1986; Labanca, 2007; Ponzanesi, 2004). Since the 1980s the rapidly escalating number of migrants, asylum seekers and refugees coming not only from the former Italian colonies in the Horn of Africa (Somalia, Eritrea, Ethiopia) but also from the Maghreb and other African countries, and from Latin America, the Middle East, and Eastern Europe (especially after the fall of the Berlin Wall and the war in Yugoslavia), has drastically changed the structure of Italian cities. This means that immigration to Italy has been received as something of a shock, framed as a national 'emergency' in alarming tones and concomitant incompetent juridical approaches.[9]

La sconosciuta does not directly touch upon the question legislations on immigration and how the tightening of borders and the reduction of legal channels of migration actually make migrant women more vulnerable to the effect of economic exploitation and social marginalization. This happens in particular when third parties see the 'economic' value of organizing illegal immigration that target women as a principal 'object' of revenue. Feminist theories that attend to the importance of locating women in positions other than that of coercion or depictions of exploitative and slavery-like conditions, show how the trafficking of women does not need to focus on the 'gender' element of exploitation but on the 'economic' one, since women are valuable commodities, not because of their sexual difference but because of the 'function' they come to fulfill in the host society. Europe therefore, and its differentiated policies towards prostitution and immigration, is not only responsible for and complicit in the trafficking of women but also for the reduction of the female subject to a sexual object, and thereby resorting to victimizing images of female bodies in their attempt to rescue them.

In her work on trafficking in women, Andrijasevic makes a case for mapping the link between trafficking and the current redefinition of European spaces and people. Her crucial point is that 'the representation of trafficking along the criminal-victim nexus is implicated in sanctioning the membership in the European community and consequently in establishing the material and symbolic boundaries of the European citizenship in the making' (Andrijasevic, 2004, p. 11). Border and immigration regimes create the conditions for the existence of trafficking and exploitation of women's labour in prostitution. Andrijasevic argues that in order to detect female agency it is important to analyze how these women come into contact with the trafficking networks and to explore the possibility of negotiations and articulations that they have within and outside them. Entering trafficked networks is often informed by women's desire for mobility, namely by their migratory project (Andrijasevic, 2010).

What is interesting in the case of migration from Eastern Europe is the issue of racialization, namely by looking at the ways in which the 'whiteness' of Eastern European women is repeatedly emphasized. This construction positions Eastern European women as racially indistinguishable from 'European' women (and therefore passing as Western) while at the same time it differentiates them from their European counterparts by identifying trafficked women as victims of patriarchal social relations. Therefore, it is relevant to quote Paul Gilroy (2004) who in his *After empire* poignantly positions the displacement mechanism which takes place in the question of immigration and racial theories. The arrival of newcomers to Europe, from Eastern Europe for example, is played around the politics of passing, by choosing to magnify whiteness to downplay foreignness:

> They [immigrants] too will seek salvation by trying to embrace and inflate the ebbing privileges of whiteness. That racialised identification is presumably the best way to prove they are not really immigrants at all but somehow already belong to the home-space in ways that the black and brown people against whom they have to compete in the labour market will never be recognized as doing. (Gilroy, 2004, pp. 110–111)

La sconosciuta has an ambivalent role in representing the Eastern migrant woman and does not proffer a very sophisticated one if we consider the debates described. Yet, it manages to forcefully address an issue that would otherwise remain taboo or restricted to police proceedings. The film falls back on forms of voyeurism (especially the already mentioned opening scenes in which women are treated like slaves in a market) and indulges in several clichéd representations of trafficking that render women's bodies as passive objects of male violence and gaze and replicates traditional stereotypes of Eastern European women's femininity. However, it also illustrates the politics of encounter between the Italians and the new immigrant, placing the position of the Eastern woman to a much more dangerous proximity than the above analyzed figures of the Muslim woman or the lesbian asylum seeker. Whiteness being one of those markers of apparent 'proximity' that makes the stranger other fatally close, and yet never fully assimilable because she is subjected to other markers of social exclusion (such as marginalized forms of work: domestic care, assistance to elderly people and prostitution).

Conclusions

The films analyzed in this article were made by fairly well established European filmmakers and do not necessarily depart from dominant cinema – they use mainstream techniques and genres to address the issue of migration, identity and gender in the different national constituencies (United Kingdom, Germany, Italy). *Yasmin*, *Fremde Haut* and *La sconosciuta* portray specific local realities that are determined by the globalization of labor forces, religious revival and the globalization of sex. The choice for European filmmakers was motivated by the desire to untangle the various representations of the 'other' circulating in the new Europe, a discourse that is obsessed with the figure of the 'Muslim', the refugee and the trafficked woman as the new marginal positions that have replaced the previous postcolonial subjects in the struggle to claim European citizenship and identity.

Migrant cinema literally gives a face and a form to those defined as strangers. The investment in the figure of the stranger involves making claims about the stranger's being. As Ahmed writes, the celebration of the stranger inevitably involves the problems of anthologizing the stranger, by giving the stranger the status as a figure that contains or has meaning. In theory we are all strangers as almost all people are displaced, become immigrants or because of globalization's increasing mobility. Ahmed cites Diken who proposes a kind of universalization of the strangers and states that 'with the strangers we find ourselves' (Diken, 1998, p. 124) proposing a journey towards the stranger that becomes a form of self-discovery. However, as Ahmed (2000, p. 6) further argues, rendering strangers internal rather than external to identity, which brings us to the conclusion that we are all strangers to ourselves as Kristeva proposes, implies avoiding the political processes which designate some others as being stranger than other others. Ahmed argues that we need to consider how the stranger is an effect of the processes of inclusion and exclusion that constitutes the boundaries of bodies and communities. She describes these processes in terms of encounters, suggesting a meeting that involves recognition but also conflict. As Ahmed further writes:

> These others cannot be simply relegated to the outside: given that the subject comes into existence as an entity only through encounters with others, then the subject's existence cannot be separated from the others who are encountered. As such, the encounter itself is ontologically prior to the question of ontology (the question of the being who encounters). (Ahmed, 2000, p. 7)

Yasmin, *Fremde Haut* and *La sconosciuta* articulate the different positions that the stranger plays in the politics of encounter as illustrated by Sarah Ahmed, both in representational and material terms. Through the illustration of three characteristic films, this article has shown how the stranger remains inassimilable and unassailable both as figuration and as a subject. The films' visual and ideological commentaries participate in the redefinition or abolition of the notion of Europe which no longer functions as a self-contained entity but searches for alternative modalities (the famous borders within and without mentioned by Balibar [1998]) that are making Europe vacillate by proposing not only the representations of the strangers within from original and unexpected positions but also by highlighting the transformation of the 'European subject' through the politics of encounter. As Bo Stråth has said: 'We should recognize that Europe can also emerge as the other from within, that is, from within what others consider to be Europe, as a kind of self-imposed exclusion' (Stråth, 2000, p. 15).

Migrant cinema in Europe is a privileged point of departure from which to explore how the 'stranger' is aurally and visually rendered, in keeping with Ahmed's idea that the stranger is opposite to but also constitutive of Europe's othered self. *Yasmin*, *Fremde Haut* and *La sconosciuta* were not chosen because they are exemplary, or representative in essentialist ways, but because they illustrate the symptomatic, and therefore significant, processes of recognition and differentiation, of inclusion and exclusion, of ideological constitution and deconstruction in the new Europe from a gendered postcolonial perspective.

Notes

1. *My son the fanatic* was released in 1992, directed by Udyan Prasad and based on a script by Hanif Kureishi. The Pakistani driver Parvez, played by Om Puri, has a relationship with the young British prostitute Bettina. While his family crumbles, Parvez's son, Farid, gradually rejects Western institutions and values and turns to Islamic fundamentalism. Kureishi's screenplay effectively dramatises the rise of fundamentalism in a Northern England town (in the wake of the Rushdie affair, 1989) with the son becoming holier than the father in the family. In his novel the *Black Album* Kureishi also tackles the issue of a young Asian man, Sahid Hasan, growing up in Britain amidst the rising forces of Islamic fundamentalism. Set in 1989, in the year the *fatwah* was declared against Salman Rushdie, the novel is a convincing portrayal of the rootlessness probably felt by many British Asians growing up with conflicting loyalties towards Islam and Western liberal culture.
2. There is a vast debate on whether multiculturalism and feminism can be seen as compatible terms. The debate, stirred in the first instance by Okin's (1999) polemical text *Is Multiculturalism Bad for Women?*, departs from a vision of gender equality as clashing with the interest of minority cultures and individual rights. The fundamental position of 'Western' feminist movements (in its more essentialist approaches) states that gender equality cannot be sacrificed in the name of group rights, which often do reinforce existing hierarchies. However, as the many responses to Okin have demonstrated, the definition of minorities can be essentialistic and universalizing, and if there is a need to account for conflicts within and among minority groups (such as the implicit and reified gender inequalities) this need should be specified and addressed within the group itself and not in the name of 'women' in the general sense (Ponzanesi, 2007).
3. Joan Scott emphasizes the conflicting approaches to sexuality that underlie the headscarf debate. She claims that French supporters of the ban view sexual openness as the standard for normalcy, emancipation, and individuality, and therefore modernisation, whereas the sexual modesty implicit in the wearing of the headscarf is proof that Muslims can never become fully French.

4. The English title *Unveiled* was conceived by the US distributor of the film. See Swartz (2005).
5. Jasmin Tabatabai moved, aged 12, with her mother and siblings from Teheran to Germany. The performance of Jasmin Tabatabai has been much praised by critics and audiences alike. She convincingly plays a 30 year old woman who has to cope not only with the loss of her own identity and cultural background but also with the denial of her sexual desires and leanings out of concern for her own safety. The film makes a connection between the homophobic legislation in Iran as much as with repressive German normality (law and order). As the actress said, the 'trousers role' already existed in Shakespeare's time, as well as in *Yentl* or *Boys don't cry* but unveiled is more than a question of identity crisis, but of the risk in living in a foreign skin for survival with all the sexual and political connotations and consequences that that entails. See interview with Jasmin Tabatabai on the film *Unveiled* and Press Release (2005).
6. From www.unhcr.org/protect/PROTECTION/3b66c2aa10.pdf. See also http://www.unhcr.se/SE/Protect_refugees/pdf/magazine.pdf. Retrieved 10 September 2009.
7. The Italian director Giuseppe Tornatore achieved international acclaim and status with his film *Nuovo cinema paradiso* (Oscar for Best Foreign Language Film, 1990). The film before *La sconosciuta*, *Malena* (2000), was badly received as a voyeuristic film which mainly focused on the sex appeal of the female actress, Monica Bellucci, and organized around the exoticising and glossy images of a touristy and picturesque Italy. *La sconosciuta* is Tornatore's comeback and was awarded numerous prizes, both nationally and internationally. Ennio Morricone, one of the world's most famous soundtrack artists, delivered the suggestive soundtrack which alternates delirious violins with a sad and mellow melody. With *La sconosciuta* Tornatore avenges himself from the previous trademarks of nostalgic sentimentalism.
8. Recent examples of movies dealing with vulnerable migrant women portrayed in their victimised status but ambivalent eroticism are Carlo Mazzacurati's *Un'altra Vita* (1992) about the Russian Alia, *Vesna va veloce* (1996) about the Czech Tereza, Corso Solani's *Occidente* (2000) about the Romanian Malvina, Silvio Soldini's *Un'Anima divisa in due* (1993) about the gypsy Pabe, Armando Manni's *Elvjs & Merilijn* (1998) about the Romanian Ileana, Gianluca Maria Tavarelli's *Portami via* (1994) about Cinzia, from Bulgaria, and Christina, a Russian, who are callgirls.
9. The various improvised laws that attempted to regulate and legislate the presence, residence and right to citizenship of the newcomers were each more inadequate and disastrous than the other (Legge Martelli, 1990, Turco-Napolitano, 1998; Bossi-Fini, 2002; pacchetto-sicurezza 2009). The sudden influx of immigration to Italy (chaotically hosted in detention centres, refugee camps and improvised 'centri di accoglienza' [hosting centres]) was not a temporary emergency but destined to continue. The short-sighted legislation did not foresee that the sudden migration to Italy was not only due to its kilometres of unguarded coasts, which made Italy susceptible to many destitute people from nearby countries such as Albania (often using Italy as a transit zone for further migration to Northern Europe), but to a complex logic of late capitalism which intersected patterns of migration with the globalization of the labour force. Migration could therefore not be thought of outside the social and economic development of Italy itself but the fear of the other, as the resurrection of the unprocessed colonial past, re-emerged in Italy with violence. As Parati very poignantly remarks: 'The beginning and end of the century locate Italians on opposite positions' (Parati, 1999, p. 39) but Italian society has not yet adjusted to this new configuration.

References

Ahmed, S. (2000). *Strange encounters. Embodied others in postcoloniality*. London: Routledge.
Andrijasevic, R. (2004). *Trafficking in women and the politics of mobility in Europe* (Unpublished doctoral dissertation). Utrecht University, The Netherlands.
Andrijasevic, R. (2010). *Migration, agency and citizenship in sex trafficking*. Houndmills, Basingstoke: Palgrave.

Asad, T. (2003). *Formations of the secular. Christianity, Islam, modernity*. Stanford, CA: Stanford University Press.
Balibar, E. (1998). The borders of Europe. In P. Cheah & B. Robbins (Eds.), *Cosmopolitics. Thinking and feeling beyond the nation* (pp. 216–229). Minneapolis, MN: University of Minnesota Press.
Balibar, E. (2004, November). *Europe as borderland*. Paper presented at the Alexander van Humboldt lecture in human geography, University of Nijmegen. Retrieved from http://socgeo.ruhosting.nl/colloquium/Europe%20as%20Borderland.pdf
Bracke, S. (2004). *Women resisting secularisation in an age of globalisation* (Unpublished doctoral dissertation). Utrecht University, The Netherlands.
Bracke, S. (2008). Conjugating the modern/religious, conceptualizing female religious agency contours of a 'post-secular' conjuncture. *Theory, Culture & Society, 25*(6), 51–67.
Braidotti, R. (2008). In spite of the times. The postsecular turn in feminism. *Theory, Culture & Society, 25*(6), 1–24.
Chadha, G. (Producer & Director). (2002). *Bend it like Beckham* [Motion picture]. United Kingdom: Kintop Pictures.
Curling, C. (Producer), & Prasad, U. (Director). (1997). *My son the fanatic* [Motion picture]. United Kingdom: Arts Council of England.
Dal Lago, A., & Mezzadra, S. (2002). I confini impensati del'Europa [The unimagined frontiers of Europe]. In H. Friese, A. Negri & P. Wagner (Eds.) *Europa politica: Ragioni di una necessità* [*Political Europe: Reasons for a necessity*] (pp. 143–157). Rome: Manifestolibri.
De Lauretis, T. (1982). *Alice doesn't: Feminism semiotics cinema*. Bloomington, IN: Indiana University Press.
Del Boca, A. (1976–1986). *Gli Italiani in Africa Orientale. Dall'unità alla marcia su Roma* [Italians in Oriental Africa. From unity to the march on Rome], vol. I; *La conquista dell'impero* [The conquest of empire], vol. II; *La caduta dell'impero* [The fall of empire], vol. III; *Nostalgia delle colonie* [The nostalgia for the colonies], vol. IV. Laterza: Bari.
Diken, B. (1998). *Strangers, ambivalence and social theory*. Aldershot: Ashgate.
Fanon, F. (1965). Unveiling Algeria. In F. Fanon, *A dying colonialism* (pp. 35–67). New York, NY: Grove Press.
Fattori, L. (Producer), & Tornatore, G. (Director). (2006). *La Sconosciuta* [*The unknown woman*] [Motion picture]. Italy: Manigolda Film/Outsider Pictures.
Fischer, M. (Producer), & Maccarone, A. (Director). (2005). *Fremde Haut* [*Unveiled*] [Motion picture]. Germany: Wolfe Releasing.
Gilroy, P. (2004). *After empire: Melancholia or convivial culture?* London and New York, NY: Routledge.
Hall, S. (1993). Cultural identity and diaspora. In P. Williams & L. Chrisman (Eds.), *Colonial discourse and post-colonial theory: A reader* (pp. 392–403). New York, NY: Harvester Wheatsheaf.
Hibbin, S. (Producer), & Glenaan, K. (Director). (2004). *Yasmin* [Motion picture]. United Kingdom: Parallax Independent.
Labanca, N. (2007). *Oltremare. Storia dell'espansione coloniale italiana* [*Overseas. The history of Italian colonial expansion*]. Bologna: Il Mulino.
Lewis, R. (1996). *Gendering orientalism: Race, femininity and representation*. London: Routledge.
Mahmood, S. (2005). *Politics of piety: The Islamic revival and the feminist subject*. Princeton, NJ: Princeton University Press.
Mezzadra, S. (2001). *Diritto di fuga. Migrazioni, cittadinanza, globalizzazione* [*Right of escape. Migration, citizenship and globalization*]. Verona: Ombre Corte.
Naficy, H. (2001). *An accented cinema: Exilic and diasporic filmmaking*. Princeton, NJ: Princeton University Press.
O'Healy, Á. (2008). Border traffic: Reimagining the voyage to Italy. In: K. Marciniak, A. Imre & A. O'Healy (Eds.), *Transnational feminism in film and media* (pp. 37–52). New York, NY: Palgrave.
Okin, S.M. (1999). *Is multiculturalism bad for women?* Princeton, NJ: Princeton University Press.

Parati, G. (1999). *Mediterranean crossroads: Migration literature in Italy.* Madison and London: Fairleigh Dickinson University Press/Associated University Press.
Ponzanesi, S. (2004). *Paradoxes of post-colonial culture. Contemporary women writers of the Indian and Afro-Italian diaspora.* Albany, NY: Suny Press.
Ponzanesi, S. (2007). Feminist theory and multiculturalism. *Feminist Theory, 8,* 91–103.
Saghal, G., & Yuval-Davis, N. (1992). *Refusing holy orders: Women and fundamentalism in Britain.* London: Virago.
Scott, J.W. (2007). *The Politics of the veil.* Princeton, NJ: Princeton University Press.
Spivak, G. (1988). Can the subaltern speak? In C. Nelson & L. Grossberg (Eds.), *Marxism and the interpretation of culture* (pp. 271–313). Urbana, IL: University of Illinois Press.
Stråth, B. (Ed.) (2000). *Europe and the other and Europe as the other.* Brussels: Peter Lang.
Swartz, S. (2005, November 17). 'Interview with *Unveiled* director Angelina Maccarone.' AfterEllen.com. Retrieved September 10, 2009, from http://www.afterellen.com/archive/ellen/Movies/2005/11/unveiled.html
Tabatabai, J. (2005). Interview and Press Release for *Unveiled*. Retrieved September 10, 2009, from http://jasmin-tabatabai.com/english/film_fremde_haut.htm.
Ticktin, M. (2005). Policing and humanitarianism in France: Immigration and the run to law as state of exception. *Interventions, 7,* 347–368.
Udwin, L. (Producer), & O'Donnell, D. (Director). (1999). *East is East* [Motion picture]. United Kingdom: Film4.
Woodhull, W. (2003). Unveiling Algeria. In R. Lewis & S. Mills (Eds.), *Feminist postcolonial theory: A reader* (pp. 567–585). Edinburgh: Edinburgh University Press.

Multiculturalism in a selection of English and Spanish fiction and artworks

Lourdes López Ropero[a] and Alejandra Moreno Álvarez[b]

[a]English Department, University of Alicante, Alicante, Spain; [b]Department of Anglogermanic and French Studies, University of Oviedo, Oviedo, Spain

> Discourses of cultural pluralism in literature, cinema and art today prove that inter-ethnic relations in Europe are moving towards, and in some spaces have already achieved, a spontaneous conviviality, in spite of the presence of racism and social injustice. Though the focus will be on the long-standing British multicultural experience, attention will also be paid to the case of Spain, a much younger country of migration. The specific histories of migration of these countries will also be tackled.

Migration, diasporic or transcultural processes which have conditioned the lives of millions of people in Europe have made it almost impossible to connect their identity to a specific and unitary location. In this context, the question 'who am I?' needs to be asked not only in connection to one's roots, which are often found in different continents, but also in relation to one's routes. The postmodern celebration of movement, travel, and rootlessness as alternative processes of identity formation has opened up unending possibilities for the de/construction of old subjectivities, once defined in relation to national and cultural attachments which no longer prove stable and valid. Likewise, the capacity of many individuals to develop a sense of identity precisely because of not being linked to a specific location or because several places serve them simultaneously as points of reference has proved a useful tool for the recognition of hybrid identities and cultural formations developed in this large contact zone which Europe has become. Quoting Rosi Braidotti (1994), Suárez Lafuente highlights, in *La historia espacial en la novela inglesa contemporánea* [The history of space in the contemporary English novel] (2007), 'that the nomadic subject is formed by various axes becoming a narrative entity and a political recreation who can surpass different categories and levels of experience diluting, at the same time, the limits of difference without burning the norm' (2007, p. 192). Critical theory and literature become the natural space where the nomadic subject becomes an entity who un/identifies itself in order to be identified. This allows the nomadic subject to negotiate all the possible norms of social implementation of these new positions of the postmodern subject. As Suárez Lafuente also argues, it was Zygmunt Baumann

(1996) who underlined that 'identity, though ostensibly a noun, behaves like a verb' (as cited in Suárez Lafuente, 2007, p. 192).[1]

Stuart Hall has talked about these issues from his perspective as a British citizen of Jamaican descent. In this sense, Hall rejects essentialist notions of the subject and admits that identity is always in process, can never be fixed and must be understood as a question of becoming, rather than of being. Yet, despite concurring with the idea that essentialist notions of the subject can no longer hold in this continuous re/formative process, Hall warns us against assuming that a post-identity stage is possible and/or desirable. Conceding that subject and identity are some of the most contested notions today, Hall stresses nonetheless that they are notions which are still in demand and have continued to proliferate under different guises (1996, p. 248). Therefore, he calls for strategic and provisional discursive positions which allow for the articulation of identitarian meaning. In the context of migration and diaspora, the need for subjects to establish positional notions of identity is directly related to the establishment of a sense of place in the host country, as a substitute for the land they have left behind and on which they continue to feed imaginatively. In this sense, migrants have to ask themselves questions about where they are before they can even begin to solve the problem related to who they are (Dong, 2004, p. 66). Natives also have to ask themselves the same questions as their Motherland has been altered into the (m)otherland due to the plurality and diversity of subjects that inhabit nowadays the multicultural territory.

In *After empire: Melancholia or convivial culture?* Gilroy defines 'conviviality' as 'the processes of cohabitation and interaction that have made multiculture an ordinary feature of social life in Britain's urban areas and in postcolonial cities elsewhere' (2004a, p. xi). It is worth noting that Gilroy uses the word *multiculture* instead of *multiculturalism*. For Gilroy, multiculturalism, understood as an 'active ideology' that involves government action, does not exist in Britain. Similarly, the Commission on the Future of Multi-Ethnic Britain, set up in 1998, and resulting in the 2000 Parekh report, concluded that even though 'the movement towards a multicultural, multi-ethnic Britain has been decisive', it is not 'yet an accomplished fact', since 'much of the country, including many significant power centres, remains untouched by it' (Bhikhu, 2000, p.15). In spite of this, Gilroy insists, there does exist in Britain a spontaneous, 'vibrant multiculture', the inevitable product of the country's 'long experience of convivial post-colonial interaction' (Gilroy, 2004b). The author also highlights in *Postcolonial melancholia* how conviviality does not erase racism or inscribe the triumph of tolerance but 'suggests a different setting for their empty, interpersonal rituals, which . . . have started to mean different things in the absence of any strong belief in absolute or integral races' (2005, p. xv). To sum up, conviviality, which does not preclude intolerance, is the inevitable result of decades of cohabitation of different races in Britain. It is spontaneous for it does not depend on the demands made on citizens by others.

This essay examines discourses of cultural pluralism through literature, cinema and art in order to prove that hybrid identities are moving towards, and in some spaces have already achieved, this conviviality. In fact, Gilroy highlights the contribution, necessary though not sufficient, of the arts, including literature, to this process (2004a, p. 157). Though the focus will be on the British experience, attention will also be paid to the experiences of another European country, Spain. Certainly, migration policies are the subject of much debate almost everywhere in

Europe nowadays and, given the increasing influence of the European Union, migration has a continental dimension that transcends national borders. In fact, this geopolitical entity is increasingly becoming a larger narrative to which its members must 're-connect' themselves, as Yasmin Alibhai-Brown remarks speaking of Britain's need to increase its commitment to its 'European future' (2000, p. 59). Our comparative approach responds to this call for re-connection. Significantly, despite Britain's and Spain's distinct histories of migration and cultural interaction, the former having a much longer tradition of immigration, the latter has encountered similar challenges, which point at the convenience of relating to a common European narrative. At this juncture, it becomes necessary to discuss the distinctive features of the British and Spanish experiences of migration.

A brief history of race relations in Britain and Spain

The 23 June 2008 edition of the newspaper *The Guardian* is very revealing of the English history of race relations and its present convivial culture. The news item features the two artists commissioned to fill the fourth plinth on London's Trafalgar Square. Named after the famous battle where the English, led by Admiral Nelson, defeated the French, the square is peopled with sculptures of English national heroes like George IV, Nelson himself, or Henry Havelock, a general famously involved in the Indian Munity. Yet, one of these plinths holds no statutes but has been used as a rotating site where, since 1999, when the Royal Society of Arts launched The Fourth Plinth project, contemporary artists exhibit their work. The two winning proposals for the coming year (2009) are from Antony Gormley and Yinka Shonibare, both of whom emphasize diversity in their works. While the former will have an ordinary person stay on the plinth for an hour, for every hour of 100 days, doing whatever they please, the latter will put up his Nelson's Ship in a Bottle, a replica of the old ship with sails made of colorful African fabric.

Even if Shonibare's hybrid ship could be approached as an overt, though somehow belated, denunciation of Britain's infamous involvement in the slave trade, or as a reminder that Britain's overseas empire and its dominance over other European nations were part of the same enterprise of national greatness, the London-born artist of Nigerian background has acknowledged that his piece is 'a reflection on, and celebration of, multiculturalism in London today' (Brown, 2008). As a reflection on multiculturalism, the artifact undermines the notion that 'postcolonial people are only unwanted alien intruders without any substantive historical, political, or cultural connections to the collective life of their fellow subjects' (Gilroy, 2004a, p. 98). By exposing Londoners to Nelson's Ship in a Bottle, and by doing it in a location with such nationalist and melancholic overtones, Shonibare reminds them that the cultural diversity found in London and in other English cities is not a random occurrence but the result of long-standing historical, cultural and political connections with other nations. On the other hand, as a celebration, Shonibare's installation testifies to the fact that, despite the enduring presence of racism and inequality in British society, a convivial culture has emerged.

At this point it should be said that, as the title of Gilroy's volume shows, discussions of multiculturalism are generally loaded with ambivalence. Britain has come a long way from the rivers of blood speeches, yet Gilroy remarks that it may sound 'naïve' to speak of living with difference in the face of 'global inequalities and conflicts over resources' (2004a, p. 5). Similarly, Vron Ware states that British multiculturalism appears 'more fragile than ever' and points at the unprecedented success of the British National Front in the local elections of 2006 (2007, p. 53). Graham Huggan goes so far as to describe British multiculturalism as a 'virtual' construction created by politics and the media, questioning the overall efficacy of multicultural policies given the xenophobia and nationalism sweeping the New Europe (2001, pp. 81–82). The same tentativeness underlies Tariq Modood's statements when he concludes that 'there is an emerging recognition that multiculturalism means a new way of being French, a new way of being German, a new way of being British, and perhaps also a new way of being European' (1997, p. 24). Similarly, in her volume, aptly titled *After multiculturalism,* Yasmin Alibhai-Brown claims that the notion of multiculturalism, dating back to 1950s Britain, needs to be upgraded. If the debate on multiculturalism has so far revolved around the entitlement of minorities – namely 1950s immigrants (2000, p. 9) – to stay in the UK and to have a voice in their hostland, 'the next phase must be about collectively *reimagining* ourselves and the society in which we live' (2000, p. 11, our emphasis). This approach involves acknowledging the complex bonds that now link Britain to the rest of the world and to its 'European future' (2000, p. 59). Indeed, the challenge of diversity that European Union countries face, stemming from the legacy of their empires or from the impact of global problems, is compounded by their membership in the EU, which entitles new members to move and work freely across the EU. As Pnina Werbner rightly points out, 'Europe today... is the product of postcoloniality: a continent of immigrants and their descendants' (1997, p. 261). EU directives, the legacy of the former empires, and global problems, all combine to make European countries increasingly multicultural and to intensify the challenge of living with difference.

The only immigration-related item featured in the 23 June 2008 edition of the Spanish newspaper *El Mundo* contrasts with that in *The Guardian*. As the Spanish national team struggled to beat Italy on penalties in a quarterfinal match of the European Championship, the news item reports, an avalanche of sub-Saharan immigrants swarmed into the Melilla border hoping to catch the Spanish local authorizes off guard and engrossed in the penalty shootout (Sánchez, 2008). Melilla is a Spanish enclave in northern Africa whose conquest dates back to 1497, a time when Spain was expanding its colonies into the New World and other places under the Catholic Monarchs Isabella and Ferdinand. This remnant of the Spanish Empire is now used by starving and war-stricken Africans, lured by illegal immigrant trafficking gangs, as a stepping stone into Spain and Southern Europe. It is equally paradoxical that the arrival of the very people who are causing us to find a new way of being Spanish should take place during a football match, a perfect occasion for national affirmation and proud display of flag and anthem. Although it is true that before they were driven out by the Catholic Monarchs in 1492 Spain was home to Muslims and Jews, it is only recently that the country's cultural make-up is becoming more diverse. Two thirds of the immigrants living in Spain in 2002 had arrived after 1995 coming from Maghreb, Central Africa, Latin America and Eastern Europe to a lesser extent (Seguí, 2002, pp. 40–41). Spain is a young country for immigration when compared with the UK, France or Germany, countries with a 'long-standing and well-established immigration experience' (Melotti, 1997, p. 85). It was not until 2000 that debates on citizenship and multiculturalism gained importance, and the issue of migration started to receive media and socio-political attention (Abella, 2007, p. 85).[2] The year 2001 witnessed the passing of the first law granting immigrants integration measures and protection against discrimination, the Act for the Rights and Freedoms of the Immigrants Living in Spain and their Social Integration.[3] Despite its youth as a country of immigration, a multicultural society is emerging in Spain to the extent that it is already being depicted in novels dealing with contemporary Spanish society. Lucía Etxebarría's *Cosmofobia*, to which we now turn, and El Hachmi's *L'últim Patriarca* are examples of these novels.

Spain's budding multiculturalism: the novels of Lucía Etxebarría and Najat El Hachmi

Etxebarría's latest novel, *Cosmofobia* [Cosmophobia] (2008), testifies to the rise of diversity in Spanish society. This is probably the most socially-oriented novel by Extebarría, who belongs to a young generation of Spanish writers from the 1990s concerned with depicting the 'ontological angst' of 'a youthful culture-in-crises' (Folkart, 2004, p. 44) with the attendant problems of alienation, lack of communication, indifference and addictions. With her new novel, Etxebarría intends to fill a void in contemporary Spanish fiction, which has produced very few novels about immigration given its penchant for looking back in time (Goyoaga, 2007). The novel has a loaded setting, the Lavapiés district in Madrid. Lavapiés was the former Jewish neighbourhood of the city until expulsion, named after the fountain where the inhabitants used to wash their feet before entering their place of worship. It seems as if Spain's suppressed multicultural past had returned with a vengeance, for Lavapiés not only shelters a large percentage of the capital's immigrant population, but has been described metaphorically as a 'laboratory where Spain's recent cultural diversity is being tested' and an anticipation of what Spain may look like in ten years' time (Pérez, n.d., p. 1).[4] Furthermore, Lavapiés is infamously known as the place where one of the ringleaders of the Madrid 3/11 terrorist attack ran a phone shop. That most of the cell phones used to trigger the bombs were traced back to this shop inevitably summons up the stereotype of the enemy within. As Etxebarría has acknowledged in an interview with the UNHCR's External Relations Officer in Spain, the title of her novel evokes an endemic problem in multicultural societies, the fear of the other, for which the media are partly to blame. The author believes that the only way for people to embrace cultural diversity is to be exposed to realities different from their own and to realize that similarities outnumber differences (Fontanini, 2007). Etxebarría's ideas resonate with Gilroy's invitation to reconsider our notions of 'sameness and difference... so that the strangeness of strangers goes out of focus and other dimensions of a basic sameness can be acknowledged and made significant' (2004a, p. 3).

In *Cosmofobia* [Cosmophobia], Etxebarría highlights the basic sameness of characters through a choral narrative where their lives are intertwined in the bustling district of Lavapiés. They range from working-class white Spaniards like Sonia, to Spanish-born of Guinean parents Susana, or African refugee Ismael. Through Susana, the author criticises the dangerous conflation of nationality with ethnicity. The white Spanish customers of the clothes shop where Susana works are shocked at her native Spanish and show incredulity when she insists that she was born in Alcalá de Henares, a town in Southern Madrid. Furthermore, they seem completely unaware of their own country's ties with Guinea, a former colony where Spanish is still the main official language (pp. 69–70). Lavapiés also hosts people like Ismael, who fled the war in his native Côte d'Ivoire in search of the European dream and now works clandestinely in a grocery shop. Ismael's dream did not come true, but neither did Sonia's, daughter to a wife-barterer, whose precarious job as a telephone operator is threatened by relocation. Even though Sonia did not experience war, she suffered domestic violence. Significantly, it is a white Spaniard and not a Muslim man that is portrayed as a wife abuser in the novel. In doing so, Etxebarría challenges the stereotype of Muslim men as wife abusers, voiced by another character in the novel who warns her daughter against her Moroccan boyfriend (p. 101). Although the novel emphasises not only the interactions among the different ethnic minorities and between the ethnic minorities and the white mainstream, but also what all these groups share, it does not offer an idealised image of convivial fusion in Spain. Running through the novel like a leitmotif is the opinion voiced by several characters that the neighbourhood is 'multicultural' as opposed to 'intercultural,' for 'communities tolerate each other, they do not mix' (p. 34). Yet it may well be, as a character says full of foreboding towards the end of the novel, that 'it's still too early and things will move fast' (p. 163).[5]

This leitmotif is also present in Najat El Hachmi's novel, *L'últim Patriarca* [The last patriarch] (2008), awarded the Ramon Llull prize.[6] El Hachmi, a writer of Moroccan origin who moved to Spain in her youth, bases her novel on the figure of Mimoun Driouch, a Moroccan migrant who moved to Barcelona to work as a bricklayer leaving his family back in Morocco. Once Mimoun is well situated his family joins him in Catalonia, where he continues his despotic manners as if he were in Morocco. A village next to Barcelona becomes a Moroccan space for the family since his wife is enclosed within the household where garments and smells are tinted with a Moroccan environment, slightly mixed with Spanish ham scent which Mimoun and his family consider disgusting. Mimoun does not mix with Spaniards except for casual sexual encounters, thus, he represents the exotic. El Hachmi lets the reader visualize how neither the Moroccans nor the Spaniards really mix and how conviviality is, then, virtual. Nevertheless, Mimoun's daughter moves towards that conviviality since she is able to break up with her father's rules and lead her own inbetween life. Mimoun's daughter does not have a name, she is just the daughter of the last despotic Driouch. When she moves to Catalonia with her parents, she spends her life within the household and the school. At home she has to help her mother, in the street she becomes her parents' translator as they do not speak Catalan, and at school she is not allowed to talk to boys. Her mother does not allow her to use tampons, as she believes they can make her lose her virginity which she is to keep intact until she marries. But she falls in love with a Moroccan drug dealer and loses her virginity and, because of that, her father allows her to marry him. Mimoun's daughter feels that she is free once she marries her lover but her husband begins to control her as her father did. He asks her to cover her head and body and not to work in bars and restaurants where she is exposed to the gaze of the others, particularly men. And thus, feeling trapped under the control of another patriarch, she decides to divorce him and live a free life where she will be the one to decide what to wear, how to sit and where to work. Mimoun's daughter frees herself from the traditional rules she was brought up with and also shows how, once in Catalonia, she hardly mixes with the others except for the Moroccans that live there. Her family has not given her the tools to do so but she, as a second generation migrant, makes a step towards a conviviality that, as in Etxebarría's novel, is still more virtual than real.

This is England

It may seem as if, while countries like Spain are still beginning the long path towards diversity, others like Britain have already come of age as multicultural societies, although as said previously, this view is contested by critics like Gilroy or Huggan who considers British multiculturalism more virtual than real. The British experience of migration and the subsequent cultural diversity that now exists in the country originated in the post-war labour shortage that attracted large numbers of colonial immigrants from the West Indies, Asia and Africa to the mother country in the late 1940s. These immigrants came under the 1948 Nationality Act which granted them full rights of citizenship. Yet the decrease in the demand for labour and the heavy influx of immigrants led to tighter immigration controls throughout the 1960s and 1970s and the concomitant rise of British nationalism as embodied in the anti-immigration speeches of Enoch Powell and the emergence of the National Front. As a result of these developments, a multiracial Britain has irresistibly risen (Phillips, 1999). The fact that the pioneering immigrants were given full rights of citizenship has provided Britain with a great deal of experience in handling cultural diversity (Lewis, 1997, p. 126). Legal protection against racial discrimination has existed in Britain since the Race Relations Act of 1976, which was enhanced by the Race Relations Amendment Act of 2000. The case of the northern industrial city of Bradford, which had an Asian Lord Mayor, Muhammad Ajeeb, in 1985 (p. 143), illustrates how minorities have entered British public life and have a share of power within political parties dominated by the white mainstream.

In keeping with the country's long-standing experience of migration, migration novels have been written in the UK since the late 1950s. In fact, London became the literary headquarters for young Caribbean writers, who found a positive critical reception and the much-needed publishing agents and reading audience that they couldn't find at home. Trinidadian Samuel Selvon was one of the pioneer writers of the so-called West Indian Renaissance. His Moses trilogy, *The Lonely Londoners* (1956), *Moses Ascending* (1975) and *Moses Migrating* (1983), is a vivid document of the development of multicultural Britain in post-war England. Nowadays, surveys of contemporary British fiction or art range widely. Richard Lane's or Philip Tew's collection of essays discuss the work of black or Asian British authors like Zadie Smith, Andrea Levy, Monica Ali, or Hanif Kureishi alongside that of Will Self, Martin Amis or Angela Carter. Likewise, the artists included in Rebecca Fortnum's *Contemporary British women artists: In their own words* (2007) range from black-British Sonia Boyce to Scottish Christine Borland. Authors and artists of immigrant background are not allocated to a specific movement but are approached as an integral part of the British literary production, reflecting the social changes that have taken place in the course of time.

Andrea Levy's award-winning novel *Small Island* (2004), in an effort to both reflect on and celebrate multiculturalism, to borrow Shonibari's words, looks back on a very early stage of British race relations. After five decades of cohabitation and interaction, Levy revisits the 1950s experience of migration in a very different light from Windrush writers like Samuel Selvon. Her reflective analysis tries to strike a delicate balance between guests and hosts, offering both sides to the story and trying to explain why the British behaved the way they did. In order to achieve this, the narration of *Small Island* is shared by four characters: Hortense Joseph, her husband

Gilbert, their landlady Queenie Bligh and Queenie's husband Bernard. An example of the explanatory drive running through Levy's novel is found very early in the Prologue to the text, which recounts Queenie's visit to the British Empire exhibition as a little girl, which only provided her with prejudiced notions of other cultures. Levy uses irony in her work to show how conviviality can take place once the constructed stereotypes have been deconstructed. That is, Hortense has to leave aside the constructed ideas she has learnt about the British and Queenie about the Caribbean immigrants. Hortense has grown up believing she is destined for a golden life, but her experience of coming to Britain is the biggest letdown. Levy portrays Hortense's shock at the ugliness of racist Britain, a place where her fair skin, white gloves and college education count for nothing. Queenie also believed she was destined for a superior life and soon learns there are limitations to what life can offer her. The author presents a binary opposition formed by these two female characters, Queen(ie) and Hortens(e)ia, creating a dichotomy where one of the elements is more powerful than the other. Queen(ie) carries the crown and, thus, the power over the colony, Jamaica, where Hortensia(e)s grew. Levy deconstructs this hierarchical dichotomy since, even though Queenie is superior to Hortense, due to her skin color, she tells her 'I'm not worried about what busybodies say. I don't mind being seen in the street with you' (Levy, 2004, p. 330). But not all the subjects Hortense encounters are similar to Queenie; many times she has to step off the pavement when she comes across English people: 'I, as a visitor to this country, should step off the pavement into the road if an English person wished to pass and there is no sufficient room on the pavement for us both' (p. 335). Levy creates two very different characters that have experienced different routes to become, at the end of the novel, subjects unified by motherhood/motherland. Queenie gives birth to a colored baby and being conscious of the discrimination he would suffer because of his skin color asks Hortense to take him as her son. In doing so Levy represents a convivial code between these two female characters but a virtual one among society.

Brick Lane (2003), Monica Ali's debut novel, attempts a panoramic view of the Bengali community as seen through the eyes of Nazneen, a young woman from a village who moves to London after her arranged marriage at the age of 18 to Chanu, a somewhat educated Bengali. Nazneen spends 15 years of her marriage raising two children and clipping her husband's corns and deferring to his wishes and ideas. The novel flashes back and forth between Nazneen's life in Brick Lane and her memories of life in the village as a child, through letters exchanged between her and her younger sister Hasina. Ali gives voice to Nazneen and also to Shahana, Nazneen's daughter born in London and brought up as a Bengali at home and as a Londoner at school. Shahana is placed in a convivial inbetweeness which, at home, neither her mother nor father have yet achieved, and thus this conviviality becomes virtual. Karim, Nazneen's lover, describes Nazneen as the 'real thing' (2003, p. 454), definition that she tries to decodify, 'How did Karim see her? The real thing, he said. She was his real thing. A Bengali wife. A Bengali mother. An idea of home. An idea of himself that he found in her' (2003, p. 454). Karim is caught up in the same inbetweeness as Shahana but since he has not reached a convivial space, he is the other in the (M)otherland. Nazneen realizes, thanks to her daughter, that her subjectivity has been created by the others; her father, who arranged her marriage with Chanu, her husband, who enclosed her within their flat in Brick Lane, and by Karim, who wanted her to be the 'real thing'. Ali makes Nazneen visualize the dominant discourse which constructed her, so that she is able, later on in the novel, to deconstruct it: 'I wasn't me, and you weren't you. From the very beginning to the very end, we didn't see things. What we did – we made each other up' (2003, p. 455). Nazneen leaves her inbetweeness aside to become a convivial subject in a virtual convivial space. Ali inscribes this conviviality moving the reader from the imagined heat of Bangladesh to the coldness of a British ice-skating ring. The novel ends up with Nazneen ice-skating in a sari to Razia's surprise: 'But you can't skate in a sari'. Razia was already lacing her boots. 'This is England,' she said. 'You can do whatever you like' (2003, p. 492). Nevertheless, the idea of the heat of Bangladesh melting the British ice and thus, forming a unified entity is still more virtual than real.

Shane Meadows's award-winning film *This is England* (2006) looks back to the early 1980s of British working-class life through the eyes of young Shaun and his new gang, and deals with the bitterness of racism and xenophobia, of mass unemployment and the Falklands War during Thatcher's Britain. Mods, New Romantics, and Skinheads of the English summer of 1983 are represented in this film, where young 12-year-old Shaun is drifting away during the start of his school holidays, until his chance meeting with Woody and his Skinhead pack, who welcome and introduce him to a new way of life. That is, until Combo, a bitter, dangerous and racist character arrives on the scene. Meadows uses repetitive sketches which Branka Arsic defines as a mirror that 'mirrors the mirror' (2003, p. 4). The film constitutes, then, a mirror for the spectator, as he or she sees what happens within and outside the screen, since what is projected is an image of the virtual conviviality in society. It is when Combo, also known as Snake, comes out of prison, that we perceive how the convivial space to which Shaun has been welcomed is virtual as it is broken abruptly. Thus, the movie is, for the spectator, a mirror that mirrors the mirror that virtual conviviality represents. Combo asks Milky, the nickname of the Jamaican character, if he considers himself English or Jamaican. Milky wonders, as though he had never asked himself this question, and ends up answering that he defines himself as English. Combo is not satisfied with this answer since he will always consider Milky a 'fucking nigger' because of his skin colour.

Meadows reflects what the dominant discourse is creating within and outside the screen. It is through loops and repetitions that Meadows highlights how vision is formed by an opposite procedure, vision 'is given to an eye that is looked at, that does not look, to an eye without gaze, to a blind eye' (Arsic, 2003, pp. 30–31). Snake and Milky become a binary opposition where Snake is the powerful being and Milky is the Other. Snake is blind, for he has interiorized the message that he is superior due to his skin colour and does not see the absurdity of considering Milky a nigger and, thus, a no one. The visible has become invisible as it has disappeared through dominant discourse. Thus, dominant discourse has to be deconstructed in order to dismantle the invisible and make it visible so that virtual conviviality can become real. Meadows, amongst others, has, therefore, described how societies are moving towards a conviviality.

Hortense, in *Small Island*, could never have dreamt that England would be like this, 'come, in what crazed reverie would a white Englishwoman be kneeling before me yearning for me to take her black child?' (2004, p. 523), but others could. Levy made it happen, and so did the 44 edition of Notting Hill. The Spanish newspaper *El País* highlights how Notting Hill's carnival has become a convivial space where hybrid identities in process gather, dancing reggae, house and garage. Tubella highlights how in 1958 the white working class of Notting Hill became the Londoner's Harlem due to the arrival of the Afro-Caribbean migrants (Tubella, 2008, p. 1). Notting Hill has changed in 50 years from 'no-coloureds' signs to tones of chicken, rice, peas, coconuts and Jamaican Ron to celebrate convivial hybridity, although under a high security control which makes conviviality virtual more than real. Claudia Jones, editor of the *West Indian Gazette*, organized the first Caribbean festival in London, which six years later became the Notting Hill festival, as a response to the racial discrimination that migrants from the colonies received at their arrival in the 1950s (Tubella, 2008, p. 2). Half a century later Etxebarría, El Hachmi, Levy, Ali and Meadows, amongst others, have voiced the strangeness of strangers so that it became sameness and thus significant (Gilroy, 2004a, p. 3) in order to achieve convivial spaces.

In the course of this paper we hope to have shown that literature and the arts contribute to the formation of a convivial culture, one that is tolerant and spontaneously at ease with its rich diversity. In addition, these texts articulate the complexities of multiculturalism, an ideology which is commonly agreed to have failed to accomplish its goals, but which remains an aspiration for the future. We have adopted a European framework, taking Spain and Britain as two case studies representing different stages of race relations in Europe. Titles like *After multiculturalism, After empire, The future of multi-ethnic Britain, Small Island* or *This is England*, all discussed above, are very revealing of the fact that enough time has elapsed for Britain to have taken a reflective turn in its analysis of race relations. Spain, on the contrary, is a much younger country of migration and the social debate on multiculturalism, as well as the development of literary reflection on it, is still in its very early stages. Both case studies evidence the fact that Europe is, to borrow Pnina Werbner's words again, the product of a postcolonial world and of immigrants and their descendants.

Notes

1. Our translation. The original reads 'El sujeto nómada contiene la presencia simultánea de muchos ejes, y, como tal, es una figuración narrativa, una recreación política que puede atravesar categorías y niveles de experiencia y diluir los límites de la diferencia sin quemar los puentes de su normalidad'.
2. Our translation. The original reads 'comienzan a cobrar importancia cuestiones relacionadas con la ciudadanía y el multiculturalismo, y la inmigración comienza a ser un asunto de relevancia mediática, política y social'.
3. Our translation. The original reads 'Ley sobre Derechos y Libertades de los Extranjeros en España y su Integración Social'.
4. Our translation. The original reads 'laboratorio de ensayo de la recién estrenada realidad multiétnica en nuestro país,' 'mapa humano de la España de dentro de 10 años'.
5. Our translation. The original reads: 'pero todo esto es muy dinámico y ha pasado poco tiempo' (p. 163).
6. The Ramon Llull prize is a literary award granted yearly to a novel originally written in Catalan. This prize was first created in 1981 by editor José Manuel Lara Hernández and it is given by Editorial Planeta. The aim of this award is to broadcast works written in Catalan as a way to expand Catalan literature worldwide. The awarded novels are translated into Spanish and published in Spain and Latin America.

References

Abella Vázquez, C.M. (2007). La aparición de los discursos sobre el multiculturalismo en España: El debate del velo en la prensa escrita [The beginning of multicultural discourses in Spain: The veil in the written press]. *Athenea Digital, 11*, 83–103.

Ali, M. (2003). *Brick Lane*. London: Black Swan.

Alibhai-Brown, Y. (2000). *After multiculturalism*. London: The Foreign Policy Centre.

Arsic, B. (2003). *The passive eye*. Stanford, CA: Stanford University Press.

Baumann, Z. (1996). From pilgrim to tourist – or a short history of identity. In S. Hall & P. Du Gay (Eds.), *Questions of cultural identity* (pp. 18–35). London: Sage.

Bhikhu, P. (2000). *The future of multi-ethnic Britain: The Parekh Report*. London: Profile Books.

Braidotti, R. (1994). *Nomadic subjects*. New York, NY: Columbia University Press.

Brown, M. (2008). *Fourth plinth: He wanted to scrap it. Now Boris Johnson could be on it*. Retrieved August 17, 2008, from http://arts.guardian.co.uk/art/news/story/0,,2287108,00.html

Dong, L. (2004). Gendered home and space for the diaspora: Gish Jen's Typical American. *Thirdspace, 4*(1), 66–86.

El Hachmi, N. (2008). *L'últim Patriarca* [*The last patriarch*]. Barcelona: Planeta.

Etxebarría, L. (2008). *Cosmofobia* [*Cosmophobia*]. Barcelona: Destino.

Folkart, J. (2004). Body talk: Space, communication, and corporeality in Lucía Etxebarría's Beatriz y Los Cuerpos Celestes. *Hispanic Review, 72*, 43–63.

Fontanini, F. (2007). *Conversamos con Lucía Etxebarría sobre su nuevo libro* Cosmofobia [*Discussing* Cosmophobia *with Lucia Extebarria*]. Retrieved August 17, 2008, from http://www.eacnur.org/01_02_01_02_01.cfm?id=1073&seccion=Testimonios

Fortnum, R. (2007). *Contemporary British women artists: In their own words*. London: I.B. Tauris.

Gilroy, P. (2004a). *After empire: Melancholia or convivial culture?* Oxford: Routledge.

Gilroy, P. (2004b). *Melancholia and multiculture*. Retrieved July 15, 2007, from http://www.opendemocracy.net/arts-multiculturalism/article_2035.jsp

Gilroy, P. (2005). *Postcolonial melancholia*. New York, NY: Columbia University Press.

Goyoaga, A. (2007). *Lucía Etxebarría Escritora: La novela española va por detrás de la realidad.* [*Lucia Extebarria, writer: The Spanish novel lags behind reality*]. Retrieved August 12, 2008, from http://medios.mugak.eu/noticias/noticia/107051

Hall, S. (1996). When was 'the post-colonial'? Thinking at the limit. In L. Curti & I. Chambers (Eds.), *The postcolonial question: Common skies, divided horizons* (pp. 242–260). London: Routledge.

Herbert, M. (Producer), & Meadows, S. (Director) (2006). *This is England* [Motion picture]. Britain: Warp Films Production.

Huggan, G. (2001). Virtual multiculturalism: The case of contemporary Britain. *European Studies, 16*, 67–85.

Levy, A. (2004). *Small Island*. London: Review.

Lewis, P. (1997). Arenas of ethnic negotiation: Cooperation and conflict in Bradford. In T. Modood & P. Werbner (Eds.), *The politics of multiculturalism in the new Europe: Racism, identity and community* (pp. 126–146). London & New York, NY: Zed Books.

Melotti, U. (1997). International migration in Europe: Social projects and political cultures. In T. Modood & P. Werbner (Eds.), *The politics of multiculturalism in the new Europe: Racism, identity and community* (pp. 73–92). London & New York, NY: Zed Books.

Modood, T. (1997). Introduction: The politics of multiculturalism in the new Europe. In T. Modood & P. Werbner (Eds.), *The politics of multiculturalism in the new Europe: Racism, identity and community* (pp. 1–25). London & New York, NY: Zed Books.

Owen, A. (Producer), & Gavron, S. (Director) (2007). *Brick Lane* [Motion picture]. Britain: Ruby Films.

Pérez López, S. (n.d.) *Lavapiés, el barrio de las mil culturas* [*Lavapiés, a multicultural neighborhood*]. Retrieved August 17, 2008, from http://geo.ya.com/lavapiesnet/paralectura.pdf

Phillips, M. (1999). *Windrush: The irresistible rise of multi-racial Britain*. London: Harpercollins.

Sánchez, P. (2008). *Un grupo de subsaharianos aprovecha la tanda de penaltis de España para intentar entrar en Melilla* [*A group of sub-Saharans' attempt to cross Melilla' border during Spanish penalty kicks*]. Retrieved August 17, 2008, from http://www.elmundo.es/papel/2008/06/23/espana/2429759.html

Seguí, L. (2002). *España ante el desafío multicultural* [*Spain confronts multicultural challenge*]. Madrid: Siglo XXI.

Suárez Lafuente, S. (2007). La historia espacial en la novela inglesa contemporánea [*The history of space in the contemporary English novel*]. *Odisea, 8,* 187–197.

Tew, P. (2007). *The contemporary British novel.* London: Continuum.

Tubella, P. (2008). *Notting Hill celebra el mestizaje. Arranca en Londres el gran carnaval que sepultó los conflictos raciales hace 50 años* [*Notting Hill celebrates mixed race. The carnival, which 50 years ago put an end to racial conflicts, is now taking place*]. Retrieved August 30, 2008, from http://www.elpais.com/articulo/Revista/Verano/Notting/Hill/celebra/mestizaje/elpepirdv/20080825elprdv_1/Tes

Ware, V. (2007). The white fear factor. *Wasafiri, 22*(2), 51–56.

Werbner, P. (2007). Afterword: Writing multiculturalism and politics in the new Europe. In T. Modood & P. Werbner (Eds.), *The politics of multiculturalism in the new Europe: Racism, identity and community* (pp. 260–267). London & New York, NY: Zed Books.

Adrift on the black Mediterranean diaspora: African migrant writing in Spain

Esther Sánchez-Pardo

Departamento de Filología Inglesa II, Universidad Complutense de Madrid, Madrid, Spain

Focusing on the strategies employed to recreate agency in the black diaspora in postcolonial Europe and taking at its basis recent narratives produced by African migrant writers in Spain – Cameroonians Inongo-vi-Makomé and Susan Akono, and Guinean Donato Ndongo – this paper explores the ways in which identity is reconstructed in diasporic situations, to answer questions such as what images of the self and the other are created and disseminated at a national level and in the wider context of globalization.

Spain, the historically homogeneous out-migration country is transforming into a site of multicultural interaction as it becomes a destination for members of several diasporas, many with their own legacies of colonialism and racism. Due to its European Union status and growing presence in the world economy, the nation is participating in a global phenomenon in which immigrants, asylum seekers, and refugees are looking towards the new Europe as an impenetrable fortress. This paper attempts to discuss these issues within the tangled web of forms of power and subjection exercised upon immigrants through Western imperialism.

Loading the trauma of difference onto the black man, the white man can delude himself that there is or might be no trouble between men (a delusion the universalists share). (Rose, 1998)

For several decades now, the fruitful synergy between postcolonial and cultural studies has brought postcolonial cultural production to the forefront of social analysis. As a subject of increased critical attention, critics have focused on the ways in which narratives, both in literature and ethnography, serve both to construct and to destabilize notions of identity at the individual, national and postnational levels. As the materials under consideration here show, texts produced by migrant writers in particular, demonstrate the malleability of subject positions, as these migrant writers interrogate their shifting roles *vis-à-vis* the metropolis as well as institutionally-dominated writing traditions.

With the insight and methods of postcolonial theory[1] and through a reading of a selection of texts by black African migrant writers residents of Spain, Inongo-vi-Makomé, Susan Akono and Donato Ndongo – *España y los Negros Africanos* [*Spain and African Blacks*, 1990], *Población Negra en Europa* [*The Blacks in Europe*,

2002], *Iris Negro* [*Black Iris*, ca. 2001], *The Weapons of my Disappointment* (2004) and *Shadows of Your Black Memory* (2007) – this paper is an attempt to disentangle the complex web of identity, community, home/land and collective and individual histories in their writing. Focusing on the strategies employed to recreate agency in the black diaspora in Europe and taking at its basis recent narratives produced by black African writers in Spain, we explore the ways in which the self is reconstructed in diasporic situations through the various overlapping and fragmented experiences represented in narrative processes, to answer questions such as what images of the self and the other are created and disseminated through narratives? We also examine the tensions between individual agency and social structure by looking at different loci of communication (language, memory, etc) as expressed in narratives which can illuminate these tensions attending to their specific locations and the power relations which rule them.

In the pages that follow, I also aim to examine issues regarding racism and exclusion in Spain, a country deeply ambivalent about its own African past. The presence of Africans blacks in Spain constitutes an unwritten chapter of Spanish history[2] and an unacknowledged fact of long-lasting consequences for recent immigrants. It was not until 1959 that blacks in Spain's last African colony, Spanish Guinea, gained equality with whites, and many migrated to the peninsula for work and higher education. The 1968 independence of the new republic of Equatorial Guinea brought political and economic instability, and Guinean exiles entered as dual citizens into Spain, where they compose the largest single national group of African descent.

In the last two decades, Spain's socioeconomic situation has changed drastically, transforming a country of emigrants in the 1950s through the 1970s into a country of immigrants in the 1980s and 1990s. The reasons for this reversal is part of a regional Mediterranean phenomenon. They include the end of guest worker programs in Northern European countries and the closing of their borders to immigrants, extensive underground economies in Europe that rely on illegal immigration, and the admission in the 1980s of Spain, Portugal and Greece into the European community, making them 'gateway' countries as well as front line states on Europe's southern border.

The country has absorbed more than three million foreigners during the past decade, and immigrants now constitute more than 10% in a total population of 44 million people. In the process, Spain has become a test of how well a modern European nation can integrate waves of strangers, frequently from radically different cultures. This comes as a remarkable change for a nation that, just a generation ago, was one of Europe's most homogenous and poor countries. Its successful transition from dictatorship to democracy and the nation's subsequent integration into the European Union transformed it from a country of emigration to a magnet for the poor from South America, Eastern Europe, and, more recently, North and sub-Saharan Africa.

Among Spain's immigrants, Moroccans –some 650,000 – are the largest group, followed by Romanians and Ecuadoreans, according to government figures. Spanish society must learn now to accept diversity. It has to learn to see immigrants through a positive prism. Instead, the opposite appears to be happening in some ultraconservative sectors in Spanish society. Sensing a nascent anti-immigrant movement, the right-wing opposition Popular Party politicized the issue for the first time during the recent parliamentary election campaign. Opposition leader Mariano Rajoy, who was defeated by the current Socialist Prime Minister José Luis R. Zapatero in the 9 March 2007 vote, called immigration a serious problem for Spanish society and proposed an 'integration contract' calling for the expulsion of immigrants convicted of crimes or who are unable to find a job and support themselves. The pact also called on immigrants to learn Spanish and respect Spanish customs.

The growth of Spain's foreign-born population over the past two decades is indeed stunning. Official government figures show that the number of foreigners with residency cards more than doubled over the past four years to almost four million, though independent experts put the real number, counting legal and illegal immigrants, at closer to five million, or nearly 12% of the total population. The increase is in large part due to the legalization in 2005 of over 578,000 illegal immigrants by the socialist government. An additional half-million illegal immigrants were given residency papers during the eight years of the previous conservative government.

If there is a group that is having particular trouble integrating, it is certainly the sub-Saharan Africans from Senegal, Mali, Mauritania, and other countries who arrived in recent years by the tens of thousands in the Canary Islands after a perilous (for some thousands, deadly) sea journey on rickety wooden fishing boats called *pateras*. With the Canary Islands unable to handle the numbers of migrants, the Africans are routinely flown to Spain and given expulsion orders, which they then ignore. Recently, Spain has promised additional economic aid to African countries if they will take back their migrants, who often arrive without any national identity papers. Africans, including Moroccans, now represent over 21% of the foreign population (compared with 30.5% for Latin Americans). Lacking knowledge of Spanish and with few skills, they survive as best they can, frequently staying in hostels and eating in dining rooms subsidized by charitable organizations.

Recent African immigration into Spain can be traced back to the emergence of democracy with the death of Franco in 1975, and the transformation of the country from a relatively poor country of immigration to one of dynamic economic growth necessitating immigrant labor to fill low-wage jobs. Immigration into Spain is clearly driven by poverty and the quest for a better life. Set in historical perspective, the colonization of Africa by empire nations like Spain in the early modern era, and most recently by the new empire nations and transnational entities in the post-industrial period following the Second World War, show a persistent pattern of exploitation that has produced massive African immigrations to Europe, with Spain serving as a main gateway nation and destination.

The Spanish government has made efforts to address the problem of immigration and the necessity for multicultural education. The 1985 immigration law, addressing the rights and freedoms of immigrants, has been followed by amendments in 1996, 1998 and 2000 in recognition of the permanent dimension of immigration. The 2000 amendment reflects a shift from policies focused on controlling immigration flows to those looking at integration. Under a Socialist government, President José Luis R. Zapatero's (2004–present) policies directed at easing legalization and family unification but also improving enforcement of laws prohibiting the hiring of illegals have been implemented. The socialist government has recently offered immigrants the opportunity to become legal residents in Spain. These events provide the country with an opportunity to reexamine the relationship between different national, ethnic and religious communities and search for new models for peaceful coexistence.

Black diasporas: the Afro–Hispanic

A considerable amount of people of African descent in Spanish-speaking countries are commonly omitted from the picture when it comes to exploring the complexities of colonialism, race and power in Latin America, the Caribbean and Spain. Their cultural production is far from being easily defined, but it does reflect and aid in understanding the black experience in these parts of the world. This minority inhabits a 'decolonial imaginary' (Pérez, 1999) occupying complex positionalities between the colonial and the postcolonial as they are located in nations within nations, in the form of 'internal colonization', as occurs with the Africans within Spain. As has been the case with multiculturalist policies, incorporation of Afro-Hispanic histories, cultures and traditions into research and university curricula can help provide both a more pluralistic outlook and work towards a better cultural understanding among communities with different national origins.

Stanley Cyrus and June Legge (1991) have attempted to provide a tentative definition of Afro-Hispanic literature, and they distinguish between those works which treat favorably the black Latin American – seen usually in a slavery situation – and those, written by non–black authors, which 'are not authentic...for they lack the true black perspective. They view from the outside and, though well meaning, too often fall prey to the apologetic and condescending attitude rightly opposed by black students and scholars' (1991, p. 92). What then constitutes Afro-Hispanic culture and literature? In the specific case of black Latin American cultures, Cyrus and Legge remind us that mestizaje is central to any understanding of the black experience in Latin America, 'Mestizaje means the blending of races, and many Latin American countries have insisted that the black, white and Indian races have blended perfectly into one' (1991, p. 92).

Mestizaje has nothing to do with the situation of the Afro-Hispanic residents in Spain since the blending alluded to never occurred. In any event, I believe that they share many features in common with those of the black diaspora: they have accepted their African origins and some insist proudly on them, reaffirming that their blackness is worthy and they also resist absorption into another culture, even though that attempt may be presented as interesting and profitable. In the case of Afro-Hispanic writers and intellectuals,[3] they all join efforts to reject racism, and are committed upon forging their own aesthetic, one which, while uncompromising in its themes, retains the concerns of the blacks all over the world and reflects the unique linguistic and cultural aspects of their societies.

In the pages that follow, my analysis revolves around a historical moment that coincides with an established democracy in Spain and it also necessarily grapples with globalization. The shift from national historic time to global time means that we have moved from a moment defined by temporal succession to one defined in terms of spatial expansions and displacements. The category of history, and an accompanying notion of memory became a nodal point for Spanish cultural imagination after the dictatorship (1936–1975). Later, under the transition to democracy, the same traditional left (and a majority of Spanish society) understood the task at hand as one in which Spanish society had to rebuild the social ties and democratic tradition that had been broken and, subsequently, to move past the wound wrought by the dictatorship. This recuperation would require suturing the gap between forgiveness and punishment, reconciling the divided community, and in so doing, engaging in a process of working through conflicting emotions. This implied an operation to uncover the past and exhume the dead, bringing them up to the light.

The relationship of Spanish society to its immigrants was effectively depolarized with the return to democracy, when society at large was reorganized around notions of compromise and inclusion in an all-too-complacent pluralism under a rhetoric of variety and diversity. The challenge under democracy has been to keep open the possibility of critical intervention within a system of institutional pluralism which tends to absorb all differences within a politics of indifferentiation.

No politics outside of history

The literature produced by African immigrant writers in Europe is rich, heterogeneous and diverse. This shows in the plurality of languages used, of the authors' African heritages, and of their European locations. Moreover, this new body of literature develops in different European countries at different times and follows very different patterns. This essay seeks to trace commonalities and differences among recent African texts produced in Spain that range from novels to essays, autobiography and testimonial in a joint effort to perform cultural critique. In the context of this emerging literature it makes quite a difference whether the language used is a mother tongue, a colonial language or a language of education, or a second (foreign) language. Language is crucial to mark the degree of integration or alienation of the author in a specific cultural location that may, in most cases, signal an ideological stance.

A conspicuous number of immigrant writers in Spain come from francophone countries and a smaller number from Anglophone countries, their choice to write in a foreign language reveals on the one hand a rejection of the old colonial language in spite of the privilege attached to it, and, on the other, a willingness to fully integrate in the host country. There is then the case of authors writing in a language other than the one of their host countries, such as the poetic and fictional work of Sidi Seck, a Senegalese resident in Spain, who originally writes in French but publishes in Spanish translation (his first novel, *Amina*, 2007, has just come out with the publishing house he has himself started).

In Spain, in spite of the large numbers of North African residents, there is a scarcity of books produced by this group.[4] From North Africa one should mention Mohamed El Gheryb's *Dormir al Raso* [*Sleeping in the Open*, 1994], a report on migration written in collaboration with a Spanish author, and Rachid Nini's important *Diario de un Ilegal* [*Journal of a Clandestine*, 2002], which was published in Arabic and only later translated into Spanish. Nini, himself an illegal immigrant in Spain, gives a detailed account of the *fiesta de moros y cristianos*[5] and further subverts its significance by comparing the head of the Moorish band to legendary Moroccan leaders. These comparisons point to a broader understanding of the close and conflicting relationship between the two countries and the necessity of addressing and confronting the underlying prejudices and stereotypes if a more neutral and balanced relation is to emerge.

The past colonial relationship with Equatorial Guinea, the only hispanophone country in sub-Saharan Africa, has favored the opening of a space for Guinean writers, but with the exception of Donato Ndongo, who published *Shadows of Your Black Memory* (1987) with a major publishing house, their works have had a very limited distribution.

In spite of the fact that a good number of Guinean writers reside at present in Spain, Equatorial Guinea remains largely an unknown land. During the 11 years of Francisco Macías's dictatorship following independence in 1968, one third of the population left the country. Later, the new regime of Teodoro Obiang Nguema did not live up to the people's expectations and the country never developed a truly democratic system. Repression and censorship continue to be common practices even today. As a consequence of these historical circumstances, hispanophone Guinean literature has been mostly produced outside the country. Among the most relevant works are Juan Balboa's *El Reencuentro* [*The Reunion*, 1985], María Nsue's *Ekomo* (1985), Eugenio Nkogo's *La Encerrona* [*The Trap*, 1993] and Francisco Zamora's *Cómo ser Negro y no Morir en Aravaca* [*How to be Black and not to Die in Aravaca*, 1994]. The main concerns of these writers range from the impact of colonization and its aftermath, the struggle between tradition and modernity and the difficult life conditions of Guineans in Spain.

As for African writers coming from other linguistic areas, very few of them have attracted the attention of major publishers and become successful. One of the most notable exceptions is Agnes Agbotom, from Benin, who published *Más Allá del Mar de Arena* [*Beyond the Sea of Sand*, 2005], an autobiographical piece in which the narrator, in the account of her life, foregrounds the culturally disparate and fragmentary perception of the world her migratory experience has put her through.

Despite the large presence of migrants from African countries very few texts have been published, although one should hope that the progressive immigration policies of the current government will bring forward a significant and fast change.

Race, gender and marginality

Susan Akono was born in Yaoundé and grew up in her native Cameroon. She obtained her BA at the University of Yaoundé and then went to Spain to complete her education. Since 2002 she has lived in the UK with her white British husband and their two children. Her book *WMD: The Weapons of my Disappointment* (2004) tackles the contradictions, dilemmas and absurdities of global politics in the form of a letter addressed to her infant son. Her novel *Black Iris*, remains unpublished. She has recently published *African Tales* (2008), a collection of short stories for children.

The popular response to politics portrayed in *Iris Negro* [*Black Iris*] is one in which the military coup and subsequent dictatorship was absorbed in an imaginary country, Nomansland, as a generalized catastrophe, not only for their society but for notions such as history so that writers and intellectuals critiqued the very media and methods of representation, taking on the very stability of meaning and the referentiality of signs. Their work epitomized Walter Benjamin's dictum that history's continuity is that of the oppressors while the history of the oppressed is discontinuous (1968, p. 260). Instead of trying to reconstruct a coherent, totalizing perspective to heal the open wound produced by the dictatorship, Akono in her novel dwells on within the decomposition of general perspectives. Instead of claiming a heroic, contestatory history, she works with subaltern memories – like those of her protagonist, a prostitute named Elsa – which interrupted or depaginated historical-national sequences, even leftist sequences in which, for example, the working class would have been the only representative of the revolutionary truth. She rather understands it instead as a web of memories, both continuous and discontinuous.

In her subsequent book, Akono argues that in *Black Iris*, she attempted to carry out a 'merciless, systematic, and fierce [critique] of African rulers' (2004, p. 4), and announces her first novel is only part of an ongoing project of oppositional critique, resistance and struggle. Years later, Akono sees similarities between her novel and her first published essay, '[D]espite the obvious dissimilarities between an essay and a novel, the *Weapons of my Disappointment* highly resembles *Black Iris*. Both are crude works triggered by a deep sense of disillusionment (in the case of the novel I was very disgusted and disappointed by the cruel treatment of African prostitutes by Spanish media, and decided to show that behind the red-coloured thick lips stands a human being)' (2004, p. 116). The novel reads as the struggle of the protagonist to come to terms with herself as a human being, in what seems the 'equality among the oppressed' as it is expressed in the marketing of black female bodies.

In *Black Iris*, Akono addresses questions of sexuality and violence through the themes of the journey, migrancy and displacement. In her opening section, 'The Damned,' the protagonist asks herself, 'When did the descent to Hell start?...What was first necessity or vice?' (p. 3), and recounts the story of her life starting with the traumatic events of her rape and subsequent secret relations with her cousin when she was six. The novel, built upon flashbacks, takes the reader from Nomansland in Africa to Spain, where Elsa Isabelle Moto has moved in a desperate attempt to make a living. Elsa also harbors good memories from her childhood, reconstructs her relationship with her father[6] – a teacher at the Institut Saint Jean in Afidia – and tells about the atmosphere of her hometown back in the 1950s. Akono provides rich descriptions of the natural world, 'a gift for your eyes and a treat for your taste' (31), and of the habits and rituals that govern the lives of her fellow countrymen.

Akono uses first-person narration to tell the story of Elsa, an illegal immigrant in Spain, who ends up working in a brothel with other immigrant women in order to send money for the costly medical treatment her daughter requires. Akono manages to deftly manipulate an otherwise sordid subject matter so that it becomes intriguing. There is a rather voyeuristic element to accompanying the narrator as she has sex with a series of men, her only means to make quick money for her daughter's treatment. Akono denounces that racism in society in general, as well as racism within the sex business, places black women in vulnerable situations. The multiple stigmas and realities of poverty, prostitution and racism weave a bleak story of women's lives, and many African women, as Elsa, answer back with their strength and pride. The protagonist finds herself in a situation of forced and economically coerced prostitution, alienated from her community and her family back in Africa.

The setting of the novel shifts from scenes in the brothel to scenes in Africa. In the African setting, the protagonist mixes childhood memories with a background of clandestine political struggle in which her own family engages. Akono provides a vivid portrait of the corrupt atmosphere that surrounds the activities not only of the military government of Nomansland but also of the resistance. This results in aborting any possibility of change.

Akono struggles to name fragments of experience that are no longer speakable in the language that survives the catastrophe of meaning, which amounts ultimately to death – the death of her former self and by the end of the novel, the death of her daughter. Her project in the wake of African dictatorships, makes tactical use of the fractured perspectives of current narrative discourse in favor of a revitalization of insurgent vocabularies that emerge from the accounts of the crisis of Western reason. According to the new situation she portrays, language and meaning are themselves shipwrecked along with African democratic regimes as a result of military coups. What language survives cannot name, cannot speak, of past or present experiences. She both uses and represents silence strategically, and her writing valorizes the local dimensions of culture as symbolic project for forming memory, constituting identities and representing subjects who actively work to promote equality and solidarity.

In her essay *The Weapons of my Disappointment* (2004), Akono speaks of the disillusionment that many Africans suffer when they come to Europe, 'I am a victim of the bitter disillusionment to which many Africans are subject when they reach Europe. However, the truth is that a seven-day stay in Spain is sufficient to wipe out any fantasy about the Western world that a naive African might harbor' (2004, pp. 1–2). In the form of a letter to her baby son, Akono writes a politically engaged critique of Western imperialist policy in the Middle East. On the back cover of her book, the text promises to tell readers, '[W]hy so many young Arabs have become willing suicide bombers; why the war on terror of George W. Bush is not making the world a safer place; why the "road map to peace" leads nowhere...'.[7]

In *WMD*, Akono advocates a perspective on the world as a zone of tensions and schisms as a way to keep from being deceived by the slogan of transparency supported by the West and its instrumental realism. Her text exemplifies the commitment between testimonial[8] and political radicalism. From her own experience, she denounces the harassment that non-white travelers suffer from when they simply try to traverse other countries' frontiers, and the negative reactions of her family to her exposure to white society's habits and to its hidden agenda. She also addresses the impact of mass migration movements from Africa to the West:

> Take the case of Sub-Saharan Africa. The response of most of the Sub-Saharan indigents to their poverty-stricken situation is massive migration to the West. Very soon, millions of them will discover what many Middle East people have discovered decades ago: in the West, most of them have no choice but to cope with low-paid jobs, racism, isolation and frustration...[Westerners] are so willing to see millions of us dead that they are sponsoring civil wars in our countries, and letting AIDS – a disease generated by Western scientists, of course – and extreme poverty – fuelled by unjust Western policies – decimate us. (Akono, 2004, pp. 66–67)

And, specifically in the case of Spain, she states:

> Spanish people, like other Westerners have been told for centuries that black people are inferior, I will never regard that as a cultural thing for three main reasons. First, it is harmful for the Spanish and all non-black people who believe this lie because it dehumanises them to such an extent that it makes them commit all kind of abuses against blacks. Second, it is harmful for blacks for obvious reasons. And third, it is very harmful for humanity as a whole because it complicates human relationships, legitimises inequality, and threatens all democratic values (equality of opportunities, common welfare, mutual respect, and so on). (2004, p. 107)

Akono's analysis of racism in Spain is lucid and shows direct knowledge of the workings of xenophobia and prejudice against foreigners. In her view, this set of anti-immigrant attitudes is not so much part of the culture but rather belongs in a social system that exhibits important class, sexual and religious inequalities.

In a similar vein, Guinean writer, Donato Ndongo, describes the changing attitude of Spanish society toward its black immigrants, from the 1960s when 'There was almost no racism since there were virtually no Blacks in Spain...an idyllic Spain where we assumed there was no such a thing' (2007, n.p.) to the 1980s and 1990s when an important amount of African and other immigrants entered the country. From then up to the present moment things have undergone a radical change and the pattern of treatment of recent African immigrants is characterized by distrust, fear, indifference to their human suffering, and marginalization and even violence.

Born in Niefang (1950) near Bata, Ndongo was sent by his family in 1965 to complete secondary education in Valencia. In 1968, a few months after independence, the country was taken over by the dictator Francisco Macías. The continuous acts of violence and violation of human rights perpetrated by Macías were known as the 'Years of Silence'.[9] Ndongo took the decision to remain out of his country as long as the dictator was in power. In 1969 he began studies of African history at the University of Barcelona, and from 1972 into the mid-1980s he worked as a journalist for several progressive newspapers during the period known as *la transición* (transition from dictatorship to democracy). In the 1970s and 1980s Ndongo devoted his efforts to write about Africa for the Spanish press, becoming an advocate of African issues and rights in Spain. The singularity of his condition as a Guinean dissident living in Spain grants him the insight necessary to expose the evils of a corrupt military system that exploits and disciplines its citizens while it suffocates any possibility of social change.

As in the case of Fanon – and that of Makomé, as we will comment below – it was only through the eyes of others then that he grew aware of his blackness. 'It was through the others that I came to discover my own blackness' (Ndongo, 2007, p. 2). He arrived in Spain from its former colony of Equatorial Guinea, a place where racism was almost non-explicit and exercised in a paternalistic way by Catholic missionaries. In his novel *Shadows of Your Black Memory*, Ndongo writes a compelling memoir, the story of a boy coming of age over the background of the last years of Spain's colonial rule over Guinea. From the perspective of a grown-up man living in Spain, the memories are themselves an exploration of how he arrived at the land that paradoxically has become an object of anxiety as well as the possibility to fulfill his emancipatory project.

Set in the 1970s, *Shadows of your Black Memory*, which is a combination of autobiographical commentary and a critique of his Catholic upbringing, follows the life of a boy subtly coerced into the way to priesthood, away from his own tradition and subject to the rule of the colonizers and to their Catholic legacy in his family. His parents, devout Catholics, have been indoctrinated as to what their country needs for the future and along the same lines, interpellate their offspring in the Althusserian (1971) sense. The novel reads as a *Bildungsroman*, in which Ndongo's deft narrative technique moves from memories of the protagonist's former self in his home country up to his present self growing up into manhood at the end of the Spanish colonial occupation of Equatorial Guinea. An exercise in introspection, the novel combines long passages narrating the protagonist's past experiences in the seminary interspersed with descriptions of the luxuriant natural world that surrounds him, and the habits of the land.

Parallel to the narrator's inner history, the text recounts much of the hidden history of Equatorial Guinea during the Franco dictatorship's colonization. Finally, the protagonist does not live out the destiny planned for him. He leaves the religious order to search instead for a secular solution to his country's problems. In J. Riquelme's view, '[T]he novel by D. Ndongo consists of a parody of the colonial superstructure, of the established ideology, especially in its religious aspect (according to the excesses of times gone by and always written with all respect)' (1986, p. 50).

Tío Abeso, an admired uncle and mentor who is not fluent in Spanish and practices polygamy, is the family's counterpart and comes to symbolize the repressed. He reveres the tribe's ancestors and repudiates the colonizer's belief system and way of life. Abeso unveils the colonizer's impostures and insists on initiating his nephew in the rituals of manhood.

The novel shows the protagonist's strenuous effort of recollection of his previous life in his homeland in order to preserve his 'Africanness' and describes his apprehension of his coming to terms with his own dislocated sense of identity. Along the novel, his profound understanding of the contradictions of his mentor, Father Ortiz, shows the flaws of the processes of indoctrination and acculturation and its disturbing effects in the psyche of the colonized. As if it were the reverse of Joseph Conrad's *Heart of Darkness* with the trip back to the metropolis, the narrator's journey finally leads to the discovery of his inner hollowness. His attempts at redefining himself by inscribing himself in his society of adoption are ultimately futile.

The novel is accompanied by a glossary in which the translator's decision to keep Guinean terms in the original clarifies their specific cultural meanings. In the novel we read passages such as, '. . . and there was your father dressed in his white clote, and Tio Meco dressed in his white clote, and Tio Abeso dressed in a white clote, and you noticed Grandfather Nguema Aseme also wearing a white clote' (p. 137). 'Clote' is a clear example of the pidgin version of 'cloth' – in the glossary, 'fabric, usually multicolored, worn by men' (172).

Yet for all the languages and dialects heard or referred to in the novel,[10] we come to understand that the precarious unity of Equatorial Guinea rests more than anything on the Spanish language, perhaps the most telling sign of the nation's bicultural condition – African and Spanish.

Ndongo's acute perception of the nuances of the language of the colonizer, his awareness of Spanish as a lingua franca in the Gulf of Guinea, and its limits bordering Gabon and Cameroon, leads readers to reflect upon creolization in this area where a multiplicity of languages and ethnicities intersect. He uses words and expressions in 'Pidgin English', the language of the Fernandinos (creole descendents of slaves from Sierra Leone and Nigeria), to 'defamiliarize' our perception of the original in Spanish, and the text of the novel plus its glossary make us aware of our biased Eurocentric positions.

Theorizing black migrant subjectivities

Cameroonian novelist, essayist and playwright Inongo-vi-Makomé (born in Kribi, south Cameroon) is a prolific writer. He went to school in his hometown and in

Santa Isabel (Equatorial Guinea), and he finished his secondary education in Valencia, Spain. He attended the universities of Valencia and Barcelona, and started publishing in the 1980s. Makomé has lived in Barcelona since 1972. Aside from his work as an author, he is a professor of African Literature and the director of Mfundi Kupa I Kribi-Itondi, an African cultural association engaged in the effort of promoting African oral tradition that organizes theatre events and African storytelling sessions for children.

He has published widely stories for children (*Benama, Akono and Belinga, The Kings of Zookala*), and several important essays on the situation of African immigrants in Spain, *España y los Negros Africanos* [*Spain and Black Africans*], *La Emigración Negroafricana: Tragedia y Esperanza* [*African Black Immigration: Tragedy and Hope*]. His novel *Rebeldía* [*Rebellion*, 1996], narrates the disillusionment of an emigré returning to his homeland after 20 years of hardship in Spain.

From the perspective of an African who has lived for more than 40 years in Spain, Makomé analyzes the changes he has perceived in his country of adoption, underlining the social transformations that occurred in these years and the increasing visibility of Africans in Spain, but denouncing the still prevalent racist attitudes, which have changed from a benevolent paternalism when the black Spanish population was basically composed of Afro-American soldiers and Equato-Guinean students to an outright rejection of the new migrants,[11] who are seen as destabilizing the social order.

In his book-long essay *España y los Negros Africanos* [*Spain and Black Africans*, 1990], Makomé reports something very similar to what Fanon in his 1952 essay 'The Fact of Blackness,' which would be more accurately translated as 'The Lived Experience of the Black Man.' Fanon explains that it was only upon arriving in France from Martinique that he became conscious of his 'blackness' – 'as it was an external stimulus that flicked over me as I passed by ... "Mama, see the Negro! I'm frightened!"' (1967, pp. 111–112). It is significant that he uses the words of a child to articulate the constructedness of race – the child's reaction is an unmediated (or faintly mediated) rearticulation of the cultural assumptions that pervade his or her world. As Fanon writes: 'I already knew that there were legends, stories and above all historicity', upon which the objectification was based, 'I was battered down by tom-toms, cannibalism, intellectual deficiency, fetishism, racial defects, slave-ships, and above all else, above all: "Sho good eating"' (1967, p. 112).

Makomé's version runs as follows, 'The Spaniard sees in the African black the image of an inferior being, a dominated man, and above all, a poor. His colour, that at first sight ties in with all these circumstances, produces contempt at first sight' (1990, p. 104, my translation). He reports the case of a Dominican professor of Anthropology at a US university whom he met in Barcelona who told him, 'he found out that he was black only upon his arrival in Europe and when later on he went back to settle in the US' (1990, pp. 36–37, my translation). He also refers to a Dominican female lawyer, who was racially very light-skinned and who told him in Barcelona, 'The first thing my mother told me upon arriving to Spain was that here we are black women' (1990, p. 37, my translation).

Albert Memmi (1990) has also argued that colonialism entailed a negative definition of the colonized by the colonizer, in order to justify domination. The colonized, having had their own culture destroyed or debased, tended to adopt this given character, the colonizer's myth. In the process of rebellion, however, these given traits were revalued positively, alongside an attempt to retrieve the lost culture.

Originally a migrant from Cameroon to Valencia, sent by his family to complete his education, Makomé, who later became a black intellectual, sees racism in Spain through a compound lens. As through a kaleidoscope, Makomé's multiple positions give him simultaneous views of the same image through different angles. This is not to say that he has more insight into white racism than do his African counterparts, rather that his insight is differently oriented. He writes, 'Spain shows a very peculiar behaviour; a specific racism "made in Spain" which differs dramatically from the racism of other neighbouring countries. I should also say it is difficult to speak of such racism without bordering on ambiguity and contradiction. Nevertheless, this difference does exist, although I wonder whether I will be able to explain it accurately here' (1990, p. 103). William E.B. DuBois articulated a similar viewpoint in *Darkwater: Voices from Within the Veil*. His experience in white dominated institutions gave him a privileged insight into the workings and actions of white Americans: 'I see these souls undressed and from the back and side. I know their thoughts and they know what I know' (1920/1969, p. 55). Makomé's compound perspective, like that of DuBois, comes from 'within the veil' of Spanish racism, not from outside. It is important to note that the multipositionality of both writers leads them to produce strikingly similar analyses of the relationships between capitalism, imperialism, and racism.

Our analysis of Makomé's treatment of race and racism must be conscious of the multiple positions that he articulates in his writings. He shows that 'African', like 'Negro', is a racialized category within Spain (and the EU) and that black-skinned Africans face both anti-black racism and anti-African racism. They are identified phenotypically as 'Negroes' and linguistically and culturally as 'Africans'. Makomé individuates each process of racialization and, at the same time, demonstrates that both are products of the same ideology of white supremacy and cultural superiority rooted in practices of global capitalism and imperialism and in the history of slavery: 'It is odd to verify the fact that the whole world has ended up confusing the black race with slavery. These so called slaves were born free like everybody else, and the words slave and slavery are but byproducts of human injustice that has nothing to do with Nature' (1990, p. 97, my translation). In several cases, Makomé carefully isolates his experiences of anti-black discrimination from anti-African discrimination. His comparisons emphasize the flexibility of the race concept, demonstrating that its construction is rooted not in biology, but in the histories of slavery, colonialism, and cultural practice, which differ from place to place.

Critics of colonialism have made the point that racism is enforced and maintained by capitalist interests which thrive and profit by their policies of divide and conquer. There is a very important phenomenon here: racism is not epiphenomenal of class exploitation, but its existence serves capitalist interests. In making this analysis, Makomé echoes W.E.B. DuBois's point in his 1920 text *Darkwater: Voices from Within the Veil*, in a chapter entitled 'The Souls of White Folk'. There, he argues that the US and Europe have profited economically from practice legitimated by the ideology of white supremacy: slavery, colonialism, and the exploitation of free black workers. Like DuBois, Makomé rejects the notion that racism is an inevitability of human nature. If racism is not an intrinsic part of human nature, if it is not natural, then there always exists a possibility for its transformation.

While DuBois' purpose in *Darkwater* is an intellectual analysis of white supremacy, Makomé's aim in his writings as a whole, is to counter racism's work by cultivating solidarity across ethnic and social groups against racism, as well as the related practices of imperialism and class exploitation, by encouraging grassroots activism, 'Solidarity, is an old legacy that the Blacks have inherited from their ancestors, even though it is despised by the powerful today' (1990, p. 93, my translation). Makomé's project seeks to re–imagine collectivity. Calling for solidarity among people of color and progressive whites, he asserts a practical ethics: the first step is challenging discrimination and hate in the world is personal reflection and transformation: examining and reexamining ourselves and our attitudes and daily relations to other races.

One of the writer and the black intellectual's tasks requires reaching out to the very people who are guilty of what he calls 'race prejudice' and 'race hatred.' The task of changing their minds is complicated. It cannot be done by just thinking that you can exorcise chauvinism from people by ridiculing, insulting, howling and calling them ignorant. Makomé rather shows that racism runs deeper than the ideas and actions of individuals and in fact, he never demonizes individual racists or capitalists. Although he argues that racism, class exploitation, and imperialism are structural problems that must be addressed through an authentic social revolution, he also demonstrates that social revolution depends on individual action, social interaction, and organizing at the micro-level.

Makomé's ideas aim at charging all members of his reading audience, of all ethnic backgrounds, with the moral responsibility to effect social change. In his view, the tragedy is not simply that widespread racial prejudice creates a barrier to human conviviality, but that it produces an internal crisis for people of color who must consider the consequences of racial violence as they make everyday decisions in accordance with their own principles. He seeks to bring all of his readers the knowledge and understanding from which to build an inter-ethnic, cross-class, transnational coalition. His efforts aim at trying to make clear the need to build community between oppressed groups regardless of political affiliation. Makomé's texts, in brief, work to bridge the separation among ethnics of every ideological persuasion – involving understanding, interpretation, and dissemination – across ethnicity, class, nationality, and political affiliation in order to create alternative imagined communities working collectively toward emancipation.

Conclusion

It is clear that the African immigrants' presence in Spanish society must confront oppressive and dominating (sexually, racially, etc.) relationships, with multiple chains of subjection. African migrant writing offers a unique vantage point to look into Spain from an observer-participant perspective. Spanish democracy and its social structures are scrutinized, the Spaniards' habits and way of life analyzed and challenged. In the context of a rising awareness of the involvement and responsibilities derived from the colonial enterprise of European minor empires in Africa, Spain is learning to see itself through the eyes of its others.

Susan Akono, Donato Ndongo and Inongo-vi-Makomé's protagonists, their migrant workers, border-crossers, asylum-seekers, and the landscapes they traverse seem to depend on fragmentary and disjunctive discourses (migrancy, displacement).

Their men and women, shown as poor and migrant, tend to disrupt the idylls of landscape, the myth of the European Promised land, and of travelling for pleasure, and are thus open to question. Their peoples-in-transit seem to represent an ambivalent identity and an ambivalent association with the land.

In Makomé's view, African society can no longer be easily represented in terms of or in response to the utopian fantasy of a project for global emancipation to the extent that it is constituted by a diversified constellation of aspirations, struggles, and contradictions, no longer reducible to a univocal conception of history. Donato Ndongo, for whom 'every form of expatriation is some sort of exile' (2007, n.p.) engages in a lucid critique of the recent history of the dictatorship and its aftermath in Guinea in an atmosphere of barbarism and corrupt politics. At the same time, he acts as a relentless critical observer of the Spanish transition from dictatorship to democracy. Susan Akono's lucid analysis of the intersections of race, gender, class and marginality, poses a profound critique of tabooed attitudes toward sexuality, and to the place black women should actually occupy in the construction of a future with hope.

As an active part of the community-in-progress of African migrant writers, Makomé, Akono and Ndongo's migrant aesthetics could thus be defined as an aesthetics shaped by the partial, the discontinuous, the marginal, and one which seeks to dislodge unifying gazes like the one that could conceive of global African emancipation. In my view, their vision beyond aesthetics alludes to a certain disdain for the typical critical theorist's preoccupation with aesthetic judgment in lieu of more appropriately cultural attention to social analysis.

As I have attempted to show, these writers and intellectuals are sensitive to questions about migrancy, exile, transnationalism, and human rights, which pose an engaged critique of the categories of class exploitation and belonging (national or otherwise). In my view, their texts are not merely critiques and do more than respond or contest dominant Western discourses, they also envision some specific *inside* space as well. Creatively these texts are also monuments to the lost histories of their ancestors in Africa, they (re)build community, bear witness, and engage audiences in an almost utopian effort to become, in Fredric Jameson's dictum, 'a representational meditation on radical difference, radical otherness' (2005, p. xii). This radical otherness and the utopian impulse Jameson brings to light are well represented in the variety of genres of black migrant writing, where History is no longer seen through the fictions of white supremacy but deconstructed and disseminated in *histories* that construct new forms of collectivity.

Notes

1. Taken at its most literal, the postcolonial (and by extension postcolonial studies and theory) comes after formal colonization has ended. I take as starting point and inspiration Stuart Hall's efforts to register the term's indeterminacy within academia and his use of it as 'under erasure' in the Derridean sense. This allows Hall to indicate the limits, silences and problems with the concept, for lack of a better term. Following the rapid institutionalization of the field in the early 1990s, one the main accusations raised was that it lacked political foundation, preferring instead a celebratory aesthetic of hybridity and diaspora. Hall moves towards an understanding of 'différance' that disrupts binary oppositional limits like here/there or then/now. And in Hall's view, the shift from

'anti-colonial' to 'post-colonial' involves a shift from one conception of difference to another (Hall, 1996).
2. For a comprehensive survey of the history of black populations in Spain, see the entry on 'Spain' in Appiah and Gates (2005). It is interesting to note that black African populations grew with the Atlantic expansion of Spain and the establishment of modern slavery. The almost exclusive African work force destined for the New World passed first to the Iberian Peninsula, provoking changes in Spanish society. At the end of the sixteenth century, most of the approximately 100,000 slaves who remained as a captive labor force were black. Most importation of African slaves ceased in the early seventeenth century, and the remaining population of African descent ceased to be a distinct group within a few generations (2005, pp. 47–48).
3. Cyrus and Legge identify the following common features of Afro–Hispanic literature, helpful in any attempt to further analyse the cultural and intellectual concerns of this transnational community in its different locations: (1) Afro–Hispanic literature contains a syncretic core: it is a composite that shows common elements, between romanticism and modernism on the one hand and negrism on the other hand, offering rich areas for further study and research; (2) a re-affirmative spirit: it is advocacy, a defiant zeal to continue what is considered as having been already established by ancestors; (3) a sense of universal fraternity: concern for transcending all ethnic groups, and emphasis on issues of social justice for the oppressed, and a desire for a just society; (4) a satirical tone: a tendency to use ironic wit to attack and expose the injustices of society; (5) nature: an emphasis on nature's beauty in a vital and telluric sense; (6) a kinesthetic emphasis: concentration on rhythmic qualities as those of the dance; (7) a romantic sentimentalism: a tendency to bare emotions and frustration in the face of harsh conditions; (8) resonant pitch: texts are replete with onomatopoeic rhythms, intensive phrasal patterns and sonorous African linguistic elements (1991, pp. 93–96).
4. In Spain, the stronger discrimination suffered by North Africans as compared with the benevolence by which Spaniards look at sub-Saharan Africans is no doubt a consequence of the repercussions of the terrorist attacks on Madrid's Atocha train station of 11 March 2004 which resulted in 200 deaths. The attacks, the worst act of terrorism on European soil in decades, have been attributed by the Spanish police to Moroccan terrorists linked to Al-Qaeda, and have Spanish Muslims 'bracing for a backlash.' Such fears could not have come at a more inopportune time for Spain's immigrants, both legal and illegal. Many of them are still adjusting to deepened fears and suspicions about immigrants in general created by the terrorist attacks of 11 September 2001. According to Human Rights Watch, in the immediate aftermath of 11 September, the Spanish government was the first in Europe to openly equate the fight against illegal immigration with the war against terrorism.
5. Known as Moors and Christian Festivals, this is a traditional popular celebration which reenacts events of the reconquest. Today a tourist attraction, it takes place on different locations along the Spanish Mediterranean coast. There is hardly a castle without a role in the struggle for supremacy over Al-Andalus, an Arabic name for the land ruled by Muslims in 711–1492. At its widest it covered modern Spain, except for Asturias, most of Portugal and the southern part of France. Parades that take the streets late in the evening show these and many other characters in fantastic dresses surrounded by skillful constructions of castles, boats and other scenes of the reconquest. They hang the Muslim or Christian symbols, coats of arms and banners, outside their houses, wear traditional costumes and dramatize various scenes in the streets. Over the centuries the Moors – constituting Arabs, but mainly Berbers of North Africa – mixed with the Christians through marriages. The first invaders brought no women with them. This way a large part of the second generation Moors were actually half Hispanic. Many Christians also converted to Muslims or adopted their customs while still maintaining their Christian rituals. Mozarabs, Renegades and Muladis were all Christians or former Christians who embraced Islam and often fought against their former compatriots.
6. The protagonist of *Black Iris* lost her mother, who died of malaria, when she was very young and her father used to call her Elsa Belle – her name Elsa Isabelle was thus changed into 'Elsa the Beautiful' (26).

7. Akono mingles testimonio with the objectivity of facts in her harsh critique of imperialism. She speaks of her family and her current situation in an effort to communicate crossculturally, 'My grandfather is extremely reluctant to mingle with the whites because he associates them with abuse of authority, injustice, excessive eagerness to humiliate, scorn, dominate, enslave, and exploit other people' (2004, p. 7).
8. George Yúdice in 'Testimonio and Postmodernism' defines the genre as referring to 'an authentic narrative, who is told by a witness who is moved to narrate by the urgency of the situation (e.g. war, oppression, revolution, etc). Emphasizing popular oral discourse, the witness portrays his or her own experience as representative of a collective memory and identity. Truth is summoned in the cause of denouncing a present situation of exploitation or exorcising and setting a right official history' (1996, p. 44).
9. This period is described in detail in Ndongo's subsequent novel *Los Poderes de la Tempestad* (*Powers of the Tempest*, 1997).
10. Even when the main ethnic groups in Equatorial Guinea, Bubi, Ndowe, Fang, Annabonese and Fernandinos, are distinguished by their own customs and languages, Spanish remains the lingua franca.
11. In Makomé's view, this rejection of the black immigrants started in the 1980s, '... by the mid-1980s, hatred against the Africans started to be felt in Spain' (1990, p. 162, my translation).

References

Akono, S. (2004). *The weapons of my disappointment*. Insch: Lipstick Publishing.
Akono, S. (n.d., c.2001). Iris negro [*Black Iris*]. Unpublished manuscript.
Althusser, L. (1971). Ideology and ideological state apparatuses. In *Lenin and philosophy and other essays* (pp. 121–176). (B. Brewster, Trans.). New York, NY: Monthly Review Press.
Appiah, K.A., & Gates Jr., H.L. (Eds.), (2005). *Africana: The encyclopedia of the African and African American experience*. Oxford: Oxford University Press.
Benjamin, W. (1968). Theses on the philosophy of history. In H. Arendt (Ed.), *Illuminations* (pp. 253–264). (H. Zohn, Trans.). New York, NY: Schocken.
Cyrus, S., & Legge, J. (1991). Afro-Hispanic literature: Cultural and literary enrichment for the foreign language classroom. In T. Robert (Ed.), *Acting on priorities: A commitment to excellence* (pp. 91–102). Southern Conference on Language Teaching, Valdosta State College. Valdosta, Georgia.
DuBois, W.E.B. (1920/1969). *Darkwater: Voices from within the veil*. New York, NY: Schocken.
Fanon, F. (1967). *Black skin, white masks*. New York, NY: Grove Press.
Hall, S. (1996). When was the postcolonial? In L. Curti & I. Chambers (Eds.), *The postcolonial question: Common skies, divided horizons* (pp. 242–260). London: Routledge.
Jameson, F. (2005). *Archaeologies of the future*. London: Verso.
Makomé, I-V. (1990). *España y los Negros Africanos* [*Spain and black Africans*]. Barcelona: La Llar del Llibre.
Makomé, I.-V. (2000). *La Emigración Negroafricana: Tragedia y Esperanza* [*African black immigration: Tragedy and hope*]. Barcelona: Carena.
Makomé, I.-V. (2002). *Población Negra en Europa. Segunda Generación, Nacionales de Ninguna Nación* [*The blacks in Europe. Second generation: nationals of no country*]. San Sebastián: Hirugarren Prentsa.
Memmi, A. (1990). *The colonizer and the colonized*. (H. Greenfeld, Trans.). London: Beacon Press.
Ndongo, D. (1997). *Los Poderes de la Tempestad* [*Powers of the tempest*]. Madrid: Morandi.
Ndongo, D. (2007). *Shadows of your black memory*. (M. Ugarte, Trans.). Chicago, IL: Swan Isle Press.
Pérez, E. (1999). *The decolonial imaginary: Writing Chicanas into history*. Bloomington, IN: Indiana University Press.
Riquelme, J. (1986). Review of *Las Tinieblas de tu memoria Negra*, *Africa, 2000*, 3(5), 46–50.
Rose, J. (1998). *States of fantasy*. Oxford: Clarendon Press.
Yúdice, G. (1996). Testimonio and postmodernism. In G. Gugelberger (Ed.), *The real thing: Testimonial discourse and Latin America* (pp. 42–57). Durham, NC: Duke University Press.

'Rented spaces': Italian postcolonial literature

Manuela Coppola

Department of Linguistics, Università della Calabria, Arcavacata di Rende, Italy

Moving from the marginal social space assigned to migrant women and from their condition of objects of enunciation, this essay analyses the literature produced by Italophone women writers, Italians of African, Eastern European or Indian ancestry as a controversial site of self-representation. Although they gain increasing visibility through access to publication, these writers still occupy ambiguous spaces of exotic objectification and limiting definitions. By choosing a postcolonial perspective as a theoretical approach which might help re-establish connections between a repressed colonial history and contemporary global migration, the essay suggests that, in their precarious occupation of Italian literary and linguistic spaces, postcolonial women writers inhabit different discursive places like a 'rented apartment' whose transitory power provides new strategies of literary and linguistic cohabitation, effectively disturbing the construction of supposedly homogeneous national and cultural spaces.

In a European context, generally engaged with debates on multicultural societies, citizenship, and questions of language, Italy has newly acknowledged the presence of a 'second generation' of migrants, people of non-Italian origin who are still striving for recognition and who are increasingly gaining access to practices of self-representation.[1] In fact, while in other European countries the legacy of colonialism and the recent global migratory flows have contributed to the redefinition of national subjectivities, only in recent years has Italy started confronting its colonial past and the consequences of global mass migration. Moving from the marginal social space assigned to migrant women and from their condition of objects – rather than of subjects – of enunciation, this essay analyses the literature produced by Italophone women writers as a controversial site of self-representation.[2] Although they gain increasing visibility through access to publication, women writers of African, Eastern European or Indian ancestry still occupy ambiguous spaces of exotic objectification and limiting definitions. In the trail of a recent strand of academic studies from different disciplines which has started to reassess the crucial role of the legacy of Italian colonialism in the contemporary experience of migration, I wish to focus on the contribution of this new literature to the re-discussion of national subjectivities and cultural spaces, contextualizing it in a European postcolonial perspective.[3] Far from implying a further labelling and limiting view of this literature, the term postcolonial suggests a confrontation with theoretical approaches which might help re-establish connections between a repressed colonial history and the emergent corpus of Italophone literature at the crossroads of European intersections.

The publication of some critical studies such as *Post-colonial Cultures in France* (Hargreaves & McKinney, 1997) testifies to a recent shift in the literary field which has partially tempered the absence of Europe within postcolonial studies lamented by a number of scholars. In the effort to turn the gaze on Europe as the site of complex entanglements of colonial and neocolonial powers, these texts provide the first attempts to investigate its literature as the product of hegemonic cultural and political practices. Although Italian studies are still a long way off a radical reconceptualization of Italy's colonial past and its present of migration, postcolonial women writers play nonetheless a crucial role in the critical exposure of spaces of cultural and material oppression. The term postcolonial will thus be used not only in reference to authors with direct connections to former Italian colonies, but it will also include writers experiencing a situation of cultural and linguistic dislocation whose postcoloniality consists in their literary response, 'explicit or implied, to mainstream practices of marginalization and objectification' (Huggan, 2008, p. 245).

Because of their urban, literary and linguistic displacement, I contend that postcolonial women writers hold an eccentric position: appropriating the term used by de Lauretis (1990) to describe the subject of enunciation of feminist theory, I argue that postcolonial migrant writers occupy a similarly multiple and precarious space which is simultaneously outside and inside the Italian social and literary system, a space 'that need[s] to be affirmed but not resolved' (de Lauretis, 1990, p. 144). In their precarious occupation of Italian literary and linguistic spaces, I suggest that postcolonial women writers inhabit these discursive places like a 'rented apartment' (de Certeau, 1984, p. xxi): the transitory power acquired from borrowing these spaces constitutes a cultural practice enabling these writers to produce knowledge from the critical re-assemblage of pre-existing elements, thus redefining boundaries and given notions of identity, literary canons, and linguistic normativeness. Just as migrants modify the urban space of Italian cities, transforming it with their presence, I suggest that postcolonial women writers in Italy similarly become both the practitioners and the chroniclers of everyday life by re-signifying literary and linguistic spaces. In this light, I wish to analyse the ways in which, repeating a pattern already explored by writers from former British and French colonies, these women writers offer strategies of cohabitation through a shared language and literature. While they engage in a creative dialogue with the canonical corpus of Italian literature, they trace genealogies and/or oppositional relations, stimulating a critical re-location of Italian culture in the spaces opened up by this writing.

Crossing identities

A multiple signifier related to social, cultural, and linguistic practices, the concept of space provides a useful metaphor to investigate politics of cohabitation in postcolonial Europe. As Paul Gilroy stated, 'the racial ontology of sovereign territory and the cultivation of bounded, 'encamped' national cultures, has been necessarily concerned with the symbolic organization of space, place, and political community' (2004, p. 328). In Fortress Europe, the relation of the migrant with space is obviously crucial: as it is closely connected with issues of legality and citizenship, space becomes the contested site of inclusions and exclusions, creating borders and regulating movement, providing or denying social recognition and cultural belonging.[4] This binary logic seems to be paralleled by the contradictory attitude Europe and national states have towards the phenomenon of migration:

> Although Europe, as a geopolitical entity and as an ideological concept, has rested on a historical process of absorbing, hybridising, and assimilating different people from diverse ethnic, religious and national groups, individual European countries have tended to view migration as challenging and threatening to their territories, to their identities, and ways of imagining themselves and others. (Loshitzky, 2006, p. 629)

Undecided as to its role, oscillating between a superficial welcoming of migrants and an indistinct fear often turning into overt xenophobia, Italy firmly holds to the fiction of a national identity constructed on religion and colour.[5]

The relation with space is particularly ambiguous in Italy as regards the troublesome 'politics of hospitality' theorized by Jacques Derrida.[6] No matter how long migrants have been living in Italy, their stay is always perceived as temporary. In what has been termed '*paradoxical inclusion*' (Yegenoglu, 2005, p. 143), the temporary migrant who has indefinitely prolonged his/her stay is caught in a contradictory space in which his/her status is problematically suspended. While it is inconceivable that they might be included as citizens in the national space, they are only – at times – tolerated as long as they provide cheap labour, pushed in the undefined condition of *non-persons* (Dal Lago, 2004). Being often denied the status of citizens, the supposed guests nonetheless settle in their new country, thus becoming 'permanent strangers' with scarce opportunities to re-define their subjectivities in institutional and legal terms.[7] Moreover, their identity is often produced through a set of negative stereotypes which are gender-related. While migrants are usually narrated and represented by the media as criminals, migrant women follow a different pattern of representation. Either as suffering mothers when they land on Italian shores after a life-risking crossing, or as mature strong domestic workers taking care of the elders, or as young women 'stealing' someone else's husband, or prostitutes, migrant women are trapped in stereotypes which are mainly informed by the spatial relations of their bodies with men and children or the elderly (Pojmann, 2006, p. 38). The framework of representation rarely includes other possibilities. Objectified and commodified, their bodies are constantly under close scrutiny: either through the arms of domestic workers or the fingertips required to be fingerprinted by the police, their subjectivities are often obfuscated and hid by the predominantly corporeal reality they have been assigned.[8] Quite paradoxically, this over-exposure of the female migrant's body resolves into her persistent invisibility in the host society at large.

While the upper-middle classes enjoy a sort of 'cosmopolitan awareness' of being citizens of a global world taking pleasure in free movement, this cosmopolitanism is denied to the masses of undocumented people for whom border-crossing is often a life-risking activity. Similarly, these contrasting attitudes are reflected by the split feelings towards migrants, caught between the intellectual praise of diversity and the systematic exclusion of foreigners from the social and political body. Literature somehow reflects and parallels this contradictory pull, bringing to the fore complex issues of representation and self-representation. Taking the name of *Migrantenliteratur* in Germany and of *littérature multiculturelle* in France, what in Italy is defined

The recent editorial strategy of publishing 'multicultural' texts can be read in part as set on the trail of the success of a well-established literary tradition in France or Great Britain and which has led to the publication of the Italian translations of successful novels such as *White Teeth* (2001) by Zadie Smith, *Brick Lane* (2003) by Monica Ali, and *Londonstani* (2006) by Gautam Malsani. But, while this literary tradition has gained scholarly attention in countries like France, The Netherlands, and the Nordic countries, where migration flows have stimulated a debate on the issues of multiculturalism, in Italy, on the contrary, this editorial success has not entailed a significant rediscussion of practices of representation nor a revision of canonical identities. Moreover, the race for political correctness – at least in intellectual circles – has in some cases led to the publication of novels by authors with no particularly interesting literary voice, apparently only to meet the expectations of the market.

Writing can sometimes provide a privileged space of recognition, and yet the growing visibility achieved by Italian postcolonial writers thanks to dedicated literary prizes and the proliferation of academic studies and anthologies indicates both an interest to promote this literature as well as a need for categorization. Accordingly, the editorial success of publications often marketed as young, trendy products, paves the way for an unproblematic assimilation of this writing into the easy label of 'migrant literature' in Italy, thus turning these authors into fashionable examples of a supposed cosmopolitan, multicultural society.[11] Although this trend has recently gained some academic attention in Italy, especially in Departments of Italian Studies, the new generation of postcolonial women writers is often seen as an exotic object of literary desire, represented within the fashionable paradigm of a world without boundaries. This very representation proves to be, quite obviously, another cage where disturbing categories of alterity (writer/artist/musician) can be enclosed. Literary critics are particularly fond of labels but, in this context, the struggle over definitions seems to respond to the urge of somehow controlling the new phenomenon of subjects of non-Italian origins claiming their space into the national literary community. In the implicit denial of multiple subjectivities and belongings, the 'liberating ordinariness' advocated by Paul Gilroy (2005) seems to be an untimely prospect. Caught in this aporia (Derrida), Italian postcolonial writers strive to negotiate a space where they strongly reject the further objectification performed by the literary market and, at the same time, refuse to be assimilated as Italian writers *tout court*, resisting a normalization which would simply erase their difference. Even though Igiaba Scego, a young writer of Somalian descent, has been described as the forerunner of a new generation of Italian writers, it may be true that we are still far from a significant redefinition of Italian literature which could take into account the plural subjectivities inhabiting contemporary Italy and avoid restraining definitions.

Literary contests and festivals have undoubtedly been useful for promotional purposes, and yet writers are increasingly calling for a different approach through the carving out of a self-managed space. The online journal *El-Ghibli. Literatures of migration* (www.El-Ghibli.org), the first literary periodical in Italy whose editorial staff consists completely of non-Italian writers, provides such a space. By assessing the crucial importance of *El-Ghibli*, the multicultural project she contributed to found in 2003, the writer Gabriella Ghermandi has convincingly claimed the possibility for writers to occupy their space without being guided by literary associations or academics.[12] While the criminalized or passive figure of the migrant woman is a treacherously reductive representation, the image of the 'successful migrant' is equally ambiguous and potentially dangerous. As Gabriella Kuruvilla suggests, the notion of 'success' sounds slightly racist as it implies conformity to and acceptance into the 'native' community. Contesting the notion of the migrant writer as a successful, glamorous figure, she strongly asserts the everyday dimension of her writing and her daily efforts to negotiate her identities:

> The first time they defined me [as a successful migrant] I was shocked... For a long time I wondered what it meant. Did it mean I looked like a white woman and not like a beige-skinned Indian? Did it mean I dressed like respectable people and that I had an extremely fashionable job? Did it mean that sometimes the newspapers talked about my stories? I don't feel I'm successful, whatever it may mean. I believe this word reveals a gap between my daily life and my public life. My daily life is made of sacrifices... for my son, for my job, for my dream of writing, while my public life shows a glamour and a success which do not really exist. (Kuruvilla, 2006)

In order to avoid the risk of creating other stereotyped representations, the image of the migrant writer as a fashionable figure travelling between worlds and cultures, moving in the dimension of the multicultural literary trend, should be radically interrogated. However, far from celebrating migration as an empowering condition, these writers are often aware of the legacy of suffering and uprootedness characterizing their condition, choosing to draw on their experience as a strategy to elaborate a critical space of intervention and agency.

The race for cultural spaces/literary spaces

Along with the questioning of stereotypes and appropriation of editorial spaces, the presence of voices from nearby crossing borders and their disturbing proximity is also contributing to intersect and re-discuss given notions of national and cultural identity. If the stranger is 'the space that wrecks our abode', according to Julia Kristeva (1991, p. 1), then writers writing in Italian effectively disturb the construction of supposedly monolithic and homogeneous cultural spaces, constituting an interrogating presence which consistently questions practices of representation.

The feminization of migration flows to Europe has prompted a shift in critical studies. While earlier studies on Italian immigration outlined migration as a mainly male enterprise, acknowledging the participation of women only in the family reunification process, the crucial role of gender has been re-assessed by ground-breaking works such as Andall (2000). By focusing on the experience of African female migrants working as domestic servants, Andall explores the impact of women migrants in Italy while documenting the transformation of social roles and domestic spaces. Usually employed as live-in domestic workers or caretakers, female migrants are often associated with the domestic space. As a controversial site of conflicting expectations deriving from the role of women as mediators, the house provides a metaphor for the interplay and intersection of private and public spaces. While they are often seen as bridges, problematically displaying an opposition between tradition and modernity, preservation and assimilation of new values, Andall also notes that 'within their own ethnic minority communities, women are frequently expected to retain and perform a particular version of "culture"' (Andall, 2003, p. 3). Moreover, while they embody the relation with 'home', migrant women also expose the collapse of spatial norms prescribing a rigid separation between the safe, private space of domesticity, and the more precarious outer space exposed to alterity and contamination.

Resisting the neat dichotomy between public and private space, female subjectivities often suggest a remapping of public spaces in a new geography of cross-cultural encounters. Public spaces in many Italian cities have been modified by the presence of migrant women: railway stations, post offices and parks, have been transformed into places of encounter, constituting 'a bridge between their new residence and home, a material and symbolic link with their distant homeland' (Curti, 2007, p. 61). In this disturbing proximity and simultaneous cohabitation of metropolitan spaces, the rigid spatial regulation which marked colonial ideology declares its failure. As Sandro Mezzadra argues, 'Confinement, ... and the resistance against it no longer organise a cartography capable of unequivocally distinguishing the metropolis from the colonies since they shatter and recompose themselves continuously on a global scale' (Mezzadra & Rahola, 2006).

As a shifting signifier, space becomes a transformative site marked by the interaction occurring within it. Not only has the urban space been re-inscribed and modified, it has also been represented, written upon and re-signified by other voices articulating what Brah (1996) has conceptualized as 'diaspora space'. New expressions of European subjectivities are produced by the changes occurring in the diaspora space inhabited 'not only by those who have migrated and their descendants, but equally by those who are constructed and represented as indigenous' (Brah, 1996, p. 209). Problematizing the subject position of the native, postcolonial women writers thus cast a critical and defamiliarizing gaze on national spaces and identities which advocates for a rediscussion of conventional borders. Institutional and unquestionably 'Italian' spaces are often experienced in these narratives with a sense of fear and inadequacy, and the spaces of Italian bureaucracy constitute of course the most significant example of this unease. In 'Documenti, prego' [Documents, please], a short story by Ingy Mubiayi, the young protagonist is the only person in the family who possesses all the required qualifications to venture in the prefecture and apply for Italian citizenship: 'good capacity to arrange and codify the Latin alphabet in written and/or oral form, familiarity with the places of bureaucracy, adult, and female – thus genetically unable to refuse' (Mubiayi, 2005a, p. 98). In a similar vein the same author engages in the ironic critique of a police station where ignorance and disorganization rule in the story 'Concorso' [Competitive examination], while the Italian contradictions are brilliantly explored by Igiaba Scego in 'La strana notte di Vito Renica [The strange night of Vito Renica]. In this short story Scego sketches out the paradoxical but quite common character of a young Neapolitan boy who turned into a supporter of the Northern League, a right-wing party expressing racist ideas and theorizing the supposed superiority of Northern Italians over Southerners. While her critical eye reveals the conflicts of Italian society, it also denounces the Italians' inability to negotiate their identities in the light of new subjectivities intersecting their national identities.

Cultural spaces are equally perceived with uneasiness. In *Amiche per la pelle* [*Close friends*], Laila Wadia's first novel, the Indian Shanti, the Albanian Lule, the Chinese Meigui and the Bosnian Marinka live with their families in Trieste, in the same run-down building of via Ungaretti 25, a microcosm of different life stories, languages, and cultures. Resolved to integrate into the host society, they pay for

Italian lessons despite their husbands' disapproval. One of their lessons takes place at the Caffè San Marco, the meeting place of intellectuals, and their teacher proposes a string concert at the Teatro Verdi. The theatre, historical symbol – as well as the café – of Trieste's cultural tradition, is approached by the four protagonists with a sense of awe. Excited and nervous, the protagonists worry about the price of the tickets and overdress for what they think is their coming out. To their disappointment, inevitably appearing naïve and out of place, they will find out that what they believed to be an impressive and splendid place is a small theatre where the audience in casual clothing attend the free rehearsal of an unbearable music.

The house often mirrors the migrant's precarious condition. In 'Il pranzo pasquale' [Easter lunch] Gabriella Ghermandi thus describes the neighbourhood of Corticella in Bologna, establishing a close link between people's condition and their homes: 'The last stretch of via Corticella, where foreigners concentrated, resembled a half-bombed city. Buildings which highlighted their precariousness overlooked roads with wrecked concrete. We lived in those buildings, precarious like our residence permits' (Ghermandi, 2006). In 'Concorso', by Ingy Mubiayi (2005b) the narrator is a 'settled' migrant whose integration in Italy is significantly embodied by the possession of a house. The 'room of one's own' is here represented by a huge bathroom, a comfortable space of female intimacy where the women of the house meet to chat and tell their secrets. By contrast, the poor house, where the newly-arrived immigrant Aziza lives, reveals the precarious situation of a lonely woman with two children who has invested all her savings to pay for the crossing. Likewise, Laila Wadia hints at the significantly different living conditions of migrants depending on their 'success'. In her novel *Amiche per la pelle*, for instance, the dark and small basement where an undefined number of Chinese illegal workers live, reveals the non-human living conditions of 'unsuccessful migrants', people who, unlike the four protagonists, are not lucky enough to rent a proper house and reproduce the model of a family in the new country.

On the other hand, the private space of the house, described as the repository of maternal culture, is often represented as a site of cultural conflict. In many short stories (see for instance Ghermandi, 2006; Muyiabi, 2005a; Scego, 2005) men are absent and the family is recreated in the domestic space through an all-female genealogy of mother, grandmother, daughter and sister. Yet, not only does the house become the space where maternal traditions and language are transmitted and preserved, but is also often articulated as the space where outside visitors bring in the tensions of the 'host' culture as in *Curry di pollo* [Chicken curry], where an adolescent girl of Indian origins lives with growing apprehension an invitation to dinner to her Italian friends, fearing their encounter with her parents (Wadia, 2005).

The experience of migration and diaspora inevitably entails a renegotiation and redefinition of the notions of home and identity as related to normative prescriptions. Igiaba Scego's short story 'Dismatria' [Dismotherland] foregrounds such issues in the protagonist's wish for roots, challenging the traditional Somalian condition of upootedness and nomadism. Unlike her mother, who stubbornly clings to her suitcases as signifiers of her temporary stay in Italy, the protagonist contends that 'if you feel Italian you don't betray Somalia' (Scego, 2005, p. 18), defending her choice to buy a house to establish a balance between her two motherlands. Orphaned of her *matria*, a neologism coined by the author in order to convey the idea of Somalia as a female homeland, a notion which in Italian is expressed by a word with a masculine root (*patria*), the protagonist implies that facing the taboo of suitcases, and finally unpacking them, represents the first step towards a possible cohabitation of her two *matrie*. In a constant bordercrossing, both geographical and metaphorical, the woman writer thus re-imagines her space and engages in a re-mapping of her personal cartographies which questions conventional definitions.

Rented spaces: language and the canon

Colonial empires like France and Great Britain have long seen their national language dislocated and taken elsewhere, appropriated and transformed under the impact of their former subjects. In recent times, migratory fluxes from different parts of the world have forced even European countries which did not have a colonial past to engage in a redefinition of their national identities and languages, whereas Italy has failed to come to terms with this 'uncanny' proximity. This is the reason why it is quite common for Italian postcolonial writers to lament, often with irony, the surprise of Italians at hearing them speaking Dante's language with propriety and awareness of their cultural tradition. In fact, whether they grew up in former Italian colonies or learnt Italian as a second language, these writers share a deeply conscious use of their plural linguistic and cultural legacy. In particular, what seems to be troubling is that these subjects may have access to practices of self-representation through the appropriation of the Italian language from a speaking position which is simultaneously inside and outside Italian society.

Insisting on the spatial metaphor, this appropriation of other texts and languages can be seen as inhabiting them 'like a rented apartment', as Michel de Certeau suggested (1984, p. xxi). By claiming the legitimate occupation of a space, Italian postcolonial writers increasingly suggest the urgency of a reconfiguration of the cohabitation in ways which do not imply a patronizing gesture of hospitality. The theorizations of the Martinican intellectual Edouard Glissant seem to be particularly relevant in this context. In his theoretical elaboration of a poetics of relation in a space where the violent contact between cultures has turned into a flux of relation, exchange and transformation, Glissant (1989) refuses a radical and sterile rejection of his colonial language, appropriating French creatively in order to dismantle its authority and question its supposedly superior status. If Frantz Fanon (1994) inextricably linked colonial language to the construction of a colonial identity, Glissant proposes a powerfully creolised language accounting for the hybrid identities of its speakers. In this respect, the rhizomatic identity he postulates in the Caribbean, an identity shaped by the proliferation of different traces and influences becomes the pattern to understand the current creolisation of European languages and cultures in the intersection of roots (Glissant, 1989).

Although Italian literature is still far from being effectively creolized, as Lidia Curti (2007, p. 66) suggests, postcolonial women writers perform a radical re-think of supposedly fixed categories such as national languages and literary canons. In a recent interview Gabriella Kuruvilla sounded surprised when the interviewer asked her about her literary models. The question was quite unusual since, as the writer argued, 'They always ask me about my parents as if I weren't a writer, but only a case study' (2006). Although they probably aspire to official literary recognition and to inclusion in the Italian literary canon, at the same time these writers acknowledge the potentiality of their writing which lies in their being multiple and displaced. Since, as

Jadelin Mabial Gangbo has argued, '[w]e are here and elsewhere at the same time. We are Italian and non-Italian at the same time' (in Kuruvilla, 2006), their multiple positionality defies and challenges easy categorizations and inclusions. In this creative 'in-betweenness', new strategies for inhabiting Italian as a language and its literature are produced in the space across linguistic, literary, and identity boundaries.

To account for their complex belonging, some writers have published bilingual short poems and novels or have committed to children's literature, embracing the didactical project of teaching the language and their culture of origin to the new generations living in Italy. The choice made by the Eritrean Ribka Sibhatu in *Aulò. Canto-poesia dall'Eritrea* [Aulò: Song-Poem from Eritrea, 1993], responds to both intents: a book for children, weaving the story of the writer's family into the troubled history of her country, *Aulò* is a bilingual text written in Italian and Tigrinya which becomes accessible to a wider community of readers. More often, the many languages the writers inhabit are condensed in a sort of 'displaced' Italian, haunted and nourished at the same time by different echoes. The formally perfect Italian of Ornela Vorpsi's novels, for instance, resonates with the rhythm of her native Albanian and of the French she speaks every day, testifying to the transnational status of European languages.

The relation of this new body of literature with the canonical corpus of Italian literature is interestingly revealed in *Amiche per la pelle*. Far from being casual, the references to poets like Ungaretti and Saba, whose names resonate in the topography of the neighbourhood as obscure markers of space, represent the controversial link with Italian culture and its repressed past. While the rude Italian neighbour, the old Mr. Rosso who indistinctly calls 'niggers' all his foreign neighbours, takes pleasure in teaching Kamla, Shanti's daughter, poems by hermetic Italian poets, the reference to Ungaretti marks a connection to Italian colonialism and immigration, since the poet was born and raised in Alexandria, in Egypt, in the years of Italian settlement in Eastern Africa. Likewise, the novel is framed by a quotation from a poem by Umberto Saba on Trieste, the cultural bridge between the west and the east, the intellectual city of Svevo and of Joyce's exile. Saba will appear again in the text when Shanti, after reading the poem, *Trieste*, confesses: 'The first time you don't quite understand it, but then it gets into your heart, just like this strange city' (Wadia, 2007, p. 35). Moreover, although the novel is set in contemporary Trieste and none of its protagonists nor the author experienced Italian colonialism, the ongoing effects of that history unpredictably emerge in the narration. At the end of the story, after Mr. Rosso's death, the repressed history will appear in the shape of his grandson from Addis Abeba, the city in which he had a love-affair with an Ethiopian woman in his youth.

While the references to canonical Italian literature provide a familiar background for the Italian reader, at the same time they bear the traces of a repressed history and offer new perspectives on a postcolonial present nourished by different cultural roots. As Cristina Lombardi-Diop interestingly notes in her afterword to Gabriella Ghermandi's first novel, *Regina di fiori e di perle* [Queen of flowers and pearls] (2007), the novel grafts African roots and perspectives onto Ennio Flaiano's *Tempo di uccidere* [Time to Kill, 1947], thus suggesting a new literary model in the convergence of past conflicts and contemporary complexities (Lombardi-Diop, 2007, p. 261). The intense allegory of Italian colonial experience in Africa triggers Gabriella Ghermandi's literary inspiration for her first novel in which she weaves together different voices and a common history. In the powerful scene of the killing of an Italian soldier by an Ethiopian girl, Ghermandi echoes and reverses Flaiano's description of the rape and eventual accidental murder of a young woman by a soldier during the 1930s Italian occupation of Ethiopia. The colonial encounter is thus re-imagined through a peculiar rewriting which dialogues with the 'canonical' Italian text in a similar quest for the re-elaboration of a shameful past and a possible form of redemption.

Although Africa is an often imaginary homeland, it is nonetheless constantly present in the texture of many narratives, unearthing the complex web of cultural relations with Italy. As an emotional space, it nurtures the narrative imagination of writers who blend the echoes of the trauma linked to colonialism, the suffering of the civil war, and the living conditions of migrants, thus forcefully creating a contiguity with the Italian readers. Focusing on orality as a strategy of narration, voice and language turn into a sort of home which offers a refuge and a sense of belonging in the diaspora. The language is the Italian spoken by the colonizers and imposed at schools to the writers' parents; yet, it is also the Italian appropriated by the writers in their diasporic lives, here interestingly traversed by echoes of other stories and other voices. As in *Regina di fiori e di perle*, where the protagonist becomes a 'cantora', telling stories from the colonial period in an Italian language powerfully inhabited by Amharic (Ghermandi, 2007); in the polyphonic *Madre piccola* [Little Mother], the first novel by Cristina Ali Farah (2007), the author collects the stories of her people in the diaspora and narrates them in a concentric movement. As she becomes a contemporary *griotte*, she invents a new and necessary word, *logicammino*, to express the traditional structure of Somali narration, providing a bridge between the Italian in which it has been written, and Somali, the language which gives the rhythm to her story.

Former colonial subjects share a common linguistic and cultural background with Italians but, as Lidia Curti notes, 'the proximity is rarely reciprocal as Somalia is an unknown in contemporary Italy' (2007, p. 64). Yet, in the forceful claim of a shared past, literature seems to advocate a relation of reciprocity between Italy and its former colonies which is still unrealized in contemporary society.[13] Not only does this reciprocity entail the cultural hybridity testified by the dialogue with the Italian literary canon, but it is especially performed in a language bearing the traces of other voices and cultures. *Madre piccola*, for instance, is punctuated by many Somali words coming from the colonial past and surprising the reader for their (unexpected) resonance with Italian, like *farmascio* for *farmacia*, or *fasoleeti* for *fazzoletti* [handkerchief] (Ali Farah, 2007). Moreover, the author uses whole sentences which, despite the presence of a glossary at the end of the text, are sometimes left untranslated. Reading the novel through Glissant's theorizations, it can be argued that Ali Farah makes Italian opaque and resists its authority through its interrogation and contamination with Somali words, thus suggesting a strategy of linguistic cohabitation.

The question of linguistic standardization in these postcolonial texts is still open. Possessing the language and mastering it has been viewed as a form of legitimation and has provided a sense of literary authority for the 'first wave' of migrant writers. According to Ali Farah (2005) their resistance to the inclusion of traces of their mother tongue in a carefully edited Italian text, cannot be compared with the situation of 'second generation' writers. It can be argued that, mastering Italian as their mother tongue, they should find it easier to come to terms with their bilingualism and explore new directions in the challenge to linguistic normativeness.

The claim made by Pap Khouma in his editorial to the first issue of *El Ghibli* might provide a suggestive metaphor of a new approach to Italian. Khouma asserts that they would inevitably 'attack' Dante's language, using the Italian verb *aggredire* in its etymological sense of *ad-gredi*, meaning to communicate, to go towards the other, to give and take back (2003). To what extent can the 'aggression', the approaching envisioned by Khouma, contribute to the enrichment of the Italian language and produce a shared linguistic space is an issue still to be addressed. However, while they precariously inhabit Italian spaces and languages, postcolonial women writers suggest new perspectives on European identities. Their in-betweenness may thus turn into an effective strategy of resistance and critical reassessment: their double insight allows for a sharp critical investigation of their cultures, resisting the reproduction of hegemonic discourses and providing a fertile ground for re-thinking and re-articulating spaces, be they institutional or familiar, public or private, geographical or emotional.

Notes

1. 'Second generation' is of course a debatable definition used here for convenience's sake but which will be questioned and discussed later in the article.
2. Although I am aware that Francophone and Anglophone are controversial and much criticized terms, the analogous term Italophone has been chosen here only in order to convey the idea of the flexibility of the Italian language, borrowed and transformed on the trail of what has already happened to English and French.
3. In the wake of the recent reassessment of Del Boca's work, a comparative and multi-disciplinary approach has emerged, confronting with the legacy of colonialism. See Palumbo (2003), Ponzanesi (2004), Andall and Duncan (2005). However, Alessandro Triulzi is critical of the celebration of a 'postcolonial moment' marked by the emergence of revisionist historiographic studies and of an Italophone literature, arguing that 'postcolonial Italy is embarking on a dangerous path of renewed amnesia which undermines a critical view of its own past' (2006, p. 441).
4. Although the concept of 'Fortress Europe' initially described the potential effects of a single European market after 1992, the term now refers to a supposedly homogeneous and guarded European space controlling and resisting the inflow of migrants.
5. The contradictions underlying the Italian approach to migration is illustrated by the uncanny cohabitation of spaces such as that occurring on the shores of Lampedusa, where tourists share the beach with migrants freshly landed after a life-risking journey across the Mediterranean. See for instance Andrijasevic (2006).
6. Derrida (2000) elaborates on the aporia of hospitality focusing on its paradoxical relation with space and sovereignty.
7. In a situation which resembles that of Turkish 'guest workers' in Germany, it can be argued that '[t]heir temporal remoteness, their strange cultural and social habits ... are to be kept at a safe distance so spatial nearness will not be turned into psychical closeness' (Yegenoglu, 2005, pp. 140–141). The spatial distance here is also connoted as a temporal distance, thus implying an unbridgeable cultural difference which should stand as a reminder of the impossibility of closer contacts.
8. The short story 'Fingerprints' by Christiana de Caldas Brito, convincingly discussed by Portelli (2006), is particularly illuminating in this sense.
9. See for instance *Princesa* (1994), written by Fernanda Farías de Albuquerque with Maurizio Jannelli; *Immigrato* (1990), by Mario Fortunato and Salah Methnani, or *Libera*, written by Fevven Abreha Tekle with the journalist Raffaele Masto (2005). At times, the Italian name appears as editor, as is the case of Laura Maritano for *Con il vento nei capelli* (1993) by Salwa Salem, or Alessandra Atti di Sarro in *Volevo diventare bianca* (1993) by Nassera Chorha. However, collaborative writing also raised the problem of legitimating

literary authority, revealing the writers' anxiety over the Italian language which was still not properly mastered.
10. Genevieve Makaping is an interesting case in point. Born in Cameroon, she has been living in Italy for more than 20 years. A researcher in Cultural Anthropology at the University of Calabria, she has been the first woman to edit the local newspaper (*Il Quotidiano*, published in Cosenza) and is a well-known writer. Her writing is not only concerned about race and migration, but it also addresses issues of gender and representation, confronting the sexist attitudes of a small provincial town of Southern Italy and reversing the readers' point of view. See for instance her *Traiettorie di sguardi. E se gli altri foste voi?* (2001), published by a small Southern Italian publishing house.
11. See the editorial case of the anthology *Pecore nere* (2005) which has reached the third reprint with Laterza. However, the term 'migrant literature' has already been questioned and replaced by multiple definitions. If Graziella Parati used the all-encompassing definition of 'Italophone literature' (1999, p. 14), Alessandro Portelli (2006) suggested 'new migrant writing' to distinguish the more recent strand of writing from the initial testimonial migrant literature. See also the interesting 'Italophone diasporic literature' chosen by Lidia Curti (2006, p. 199), which includes authors from the former Italian colonies and those by other countries, all sharing a transcultural condition.
12. Institutional spaces in general are hardly to be found in a context of social invisibility, but it is interesting to note that the ground-stepping web platform for migrant voices in Italy is hosted by the Province of Bologna website.
13. See for instance the reciprocity foregrounded by A. Ali Mumin and V. Gerrand in the literature of the Somalian diaspora which develops 'critical insight into Italy's recent colonial past and its role in contemporary Italian culture' (2004, p. 19).

References

Ali Farah, U.C. (2005). Dissacrare la lingua [To desecrate language]. *El Ghibli, 1*. Retrieved October 29, 2010, from http://www.el-ghibli.provincia.bologna.it/index.php?id=0&issue=01_07
Ali Farah, U.C. (2007). *Madre piccola* [*Little mother*]. Milano: Frassinelli.
Ali Mumin, A., & Gerrand, V. (2004). Italian cultural influences in Somalia. *Quaderni del Novecento, IV*, 13–24.
Andall, J. (2000). *Gender, migration and domestic service: The politics of black women in Italy*. Aldershot: Ashgate.
Andall, J. (2003). *Gender and ethnicity in contemporary Europe*. Oxford: Berg.
Andall, J., & Duncan, D. (Eds.). (2005). *Italian colonialism: Legacy and memory*. Oxford: Berg.
Andrijasevic, R. (2006). Lampedusa in focus: Migrants caught between the Libyan desert and the deep sea. *Feminist Review, 82*, 120–125.
Bhabha, H. (1994). *The location of culture*. London and New York, NY: Routledge.
Brah, A. (1996). *Cartographies of diaspora: Contesting identities*. London: Routledge.
Caldas Brito, C. (2004). Io, polpastrello 5423 [I, Fingertip 5423]. In *Qui e là*. Cosenza: Cosmo Iannone.
Curti, L. (2006). *La voce dell'altra* [*The voice of the other woman*]. Roma: Meltemi.
Curti, L. (2007). Female literature of migration in Italy. *Feminist Review, 87*, 60–75.
Dal Lago, A. (2004). *Non-persone: L'esclusione dei migranti in una società globale* [*Non-persons. The exclusion of migrants in a global society*]. Milano: Feltrinelli.
De Certeau, M. (1984). *The practice of everyday life* (S. Randall, Trans.). Berkeley, CA and London: University of California Press.
De Lauretis, T. (1990). Eccentric subjects: Feminist theory and historical consciousness. *Feminist Studies, 16*, 115–150.
Derrida, J. (2000). *Of hospitality*. Stanford, CA: Stanford University Press.
Fanon, F. (1994). *Black skin, white masks*. London: Grove Press.
Flaiano, E. (1947). *Tempo di uccidere* [*Time to kill*]. Milano: Longanesi.
Ghermandi, G. (2006). Il pranzo pasquale [Easter lunch]. *El Ghibli, 14*. Retrieved October 29, 2010, from http://www.el-ghibli.provincia.bologna.it/index.php?id=0&issue=03_14
Ghermandi, G. (2007). *Regina di fiori e di perle* [*Queen of flowers and pearls*]. Roma: Donzelli.

Gilroy, P. (2004). *Between camps: Nations, cultures and the allure of race.* London & New York, NY: Routledge.
Gilroy, P. (2005). *Postcolonial melancholia.* New York, NY: Columbia University Press.
Glissant, E. (1989). *Caribbean discourse: Selected essays.* Charlottesville, VA and London: University of Virginia Press.
Hargreaves, A., & McKinney, M. (1997). *Post-colonial cultures in France.* London: Routledge.
Huggan, G. (2008). Perspectives on postcolonial Europe. *Journal of Postcolonial Writing, 44,* 241–249.
Khouma, P. (2003). Editoriale. *El Ghibli, 0.* Retrieved October 29, 2010, from http://www.el-ghibli.provincia.bologna.it/index.php?id=0&issue=00_00
Kristeva, J. (1991). *Strangers to ourselves.* New York, NY: Columbia University Press.
Kuruvilla, G. (2006, February 28). Migranti o vincenti, ma scrittori. Colloquio con gli scrittori migranti Jadelin Mabial Gangbo e Gabriella Kuruvilla [Migrants or winners, but writers: Conversation with migrant writers Jadelin Mabial Gangbo and Gabriella Kuruvilla]. *Il Manifesto,* p. 13.
Lombardi-Diop, C. (2007). Postfazione [Afterword]. In G. Ghermandi (Ed.), *Regina di fiori e di perle* [*Queens of flowers and pearls*] (pp. 257–264). Rome: Donzelli.
Loshitzky, Y. (2006). Fortress Europe: Introduction. *Third Text, 20,* 629–634.
Mauceri, M.C. (2004). Igiaba Scego: La seconda generazione di autori transnazionali sta già emergendo [The emergence of the second generation of transnational writers]. *El Ghibli, 1.* Retrieved October 29, 2010, from http://www.el-ghibli.provincia.bologna.it/index.php?id=0&issue=01_04
Mezzadra, S., & Rahola, F. (2006). The postcolonial condition: A few notes on the quality of historical time in the global present. *Postcolonial Text, 2.* Retrieved October 29, 2010, from http://www.postcolonial.org/index.php/pct/article/viewArticle/393/819
Mubiayi, I. (2005a). Documenti, prego [Documents, please]. In I. Scego, I. Mubiayi, G. Kuruvilla & L. Wadia (Eds.), *Pecore nere* [*Black sheep*] (pp. 97–108). Bari: Laterza.
Mubiayi, I. (2005b). Concorso [Competitive examination]. In I. Scego, I. Mubiayi, G. Kuruvilla & L. Wadia (Eds.), *Pecore nere* [*Black sheep*] (pp. 109–138). Bari: Laterza.
Palumbo, P. (Ed.). (2003). *A place in the sun: Africa in Italian colonial culture from post-unification to the present.* Berkeley, CA: University of California Press.
Parati, G. (Ed.). (1999). *Mediterranean crossroads: Migration literature in Italy.* London: Associated University Press.
Pojmann, W. (2006). *Immigrant women and feminism in Italy.* Aldershot: Ashgate.
Ponzanesi, S., & Merolla, D. (Eds.). (2005). *Migrant cartographies: New cultural and literary spaces in post-colonial Europe.* Oxford: Lexington Books.
Ponzanesi, S. (2004). *Paradoxes of postcolonial culture: Contemporary women writing of the Indian and Afro-Italian diaspora.* Albany, NY: Suny Press.
Portelli, A. (2006). Fingertips stained with ink: Notes on new 'migrant writing' in Italy. *Interventions, 8,* 472–483.
Scego, I. (2004). *La strana notte di Vito Renica, leghista meridionale. El Ghibli, 3.* [*The strange night of Vito Renica*]. Retrieved October 29, 2010, from http://www.el-ghibli.provincia.bologna.it/id_1-issue_00_03-section_1-index_pos_1.html
Scego, I. (2005). Dismatria [Dismotherland]. In I. Scego, I. Muyabi, G. Kuruvilla & L. Wadia (Eds.), *Pecore nere* [*Black sheep*] (pp. 5–22). Bari: Laterza.
Sibhatu, R. (1993). *Aulò. Canto-poesia dall'Eritrea* [*Aulò: Song-poem from Eritrea*]. Roma: Sinnos.
Triulzi, A. (2006). Displacing the colonial event. Hybrid memories of postcolonial Italy. *Interventions, 8,* 430–443.
Vorpsi, O. (2005). *Il paese dove non si muore mai* [*The country where one never dies*]. Torino: Einaudi.
Wadia, L. (2007). *Amiche per la pelle* [*Close friends*]. Roma: Edizioni e/o.
Yegenoglu, M. (2005). From guest worker to hybrid immigrant: Changing themes of German-Turkish literature. In S. Ponzanesi & D. Merolla (Eds.), *Migrant cartographies: New cultural and literary spaces in post-colonial Europe* (pp. 137–149). Oxford: Lexington Books.

'Dubbing di diaspora': gender and reggae music inna Babylon

Sonia Sabelli

Dipartimento di Studi Filologici, Linguistici e Letterari, Università La Sapienza, Rome, Italy

European countries have always used gendered concepts and stereotypes to legitimize and perpetuate their colonial governance and their exercise of command and subordination. Metaphors of masculinity and femininity have often been used (by the colonizers and the colonized) to underscore relations of authority/obedience, or of strength/weakness, on the basis of the equation between racist supremacy and the loss of black masculinity. This article explores how reggae performers and audiences responded to this colonial strategy. Whether identifying black liberation with virility, and male control on women's bodies, therefore coming to perpetuate sexist images and concepts, and homophobic attitudes; or, re-visioning their struggle for freedom in forms which do not support or perpetuate phallocentrism and patriarchal control.

This article analyzes gender representations in reggae music within postcolonial Europe, in the context of the process of global consumption of reggae music and the international appropriation, by white musicians, of a musical genre which was usually identified with black identity. The author considers reggae music produced in the UK as a result of the encounter between white youth subcultures and the massive black immigrant community from Jamaica and compares it with reggae music spread through sound systems in Italian social centers by white youth countercultures. In both contexts, the postcolonial encounter between black and white youths has given rise to complex reactions grounded in the diverse historical, cultural, religious, social and political backgrounds.

'They nu want gi we credit fi we invention/Reggae music invent by the Jamaican/ UB40 tek it and a make the most million':[1] in these lines Macka B, a Jamaican singer living in the UK, complains about the global consumption of reggae music and the international appropriation, by white musicians, of a musical genre which was usually identified exclusively with Jamaican (i.e. black) identity. This nationalistic claim is a common reaction to the dislocation of reggae music and its consequent relocation to postcolonial Europe, since black music has often been considered a symbol of racial authenticity. According to Paul Gilroy, at a certain moment reggae 'ceased, in Britain, to signify an exclusively ethnic, Jamaican style, and derived a different kind of cultural legitimacy both from a new global status and from its expression of what might be termed a pan-Caribbean culture' (1993, p. 82). To be precise, in the last 30 years, reggae spread from its Caribbean origins, shifting from being the cry for peace and justice of black sufferers in the colonized countries to being the cry for pride and redemption of black immigrants in the overdeveloped countries. Subsequently, reggae has attracted a new generation of white European youth inspired by the critical and subversive potential of this musical genre, which, in this process, also amplifies the voice of white Italian youth countercultures. I will start from this international dissemination, and the new cultural and political possibilities produced by this global flow, to analyze how gender and national identity are represented in reggae music within postcolonial Europe.

Along with Gilroy (1993, p. 83), I will argue that 'the conflictual representation of sexuality has vied with the discourse of racial emancipation to constitute the inner core of black expressive cultures' because European countries have always used gendered concepts and stereotypes to legitimize and perpetuate their colonial governance and their exercise of command and subordination. Therefore, metaphors of masculinity and femininity have often been used, both by the colonizers and the colonized, to underscore relations of authority/obedience, or of strength/weakness, on the basis of the equation between racist supremacy and the loss of black masculinity. The scope of this research is to explore how reggae performers and audiences responded to this colonial strategy. Did the identification of black liberation with virility, and virility with male control of women's bodies, perpetuate sexist images and concepts and homophobic attitudes? Or, on the contrary, did the re-visioning of their struggle for freedom in forms which do not support or perpetuate phallocentrism and patriarchal control, open up the possibility for new social relations and new forms of empowerment which do not reproduce hierarchical subordination, but are grounded on a revolutionary vision of liberation, arising from a feminist perspective?

I will use an intersectional approach, connecting race and gender, ethnicity and sexual preferences, to see how sexual and power relations are represented in lyrics, poetics and performances by black and white, male and female singers/djs/selectors/sound operators and audiences coming from two different postcolonial contexts, namely the UK and Italy. I will focus not only on language but on dance and gesture, as a merely textual approach is not sufficient for an aesthetic form grounded in oral structures: a form which is clearly oriented towards specific dynamics of performance and the use of the body rather than verbal communication.

I will compare reggae music produced in the UK, considered a result of the postcolonial encounter between white youth subcultures and the massive black immigrant community from Jamaica, with reggae music which was spread across Italian social centers by white youth countercultures with the help of self-built sound systems. In Italy as well as in the UK, this encounter between black and white youths has given rise to complex reactions, especially in the case of increasing machismo and homophobia, which are grounded in the diverse historical, cultural, religious, social and political backgrounds. What is at stake here is the process of black and white subcultures identifying with a 'rebel music', which could either contribute to their struggle for liberation or continue to oppress them. How do these subcultures re-articulate the same expressive forms in their own specific local context? What changes take place if the performer or the audience is black or white? Colonizer or colonized? Migrant or native? How does gender fit in this picture? I will answer these questions using feminist scholarship and postcolonial discourses, starting from my personal position as a white feminist woman who grew up being directly involved in Rome's reggae scene.

The way gender roles are performed in the dancehall 'yard' can be read in the light of the legacy of slavery, colonialism and diaspora. Therefore, to analyze how sexual conflicts are represented nowadays, and how they are still shaped by this imperial and colonial past, it is useful to go back to the flows of people, goods and records that have transported reggae music from the Caribbean to Europe, and thus to identify the gendered *topoi* and stereotypes played by reggae musicians and their followers. These gendered stereotypes induce powerful, recurring, and conventional models of behavior, usually experienced as rigidly fixed gendered roles. In order to be accepted and valued, people are expected to conform to such models of behavior, which cannot be questioned because they assure a collective sense of belonging to a common national identity.

It dread inna Inglan: reggae music from Jamaica to Babylon system

After the Second World War, a massive emigration began from the British Caribbean to the UK. Jamaican poet Louise Bennett comments on this exodus by stating that Jamaican people are 'colonizin/Englan in Reverse'; since every poor Jamaican's future plan is to 'get a big-time job/An settle in de mother lan', thus 'Man an woman, old an young/just pack dem bag an baggage/An turn history upside dung!' (1982, p. 106). The early immigration to the UK included mainly young men without job prospects and money, who were rejected and looked down upon by the British society because of their skin color. Furthermore, to make matters worse, these men, in order to survive, were not over-particular in their choices. As the Black Uhuru state, there is 'A very thin line to start the crime', thus 'The youth of Eglington/Won't put down their Remington', as well as 'the youth of Kingston', because 'They are responsible for a lot of children/And they need food/And they want to go to school'.[2] This song is the forerunner of the *topos* of the 'bad man', whose violence is justified because he is a 'victim' of the system. This is also the case in Buju Banton's *Circumstances* ('Was I born a violent man/Circumstances made me what I am') and in Beenie Man's *Bad Man* ('Bad man and dat is who I am/Bad man I hope you'll overstand/That circumstances made me who I am').

One of the most significant items packed in the suitcases of the Jamaicans who ventured into the 'Babylon system', i.e. the corruption of the white consumerist society, was their music. They took reggae to the US, Canada and Britain, opening the way for its incorporation into the global economy of the multinational entertainment industry. Jamaican emigration had ensured a major market to the island's music: the musical tastes of immigrants provided an impetus for the development of its recording industry, insofar as by the 1950s records were produced with export principally in mind. Soon British Jamaicans turned to recording music themselves and playing for multiracial audiences. The sound systems were their main means of maintaining a link with the motherland, though their music came out filtered through its exposure to a new culture. Actually, sound systems are the easiest way to make music, whenever a few friends get together in a yard: all you need is a box of records to scratch and big and powerful speakers to spread your off-beat sound.[3] This is one of the reasons why sound systems became so popular in Italy, several years later.

The emergence of new subcultures in Britain, at the end of the 1960s, has been interpreted as the response given by the white youth to the presence of a black community.[4] In this scene Dandy Livingston, a Jamaican singer who emigrated to

England in 1959, recorded a popular song that will become a skinhead favorite, *Rudy, A Message To You*,[5] where the figure of the 'rude boy' made its first appearance. This archetype of rebellion will pave the way for the role model of the 'bad man' with a gun, who will 'shoot the batty boy'[6] during the 1990s, provoking an international debate between the advocates of singers' freedom of speech and Jamaicans' cultural sovereignty on one hand, and the defenders of human rights on the other (Oumano, 2005). This archetype, which embodies the antagonist of the sheriff (that Bob Marley wanted to shoot), also is one of the elements which contributes to the involvement of white European youth with reggae music. Reggae music is thus perceived as asking for equal rights and justice, assuring that it is possible not to conform to the Babylon system, and pushes for one's emancipation from mental slavery. Reggae voices the global ghetto youth's claim for redemption and amplifies their local practices of resistance against the system. It possesses the unique ability to cross the color line and to connect all the oppressed people on the two sides of the Atlantic, whether black or white.

Moreover, the explosion of sound system culture in Italy was marked by a strong militant and political stance, since it arose simultaneously with the Posse movement[7] in occupied and self-organized social centers (at the end of the 1980s), on the one hand, and the student protest against the privatization of the university, which took place in 1990 and carried the name of 'Pantera', on the other. To build one's own sound system meant to create a space, the dancehall yard, that operated purposefully outside of the rules set up by the entertainment industry and outside of the 'slavery' of paid work in a capitalist society. The dancehall yard was thus a space where one could be free and express oneself without a stage separating the performer from the audience. There was no need to invent a similitude between Jamaican reggae and the Italian popular tradition, because this similitude already existed. Especially in Southern Italy, perceived as part of the global South, as is Jamaica, there was a similar musical attitude, the same ability to face social problems (such as internal migration, exploitation, unemployment and political corruption), and it was common to use the regional dialects.[8]

Meanwhile, in Jamaica, Rastafarianism[9] and homophobia re-emerged as a consequence of what was perceived as a misappropriation of an exclusively ethnic Jamaican style, by white people who, unlike British youth, had not yet faced an immigrant community, nor a black subculture in their own country.

During the 1960s, much of the UK's reggae output was less accomplished than the Jamaican 'originals'. Only by the 1970s, talented musicians and singers emerged from the expatriate communities in all UK cities with sizeable migrant presence. These diasporic subjects formed strong and self-contained bands, more in line with the established conventions of youth music in Britain, whose records were quite different from those recorded in Kingston, Jamaica. These UK reggae bands found it easier, compared with singers recording with session musicians, to earn money playing live, boosted by the crossover success of Marley. This meant a move from community halls in migrant areas to student union venues and support slots at large capacity halls. These bands were equipped with their own instruments and were used to playing in front of a variety of audiences, ranging from dreadlocks to white university students. One of the results of working as a band was the development of sounds different from the Jamaican model. Moreover, these musicians had a different generation of black youth as their audience, namely largely second generation immigrants, as well as a real ideology, Rastafarianism, that gave them and their followers a new self-affirming identity.

Conversely, Rastafarianism prevented women's participation in social and political life and their achievements in the musical scene. Notably, the traditional Rastafarian beliefs impose many restrictions on women's behavior: during the menstrual cycle they are segregated, forbidden to cook and not allowed to participate in public meetings because they are considered impure; women's bodies need to be covered, as well as their heads, as they are not supposed to seduce men; they are supposed to serve their brothers, husbands and children, and to engage in sex only for the purpose of reproduction. Any other sexual practice, such as oral or anal sex, is forbidden, and homosexual relations are considered unnatural. Undoubtedly, the Rastafarian movement does not allow the empowerment of women, lesbians and gays. The reason behind this may be the following:

> The Rastafari beliefs regarding the female are clearly based on the Bible and fall in line with the premise that Rastafari is a patriarchal movement. The Rastafarian 'Reasonings', the traditional way of sharing information, cementing views or interpreting the Bible, take place primarily among the males. (Barrett, 1997, pp. 241–242)

Given these premises, the lack or marginalization of women's voices in reggae music both in Jamaica and in the diaspora should not come as a surprise, nor should the homophobic attitude of the scene, even though it is expressed, or hidden, in different ways, according to the context of its production. A few exceptions to this rule exist which will be mentioned later, in order to better understand the contradictions at stake in the contemporary scene.

The imagery of Rastafarianism meant something different to the second generation of black British. The sense of belonging to an African diaspora expressed in lyrics inspired by Marcus Garvey's words, like 'It's repatriation/black liberation', was felt as a sense of belonging to a Jamaican diaspora.[10] While some British-born youth shared the ideal of Africa as their spiritual homeland, many others dreamed of returning to a Jamaica known only through their parents' memories, or through reggae records. Around this time, increasing numbers of UK black youth were beginning to style their hair in dreadlocks, and the image of the dreadlocked Rastaman entered decisively into popular iconography. Just as the afro was a declaration of Africa-ness to African Americans, dreadlocks were a strategy of resistance for those who have always been taught by the colonizers to deny their African roots and the legacy of slavery. Only in recent years, dreadlocks have become so fashionable that in 1999 the reggae band Morgan Heritage claimed that 'You don't haffi dread to be Rasta', in order to show that one does not need dreadlocks or other superficial trappings to demonstrate one's spiritual commitment.

At the end of the 1970s the 'dread youth' became the icon of the black British who 'stan firm inna Inglan', the black British who 'are here to stay', as in Linton Kwesi Johnson (LKJ)'s poem *It Dread Inna Inglan* (Johnson, 1975).[11] But 'dread' is also the adjective chosen by LKJ to describe their music, namely as 'a dread beat pulsing fire, burning' and white people's fear of bloody rebellions resulting in the consciousness rising of an entire generation. While the UK was still struggling with its postcolonial role in the world and while its society was fighting to accept that those who were considered cheap colonial labor had now become members of the

UK society, the Notting Hill riots of 1976 reflected the inability of the government to realize that society had changed. This historical moment is portrayed in LKJ's first album, *Dread Beat and Blood* (1977), which reveals the reality of everyday-life of young black Jamaicans in Britain during the 1970s, anticipating the bloody rebellions of the 1980s. In the poem *Yout rebels*, LKJ describe them as 'a brand *new breed* of blacks', who say 'to capital neva/moving forwud hevva' (Johnson, 1975, emphasis added). They are 'new in age/but not in rage'. They do not need the counseling of 'sage in chain', because they are 'new shapes/shapin/new patterns/creatin new links'. They are carving 'a new path,/moving forwud to freedom'. With these lines LKJ anticipates what Hanif Kureishi will write in *The Buddha of Suburbia* about Karim Amir, describing him as 'a funny kind of Englishman, a *new breed* as it were, having emerged from two old histories' (p. 3), and what Zadie Smith will write in *White Teeth* about the 'Raggastani': 'It was a *new breed*, just recently joining the ranks of the other street crews' (p. 192). After the failure of many attempts by expatriate communities to create an original sound, LKJ was probably the first Jamaican artist to take existing traditions and successfully transplant them to another country, creating new expressive forms and inventing a new genre called dub poetry, which according to LKJ 'is a deconstructive art' (Ludes, 1998).

I suggest that dub poetry was created by LKJ in order to represent, both through music and language, the emergence of a new notion of subjectivity as a result of immigration: it is a means to deconstruct English national identity through the representation of the encounter between the colonizer and the colonized. Now, for the first time, colonizer and colonized have to face one another not in the colony but in the space of the metropolis, belying the colonial assumption that postcolonialism is concerned only with the margin and not with the centre of the empire. One meaningful novelty is the use of the language spoken by black Caribbean immigrants in London, which, for the first time, was put in print. It has been defined by others as 'London-Jamaican patois' but LKJ refuses this definition: 'Patois is a term which really refers to broken French... The language I'm writing is mostly Jamaican'. The term 'patois' suggests that Jamaican is a broken and subaltern version of the Standard English, while LKJ's claim for a 'national language' is a strategy of cultural resistance against colonial mentality (such as the use of black English by African American rappers, and the use of regional dialects in Italian raggamuffin), in order to deprive the language spoken by the master of its supremacy.

A few years later, in 1982, a second-generation singer called Ranking Ann clearly asserts her identity as the result of the mixture of her multiplex roots (Jamaican, British and African) through the legacy of slavery and diaspora. She claims 'Mi seh don't call me no English gal/Just call me by name', because 'Mi seh mi mama an mi papa seh dem born in Jamaica/Gimme roots'n'culture seh dem gone inna Africa', and thus 'Mi seh mi born inna Englan/But mi feel like a true born Jamaican'.[12] In spite of her demand not to be defined as an 'English gal', Ranking Ann titles this song (and the entire LP) *A Slice of English Toast*, assuring a continuity between the Jamaican tradition of 'toasting', the act of chatting on the microphone over the records' instrumental versions, and the English habit to eat toasted bread, which are both everyday gestures in the two different cultures. It is significant that 'toasting', the art of Jamaican 'deejaying', is similar to the 'MCing' in US rap, and that in reggae music the one who chooses which record to play next is not called 'deejay', but 'selector'. The record-sleeve of *A Slice of English Toast* portrays a black woman slicing a loaf of bread which is in fact a vinyl cylinder, so that the bread slices are revealed to be several records that her son is putting inside the 'toaster', which is also the Jamaican definition for deejay, while the act of slicing bread coincides with the act of 'cutting' records (to view this record sleeve, please visit http://www.strictly-vibes.com/ranking-ann-a-slice-of-english-toast-1982-vt1049.html). Thus, once again, Ranking Ann is a 'new breed'. She is neither British, nor Jamaican, but a new combination of both: she is the 'English toaster' that will dominate UK reggae during the 1980s. If the lyrics seem to recall an essentialist conception of ethnic identity, the meta-textual discourse introduced by the record-sleeve suggests the attempt to give a 'more pluralistic, post-colonial sense of British culture and national identity', connecting blackness and Englishness which usually appeared to be 'mutually exclusive attributes' and asserting the 'internality' of black people to postcolonial Europe (Gilroy, 1993, pp. 10–11).

During the 1980s, Birmingham's lively multiracial culture produced an explosion of talents which demonstrated vitality and invention similar to their counterparts in Kingston, such as deejays Pato Banton and Macka B. The latter was also highly popular in Italy, due to his conscious lyrics against racism and apartheid, his sharp criticism of the Thatcher government, and his ironical claim for black pride. In the early 1990s, a Birmingham-born singer of Asian origins, Apache Indian, started to combine raggamuffin style with *bhangra*[13] music, climbing the UK pop charts. Carolyn Cooper's article (2004, pp. 251–277) about the coming of 'Rajamuffin Sounds' is an interesting analysis of Apache Indian's ability of mixing 'the Indian [language] with all the Patwa', that clearly prefigures how the musical forms originated by black people are no longer their 'exclusive property', as in the case of the appropriation of sound system's culture by white Italian youth (Gilroy, 1993, p. 3).

During the second half of the 1980s, UK reggae also started a new roots and dub revival scene, which is still alive today, with small following in Jamaica. Both black and white followers of roots reggae will start to form their own sound systems and to produce their own rhythms. It is not accidental that these new roots sounds have focused more on instrumental excursions than on vocal acrobatics, 'because of the understandable reluctance of these musicians, far removed from the Kingston ghettos, to sing about *slavery days*' (Barrow & Dalton, 1997, p. 356).[14]

'Mothers of the nation', 'bitches', or neither of the two?

Although women are the main topic in reggae music, at least in dancehall songs, the perspective is usually predominantly male (and sexist) even if the one who speaks is a woman. Dawn Penn (a Jamaican singer now living in London) states that 'It's a male dominated business!', complaining that in reggae music there are only a few female artists (Women in Reggae, 2005). In fact, at least until the explosion of the 'dancehall queens' in the early 1990s, the role of women has always been misrepresented and undervalued in the history of reggae music, with female voices consigned to the status of one-offs, or relegated in the position of backing vocals for their male counterparts. Even though gender relationships have always been the core of reggae music, usually the lyrics provide a male-oriented point of view, reflecting the inequalities that affect the everyday lives of Jamaican women, and never questioning the universal norms of patriarchal authority and compulsory heterosexuality. Did women have a role in the building of the national identity of an island dominated by four hundred years of slavery and colonization? Have they ever gained access, as subjects, to the place of enunciation? Or will they always remain objects in a male representation of gender relations? How does homosexuality fit in this picture? And how do gender relations change when reggae music moves from this little Caribbean island to the dancehall yards in Europe? Would we find any difference in dealing with gender roles when reggae music shifts from Jamaica to the Babylon system?

In order to answer these questions, I will go back to the days of slavery in Jamaica, and to the rise of Rastafarianism as a strategy of resistance against racism and colonialism as this history still permeates beliefs and attitudes both of reggae performers and audiences today, both in Jamaica and Europe.

The only woman who has been awarded the Jamaican 'Order of National Hero' for having challenged the institutions of colonialism, thereby changing the course of Jamaica's history from slavery to emancipation is Nanny of the Maroons.[15] Immortalized in several popular songs, she was a political organizer and military leader of the Maroons at the beginning of the eighteenth century. Defeating the British colonizers in numerous battles, she possessed that fierce fighting spirit generally associated with the courage of men. Paradoxically enough, she was known as the 'mother of the people', but she has also been referred to as one of the 'founding fathers' of the nation (both in Stone, n.d., and in Meyler, n.d.). Even though a disagreement exists about the gendering of the Jamaican homeland, Nanny's legend inaugurates an absolute sense of ethnic difference, maximized through other female figures in order to distinguish people from one another, and to construct the nation as an ethnically homogeneous object.

Another woman who had a strong impact on Jamaican culture is Haile Selassie's wife; Empress Menem, also known as Queen Omega, is still considered a role model to many Rastafarian women. The name 'Queen Omega' means 'mother of creation' and suggests that Rasta women deserve respect from Rasta men, since they are told to treat women as they would treat Queen Omega. The traditional formula 'I and I' is often referred to 'the Alpha and the Omega' as well, meaning that god is 'in all men' (sic) and implying that no one is better than anyone else, because both persons are united under the love of Jah (God). Nevertheless, this is still a controversial issue because, in traditional Rastafarian belief, women are always equal *but* subaltern to men. Moreover, the figuration of the 'mother of creation' is crucial and widespread in a large number of songs, both in Jamaica and in the diaspora, where female subjectivity is always identified with motherhood (or with the act of giving birth to a gender neutral, that is to say, male subject) and the motherland: whether it is identified with the African land which has given birth to all humanity (as in Garnett Silk's *Mama Africa*), or with the Jamaican land in search for its national identity after the independence (as in Anthony B's *Woman Of The Nation*), or with one woman in flesh and blood (as in Macka B's *Respect Our Mothers*).

One of the first women within Jamaican reggae who wrote and produced her own songs was Judy Mowatt, who worked with Marcia Griffith and Rita Marley to form the I-Threes. They sang backing vocals for Marley's Wailers on their tours, but were able to step out of Marley's shadow, getting a solo career after his death. In 1978 Judy Mowatt produced *Black Woman,* and in 1982 she asked 'Why treat us inhuman/Just because we're only woman?', stating that 'We're not weak/We are strong'. She complained that 'We've been held back/For too long', claiming 'Open the door and let us through', because 'We've got our God-given talents just like you'.[16] Afterwards, other talented women asserted themselves on the reggae scene. Sister Nancy's, *Bam Bam* is an answer to all the men who have questioned her place in the dancehall: 'One thing Nancy cyaan understan/wha' dem a ask me 'bout mi ambishan?... I'm a lady, I'm not a man/MC is my ambishan'.[17] Lady G's warning in *Nuff Respect* – 'Nuh carry mi name/Nuh spread no rumours/Show me nuff respect' – was known word-for-word by all the female dancehall fans.[18]

Sister Carol was another woman who found a way to escape from Kingston ghetto, establishing her place in the dancehall. She is also known as 'Mother Nature' because of the homonymous song in which she introduces herself as 'Mother Culure pon the mic', saying they call her the 'DeeJay Mammie', not only because 'she is dynamite', but also because she 'graduated as a school teacher/to teach the Africans about their culture'. According to Sister Carol, the role of the Rasta Girl is 'to emphasize the reality of our feministic side and how important it is in terms of the whole *creation* of *civilization* and *motherhood* and all that comes with it', because '*all men came through the womb*' and 'if you disrespect me, and you keep on disrespecting *Mother Africa, Mother Nature*, the *mother of the universe*'.[19]

Sister Carol's statements about women into Rastafarian beliefs still resonate several years later in Anthony B's *Woman of the Nation* as 'Oh dis the woman of di nation/mother of civilization' where the Jamaican singer ascribes women the role of building the national identity and preserving its culture and traditions. And they still resound over the ocean, when we move to reggae music in the diaspora. As a matter of fact, one of the songs usually played by the sound systems in Rome during the Pantera movement, particularly appreciated by the female audience, was Macka B's invitation to 'Respect to the mothers/Respect to all the mothers in every country and town', with its powerful and incessantly repeated refrain: 'Ma-ma ma-ma ma/A so we love you/Ma-ma ma-ma ma/A so we love you'. Here he states that 'We must remember Africa/Because she is the mother of civilization/She is the mother of nature'.[20] Even when he addresses male violence against women, he asserts 'Don't bother beat, don't bother beat/Don't bother beat *your* woman', as if woman was only a male's property.[21]

The only exception to this rule seems to be Ranking Ann who probably offers the strongest assertion of womanliness in the history of reggae music, namely in *Liberated Woman* ('I am a liberated woman/You can no control mi life/I'm free like a bird inna di air') and in *Feminine Gender* ('Remember all them always try fi keep we under/And treat we like we are stupid and inferior/But no! me come fi tell ya we are superior') even though she explicitly refuses to be called 'feminist':

> Let me tell you something, when happened to me/Seh one friday night, me inna party/Seh here come a dread/Him a walk up to me/'Hear Ranking Ann, tell me dis: is it true what them say, that you are feminist?'/Me seh no Rasta/Me are individualist/Seh open your eyes and you must realize/You can't come and try fe cathegorize/When you call me 'feminist', me know where you mean/The thing that you want do is a different kind of sin/Seh god create woman/And god create man/And inna this time they have their function/So I don't put them down/So don't get me wrong/It's just feminine, a feminine, seh feminine gender-genda/Mi seh we no go surrender-renda.[22]

This song is an interesting response to the male chauvinism widespread in the dancehall yards, where a woman acting independently is considered synonymous to a 'male-basher', while the term 'feminist' is a simple way to dismiss a woman who refuses to make herself available to male advances. Even if it cannot be considered an explicit feminist claim, it is still certainly an unprecedented statement of women pride.

Back in Jamaica in 1996, Marcia Griffiths and Lady G recorded the single *Woman*, which was dedicated to all the women 'who are fighting' for freedom, women 'who are struggling' in a 'world of discrimination', women 'who are lawyers ... doctors ... teachers' or women 'who are ignorant', and women who are 'stronger then a roaring lion'. But, beginning from the intro, Lady G tells us that 'with a woman's help/a man can move mountains', and once again, when Marcia Griffiths starts singing the refrain, women are represented as 'mothers of the greatest nation/teachers of the young generation'.[23] Also in this case, women represent themselves as subaltern to a male subject. Subsequently, women continue to embody the same old stereotypes: both as mothers, in charge of passing down the national language and traditions, and as symbols of the nation, in charge of defining the borders of Jamaican national culture after the independence from the British Empire.

Apart from a few exceptions, gender relationships represented in reggae music are always grounded on a 'colonial mentality' which reflects the master/slave paradigm, whether in Jamaica or in Europe, whether the singer is male or female. Masculinity is overemphasized through the stereotype of the 'bad man' who wants to shoot the 'batty boy' and functions as a response to the colonial strategy of feminizing the colonized men in order to dominate them. Alternately, women are confined to the role of mothers and wives in charge of embodying the national language and traditions in opposition to the colonizing country. If they transgress this role they are considered 'bitches'. Furthermore, continuing to confine women to roles which always position them in a hierarchical relation to men, without putting into question compulsory heterosexuality, the stereotype of the 'mother of creation' is to the sex-gender system as the 'house nigger' is to the economy of the plantation: it does not reverse the power relationships inscribed in this system but rather contributes to its nourishment and preservation.

According to bell hooks, contemporary cinema continues to divide black women into two categories: 'mammies' or 'hot bitches' and, from time to time, a combination of both (hooks, 1992, chap. 4). And what about popular music? Can we recognize the same stereotypes? After having focused on the 'mammies' it is time to look for the 'bitches'. According to LKJ, 'Inglan is a bitch/dere's no escapin it'.[24] In his classic about the difficulties incurred by the first generation of Jamaican immigrants entering the British labor market, the poet uses a sexist derogatory term to define the colonizing nation. In doing so he reverses the gendered and parental rhetoric of colonial rule, consisting of a 'maternal model of caring for the welfare of indigenous people' and a 'paternalistic model of the rigorous disciplining of native children', both used as a strategy to infantilize and feminize the colonized in order to dominate them (Gouda, 2001, p. 11). To justify and perpetuate their imperialism, Europeans had always 'emasculated' the colonized men, who consequently responded by mimicking and enhancing the manly prerogatives generally associated with the masters. Just as 'the liberation of Indian men from European imperialism demanded a process of mimicking, even enhancing, those aspects of the "self" they could share with their masters' (Gouda, 2001, p. 10), the Jamaican tradition of toasting has always focused on the glorification of the 'big bamboo', overemphasizing the virility of the male performer on the stage. This representation of hypermasculinity is completely in line with the representation of women as sexual objects, so that Macka B simply had to state that 'Woman is not a sex machine/Woman is a human being'.[25] When male singers celebrate femininity, they are expected to identify gender and ethnicity, as well as their own control of women's bodies with the possession of the land, so that women's role is to assure the preservation of racial/national identity. This is the reason for the controversy raised in 1992 by Buju Banton's *Love Me Browning*, in which the Jamaican singer expressed his preference for light-skinned women. After the audience accused him of denigrating the beauty of black women and promoting a colonialist attitude, he answered by releasing *Love Black Woman*, where he sings: 'Mi nuh Stop cry/Fi all black women/Respect all the girls dem with dark complexion'.[26]

What happens when the woman is the one who consciously acts and performs as a 'bitch'? Jamaican singer Lady Saw usually sings sexually explicit lyrics with her hand touching her vagina, or straddling one of her male fans. She has always been criticized for the 'slackness' of her language and gestures, but I would suggest that we should interpret her use of the body on the stage as a way to ironically mime the hyper-masculinity of her male counterparts, reversing it in a celebration of hyper-femininity, or in a 'female fertility ritual' (Cooper, 2004, chap. 3). Lady Saw's performance of the erotic has no equivalent in European reggae music where the performers are predominantly male, and the audience seems to accept uncritically everything that comes from the island, except for its open eroticism. Usually her performances make white European audiences uneasy. Nonetheless, it is a strong assertion of the life-force of women 'in the face of a racist, patriarchal, and anti-erotic society', where women have always been taught to suppress the erotic because it is a profoundly creative source (Lorde, 1984, p. 59). Furthermore, the way male singers perform their masculinity on the stage, that is through their own use of the erotic, usually assumes women only as objects of male desire and 'use without consent of the used is abuse' while Lady Saw's performances seem to 'share the power of each other's feelings', that 'is different from using another's feelings as we would use a Kleenex' (Lorde, 1984, p. 58).

The 'bad man' and the 'batty boy' in the debate on homophobia

The nationalist ideology expressed in reggae attributes to women specific functions: mothers, reproducing the nation's population; keepers of traditional culture; and symbols of the nation to be protected (Hill Collins, 2006, p. 17). Additionally, this ideology also provides a role model for masculinity: men are supposed to defend the nation as well as their own families, consisting of heterosexual couples who produce their own biological children. In this scene, the existence of homosexuality challenges the entire system of race, gender, nationality and heterosexism, which popular music is supposed to reproduce and support.

An apparent distinction between Jamaican reggae and its diasporic expressive forms emerged only recently, owing to the explosion of the controversy over homophobia, starting with Buju Banton's release of *Boom Bye Bye* in 1993, and renewing with his charge of beating a gay man in 2004. In this song the Jamaican singer incited to kill homosexuals with a gun shot ('boom bye bye on a batty boy head'), voicing the homophobic attitude widespread in Jamaican society, where homosexuality is considered a legal crime. According to the Jamaican 'Offences Against the Person Act', male homosexuality can be punished with 10 years of hard labor. In fact, this law, which had given rise to protests, petitions and campaigns by several international organizations for human and LGBITQ rights, is the inheritance of Victorian domination of its church, Bible and sodomy laws. Now that these Western organizations are pushing the Jamaican government to change the law, their pressure is perceived as a the umpteenth imperialist intervention against the island's cultural sovereignty, as if they are pretending once again, to take on 'the white man's burden', to civilize a Third World country incapable of self-determination.

To understand how sexual relations are represented in reggae music today, it is necessary to recognize the 'two cultures' that 'were boiling in the Caribbean' during the days of slavery. One culture was carried out by imposing Christian religion on black slaves, evoking the fire of Sodom and Gomorra, and it was 'one of domination and subjugation'. Another culture, Rastafarianism, was 'a culture of resistance', developing from African roots and from the refusal of Western values, paradoxically identified with another biblical image, the Babylonian inhabitants as the representation of absolute evil and immorality (Campbell, 1985, p. 19). Even if Jamaican culture and music cannot be entirely identified with Rastafarianism, reggae lyrics have always been informed by biblical language and Rastafarian faith. Since contemporary stars of Jamaican reggae, such as Sizzla and Capleton, are mostly Rastafarians who invoke the biblical fire to 'burn' all homosexuals, I would argue that Rastafarianism, initially arising as a strategy of resistance against colonialism, revealed itself to be a fundamentalist religion, which continues to oppress through enslavement rather than freeing minds. Using the Bible, i.e that which has often been used as one of the many tools of colonial power, could allow the Rastaman to temporarily beat the master at his own game, but could not enable him to bring about a genuine change, 'for the master's tools will never dismantle the master's house' (Lorde, 1984, p. 112).[27] However, some reggae singers do support secularism and do not want to be identified with Rastafarianism. For instance, LKJ states that he is not a Rasta, even if he considers Rastafarianism as 'an important antidote to four hundred years of colonial brainwashing which made a lot of black people feel inferior about their blackness', as when 'wi can't face reality', 'some get vision/start preach relijan' and 'shout 'bout sin/instead a fite fi win'.[28]

Reggae musicians used the stereotype of the 'bad man' from the ghetto to nourish the cult of virility and affirm the superiority of the black male. According to Public Enemy's leader Chuck D, 'black men cannot afford themselves to be queer', for 'by now there are already many things pushing us back', and children need a paternal figure, since if they 'don't learn to respect the male, they will never respect anyone' (cited in Adinolfi, 1989, p. 120). Black men regaining virility was interpreted by Malcolm X (1983, p. 300) as the first step to revenge the historical castration they suffered during slavery, while Angela Davis (1983, pp. 7–8) points out that black men felt unable to defend black women from the rapist master, having serious doubts about their own oppositional capacity. These beliefs, rooted in the experience of the plantation system, where sexuality was subordinated to the reproduction of the slave population, have converged in reggae music, making way for its increasing machismo and homophobia. Only one Jamaican singer was able to challenge the colonial assumption that black sexuality must be based solely on 'power relationships which mirror master/slave paradigms' (as wished by bell hooks, 1992, p. 74), releasing a song that unequivocally takes the side against homophobia.[29] Actually, Tanya Stephens compares the bushings undergone by gays in Jamaica with the KKK's hangings of black people, demonstrating that racism and compulsory heterosexuality are two systems of power which reinforce and support each other.

When European reggae followers realized how much brutality came from their icons' mouths, supposed to spread positive vibes, it was too late. Scotland Yard already held an inquiry about homophobic singers, Outrage had launched the 'Stop Murder Music' campaign, and international protests provoked the cancellations of several concerts (in Europe and in the US), the denial of visas to some Jamaican artists supposed to perform in Europe, their exclusion from the Mobo Awards and their censorship from the iTunes catalogue.

Even if anti-gay lyrics are the easiest way to ensure an enthusiastic approval from a Jamaican audience, one could argue that inciting to kill gays in white postcolonial Europe is not acceptable. But this would only reproduce a racial and cultural binary: the fiction of Europe as the cradle of civilization and human rights still perpetuates old and new power relations. Even if European reggae followers state they are not homophobic, they are content with very little: if the singer adapts his repertory to the European audience, cutting the controversial lyrics for one night only, they will continue to buy his records. Moreover, reggae followers continue to justify their heroes because of colonial exploitation (that is to say, they cannot overcome their prejudices, because they are not 'civilized' enough), or they refuse to face the issue directly because Jamaican language is so difficult to understand. As Oumano commented: 'why pay mind to the words when the riddim and the vibe sweet yuh so?' (2005).

In 2007 I was involved in organizing a concert to celebrate Radio OndaRossa 30th anniversary, where Top Cat was expected to perform. After discovering that in 1994 he released a song titled *Shot A Batty Boy*, we asked him to clarify his stance on this matter. He answered:

> In some countries to kill a cow is normal in some it is sacrilegious. I am from a West Indian family and have been brought up predominantly with a West Indian philosophy. I have also grown up in the UK which has different philosophies. As a straight individual and one of West Indian heritage, homosexuality isn't accepted and is personally offensive, but as someone who also believes in Equal Opportunities and tolerance I don't condone violence to any group. That song was recorded in my youthful days and was in defence of my friend Buju Banton who was being attacked by the Gay Rights Movement ... Don't force your beliefs on me and I won't force my beliefs on you. (Top Cat, personal communication, 16 May 2007)

After this statement of 'cultural relativism', the concert was cancelled, since the same Radio had just promoted a national campaign to boycott homophobic reggae, together with several social centers and activists from the LGBITQ movement, and wanted to be consistent with its position.[30] But this decision drew criticism from many reggae followers, who perceived this political choice as a form of censorship. Only one Italian reggae band, Radici nel Cemento, supported the campaign, afterwards releasing a song titled *Siamo tutti omosessuali* (We are all homosexuals), where they condemn homophobic prejudice, reminding us that the celebration of 'Italian virility' was a legacy of the Fascist Empire.

But my point is that homophobia is not only confined to right-wing mentality: it also affects Italian left-wing activists, which usually accept uncritically the macho and aggressive attitude of rappers and reggae singers. This is because the 'bad man' from the ghetto has become a role model for social movement activists, who has never questioned his own machismo and homophobia (Marcasciano, 2007, p. 102). Since the 'bad man' belongs to the working class, he is a revolutionary, so we are all supposed to feel solidarity with him and we must accept him as he is, without any critical reflection, even when he preaches to 'shoot a batty boy'.

Despite the fact that European reggae followers cannot hide behind the shadows of colonialism (since they have been colonizers, rather than colonized, even though they easily identify with Kingston's ghetto youth), and the fact that social centers are supposed to be spaces where people are free to express themselves regardless of their gender or sexual preferences, there is still no consciousness about the power of words. Bob Marley used to say that one good thing about reggae music is that when it hits you, you feel no pain. But what happens if a gay man or a lesbian enters a dancehall yard? Most likely, they will not feel comfortable in that space. Moreover, no activist of the radical left promoting reggae in occupied social centers, nor any reggae follower in Italy, could easily assert to be exempt from sexism and homophobia, since both permeate Italian popular culture. This culture is still informed by the Catholic Church, which like Rastafarianism, considers homosexuality unnatural and gays or lesbians as sinners. Contemporary reggae music in Italy, which for years has been the soundtrack of political demonstrations, now shows all its limits: neither promoters nor consumers mind the message it sends out, they are not interested in experimenting, transforming and desiring; they limit themselves to aping Jamaican attitudes and behaviors, thus reducing this musical form to another product to market for Western consumption. 'Jamaican style is so exotic, and so cool...'.

When reggae music emerged in Italy, it was perceived as a form of 'exodus' from capitalism, from the careerism and the competition typical of the musical market, as a way to create new aesthetic forms and to build a new sense of collective belonging. In this sense the Italian reggae scene possessed all the features of a real 'counter-culture': an explicit political and ideological opposition to the dominant culture, an attempt at building alternative 'institutions' (occupied and self-organized social spaces, underground reviews, record labels, distributions and cooperatives), and an ability to blur the distinction between work and spare time (Hebdige, 1979, p. 148). Now that this countercultural phase is over, and reggae has gone mainstream by becoming a potential business opportunity for a few people, it is apparent that the Italian reggae audience has always identified with a musical genre and a particular lifestyle, without confronting the material and historical conditions of its production. Essentially, this is how 'commodity fetishism' works (Huggan, 2001, p. 19). In this process of identification and mimesis, of appropriation, exchange and consumption, reggae audiences and promoters can sing antiracist lyrics, without addressing their own racism; they can sing antifascist songs, without defining themselves as antifascists; they can say they are not sexist, while playing sexist and homophobic records. While Jamaican labels release records aimed at them, available and palatable for their target, because the homophobic lyrics (that won't be 'acceptable') have been censored, the majority of white European followers can freely consume this 'exotic product' with a superficial attitude, rather than a critical comprehension thereof. Through adapting a particular aesthetic form to their own specific experience, they would have been able to transform themselves from consumers into producers of their own subjectivity. On the contrary, instead of gaining access to another culture, they only reify people and cultures into exchangeable aesthetic objects. But this 'exotic product' still has much to reveal about its own consumers. At least, it tells us that the recurrent statements of being antiracist, antifascist, and antisexist are nothing more than an empty *formula*. This *formula* doesn't make any sense, unless it leads those who pronounce it to practices which address and dismantle the power relations inscribed in the forms of oppression they are supposed to contrast.

Notes

1. Macka B. (1990). Blackman. On *Natural Suntan* [LP]. London: Ariwa.
2. Black Uhuru. (1981). Youth of Eglington. On *Red* [LP]. London: Mango.
3. See Franco Rosso (Director). (1980). *Babylon* [Fiction]. UK: Diversity Music, National Film Finance Corporation, Chrysalis Group and Lee Electric (Lighting).
4. The shift from rocksteady to reggae, at the end of the 1960s, coincided with changes in the British youth culture, such as the emergence of mods, punks and skinheads. According to Hebdige, these subcultures represent the responses given by the white youth to the presence of a sizeable black community in England. It was mods and skinheads who embraced the sounds emerging from Kingston studios, with their appendix of ganja smoking, dreadlocks and calls for 'peace and love'. In the second half of the 1970s, some punk DJs played reggae records during their dj-sets, while *The Clash* incorporated reggae influences into their music (Hebdige, 1979, p. 74).
5. Dandy Livingston. (1967). *Rudy, A Message To You* [7"]. London: JB.
6. 'Batty boy' is the derogatory term for gay men (it is the Jamaican abbreviation of the word 'bottom' into 'batty').
7. During the late 1980s and the early 1990s (when students and workers squatted abandoned buildings to create sites that were autonomous from the influence of the state and the market place) the Italian Posse were the soundtrack of the social centers, addressing social problems and blending rap, reggae, and dub with the Italian traditional musical forms.
8. Sud Sound System. (1996). *Tradizione* [CD]. Lecce: Ritmo vitale. See the booklet.
9. Rastafarianism is both a religion and a movement of resistance, which developed in Jamaica in the 1930s, following the coronation of Haile Selassie as King of Ethiopia. Rastafarians believe that Haile Selassie is god, and that he will return to Africa members of the black community who are living in exile as the result of colonization and the slave trade. To explore the history and beliefs of the Rastafarians, see Barrett (1997). To investigate the way Rastafarianism comes to terms with the history of slavery and colonialism, the reality of white racism and the thrust for self-respect by black people, see Campbell (1985).
10. Fred Locks. (1975). Black Star Liners. On *Black Star Liner* [LP]. Kingston: Vulcan. Marcus Garvey, considered one of Jamaican National Heroes, promoted the idea that black people should migrate voluntarily to the promised land, Africa, to connect with their roots. Repatriation may be experienced as literal or physical, symbolic or cultural.
11. LKJ. (1977). It Dread Inna Inglan. On *Dread Beat and Blood* [LP]. London: Island.
12. Ranking Ann. (1982), *A Slice of English Toast* [LP]. London: Ariwa.
13. *Bhangra* is a form of music and dance that originated in the Punjab region of India and Pakistan.
14. Burning Spear. (1975). Slavery Days. On *Marcus Garvey* [LP]. Kingston: Island.
15. The Maroons were runaway slaves left behind by the Spanish colonizers when the English captured Jamaica in 1655. They formed the independent communities in the hills which gave refuge to the runaway slaves during the uprisings in 1673 and 1685. These slaves carried out a system of guerrilla warfare, attacking the plantations at night, which 'undermined the whole system of slavery' (Campbell, 1985, chap. 1). To this day, the Jamaican Maroons are to a significant extent autonomous and separate from Jamaican society (Zips, 1999).
16. Judy Mowatt. (1982). Only a Woman. On *Only a Woman* [LP]. Newton, NJ: Shanachie.
17. Sister Nancy. (1982). Bam Bam. On *One Two* [LP]. Kingston: Techniques.
18. Lady G. (1989). *Nuff Respect* [12']. New York, NY: Pow Wow Records.
19. *Ireggae.com interviews Sister Carol*, 1999 (Italics mine).

20. Macka B. (1989). Respect Our Mothers. On *Buppie Culture* [LP]. London: Ariwa.
21. Macka B. (1990). Don't Beat Her. On *Natural Suntan* [LP]. London: Ariwa.
22. Ranking Ann. (1982). Liberated Woman. On *A Slice of English Toast* [LP]. London: Ariwa. (1985). Feminine Gender. On *Feminine Gender* [LP] London: Ariwa.
23. Marcia Griffiths & Lady G. (1996). *Woman* [7"]. Kingston: Penthouse.
24. LKJ. (1980). Inglan is a Bitch. On *Bass Culture*. London: Island.
25. Macka B. (1999). Sex Machine. On *Roots & Culture*. London: Ariwa.
26. Buju Banton. (1992). *Love Me Browning* [7"]. Kingston: Penthouse. (1992). *Love Black Woman* [7"]. Kingston: Penthouse.
27. See also Gopaul, Lina [Producer] & Julien, Isaac [Director]. (1993). *The Darker Side of Black* [Documentary]. UK: Concord Media.
28. *Classical reggae interviews LKJ,* 1998. LKJ (1979). Reality Poem. On *Forces of Victory* [LP], London: Island.
29. Tanya Stephens. (2006). Do you still care. On *Rebelution* [CD]. New York, NY: VP.
30. See http:// nonsoloreggae.noblogs.org

References

Adinolfi, F. (1989). *Suoni dal ghetto.* Genova: Costa&Nolan.
Barrett, L.E. (1997). *The Rastafarians.* Boston, MA: Beacon Press.
Barrow, S., & Dalton, P. (1997). *Reggae, the rough guide.* London: Penguin Books.
Bennett, L. (1982). *Selected poems.* Kingston: Sangster's.
Campbell, H. (1985). *Rasta and resistance.* London: Hansib.
Classical reggae. (1998). *Classical reggae interviews LKJ.* Retrieved October 27, 2010, from http://www.classical-reggae-interviews.org/lkj-ras1.htm
Cooper, C. (2004). *Sound clash.* New York, NY: Palgrave Macmillan.
Davis, A.Y. (1983). *Women, race and class.* New York, NY: Vintage.
Gilroy, P. (1993). *The Black Atlantic.* Cambridge, MA: Harvard University.
Gouda, F. (2001). *What's to be done with gender and post-colonial studies?* Amsterdam: Vossiuspers UvA.
Hebdige, D. (1979). *Subculture.* New York, NY: Metheun.
Hill Collins, P. (2006). *From black power to hip hop.* Philadelphia, PA: Temple.
hooks, b. (1992). *Black looks.* Boston, MA: South End.
Huggan, G. (2001). *The postcolonial exotic.* London: Routledge.
Ireggae.com interviews Sister Carol, 1999. Retrieved October 27, 2010, from http://www.ireggae.com/sister.htm
Johnson, L.K. (1975). Dread beat and blood. London: Bogle-L'Ouverture.
Johnson, L.K. (1977). *Dread beat and blood* [LP]. London: Island.
Kureishi, H. (1990). *The Buddha of suburbia.* London: Faber.
Lorde, A. (1984). *Sister outsider.* New York, NY: Crossing.
Ludes, K. (1998). *Interview with LKJ.* Retrieved October 27, 2010, from http://www.classical-reggae-interviews.org
Malcolm X with the assistance of Haley, A. (1983). *The autobiography of Malcolm X.* London: Penguin.
Marcasciano, P. (2007). *Antologaia.* Milano: Il dito e la luna.
Meyler, D. (n.d.). *The story of Grandy Nanny: The woman who became one of Jamaica's founding 'fathers'!* Retrieved October 27, 2010, from http://www.noamies-negril.com/id79.htm
Oumano, E. (2005, February 8). Jah Division: Free speech, cultural sovereignty and human rights clash in reggae dancehall homophobia debate. *Village Voice.* Retrieved October 27, 2010, from http://www.villagevoice.com
Smith, Z. (2001). *White teeth.* New York, NY: Vintage.
Stone, T.S. (n.d.). *Jamaican women: Their politics, economics, roles, and religions.* Retrieved October 27, 2010, from http://debate.uvm.edu/dreadlibrary/stone.html
Women in Reggae. (2005). Il reggae è davvero solo un affare di uomini? *Infoxoa,* 19, 111–114.
Zips, W. (1999). *Black rebels.* Kingston: Ian Randle.

Workings of whiteness: interview with Vron Ware

Bolette B. Blaagaard

Centre for Law, Justice and Journalism, City University London, London, UK

In this edited interview, Vron Ware talks honestly about the political inspiration and personal engagement that flows through her entire body of work. From *Beyond the Pale* (1992) which introduced a new and challenging approach to the intersecting discussions on feminism and anti-racism, to *Out of Whiteness* (2001) which was written with sociologist Les Back and critiqued what the field of critical whiteness studies had become, to Ware's latest work on Britishness (*Who Cares about Britishness?* 2007) and the British military (forthcoming). Ware's political, feminist and anti-racist engagement not only keeps her alert and attuned to the undercurrent of racist attitudes in multicultural Britain, but also informs her methodology and her approach to doing research and to thinking through conversations with colleagues all over the world.

Beyond the Pale *[BTP] was one of the path-breaking publications asking questions about whiteness, femininity and power in colonial as well as contemporary times. What context did this work emerge from in terms of politics and academic traditions?*

I was working on a magazine monitoring the Far Right from 1977 to 1983, and it was clear from their propaganda they were using very crude images of white women and black men to claim that immigrants were more likely to terrorize, to rob, and to rape. This made me curious as to why that combination of figures – the predatory black male and the white female victim – had such a strong hold on people's imaginations. So then I started to do historical research to find examples of how particular radicalized fears of rape and sexual assault had emerged in colonial settings – not necessarily all the time but during periods of crisis or political tension. I discovered, for example, that in Papua New Guinea the colonial administration passed something called the White Women's Protection Ordinance in 1926 just at the point where people were beginning to organize for political participation. Another example was when the British public was persuaded to support brutal repression in India after the 1857 National Uprising as a result of graphic reports, rumors and images showing the rape and killing of English women and children.

You could see it in fiction too, both in film and in literature, where writers like E.M. Forster and J.M. Coetzee used fear of rape as a device to expose the violence underpinning colonial society. In the 1980s there seemed to be a surge of films set in the Raj or in colonial Africa, and this was a constant theme. So that was one context for BTP, following a trail back through colonial history to find out how gendered forms of whiteness had been articulated in relation to blackness, when and where these radicalized and gendered constructs were mobilized politically, and challenged as well.

But there was another whole set of images of white femininity that seemed to express quite different ideas about race and culture. I remember, for example, when Princess Diana was a young bride she went to Saudi Arabia and sat in a tent with the wives of the sheiks. Photos of that encounter were very striking; although they pointed to the clichéd contrast between this glamorous English woman and her veiled Arab counterparts, the conversation that reportedly took place was all about shopping in Harrods. But the juxtaposition opened up another strand of colonial history in which the figure of the white woman exemplified the superiority of Western Christian civilization, because she was independent, she was liberated, she could wear what she liked and she could vote, and so on and so forth.

So, different constructions of white femininity were jumping out at me, and it was exciting to trace the source of their power in colonial history once I started to look. But the information wasn't always there in the history books – it also required digging around and rethinking conventional accounts. It was part of a feminist critique of the way that history had been written without addressing gender. But at the same time I wanted to show how a gender perspective was inadequate on its own.

But the point of the book was to address what was going on at the time, rather than just deal with history. In the late 1970s there was a significant anti-racist movement in the UK, and I was involved in a women's group where we rather struggled to find the links between racism and sexism. There was very little material on gender and racism at that time, and almost nothing on the concept of whiteness. Most of the writing on feminism and anti-racism came out of parallel debates between feminists in the States. The work of writers like bell hooks and Angela Davis was influential in the UK, but in both countries questions of race and racism were assumed to be the preserve of black women. At that time, in England, if you tried to write about race and you weren't black, identity politics demanded that you confessed your own racism first, 'as-a-white-woman'. But there was also an argument that white women were absolved from the history of racism and imperialism because they were also victims of patriarchal power, along with black people.

I found the poet Adrienne Rich really helpful, especially her essay 'Disloyal to Civilization' when she introduced the concept of female racism. It seemed to me to be a useful, provocative idea that 'yes, women have been complicit with racism' that was unusual in that period. But it wasn't just that. It was exciting to learn about the role American women had played in the abolition of slavery, and to find out that feminism had grown out of the struggle for emancipation. The idea that women who took a stand against slavery and segregation were in effect being disloyal to a civilization based on white supremacy... So I became interested in thinking about questions of agency, accountability and complicity in the context of British feminist politics, going back to the anti-slavery movement to find out how that played out there.

So going back to your question about where BTP came from in terms of both politics and academic traditions, it was absolutely rooted in the transatlantic history of race and gender. But there are such big differences between the US and the UK that it has often been hard to use the same arguments in both places. The first time I gave a lecture on BTP in the US it was very much addressed to a contemporary feminist politics and, of course, it had a strong historical component. When I finished, Donna Haraway was in the audience – this was in Santa Cruz – and she put her hand up and asked: 'When did English women first think of themselves as white?' It was a deceptively simple question but I was completely thrown because it spoke more about the history of racial categories in America than the discursive way in which the English had historically named themselves as 'white'. The whole notion of racial hierarchy as a scientific discourse was devised in Europe where the concept of whiteness was aligned with European imperial power. In 1992, when the book came out, there was very little work done on what we now call 'the making of whiteness' either there in the US (apart from David Roediger's *The Wages of Whiteness*) or in the UK. Haraway's question stayed with me, and of course it was a failure on my part to really spell out what I meant, but at the same time it was a moment when the difference between the US and Britain was really apparent. Since then there has been some fantastic work done on whiteness in the context of the US that looks exactly at that how the category changed over time: What did 'white' mean in that period? Who was 'white' and who wasn't? When did the Italians become 'white', or the Irish? And so on. But that doesn't necessarily work in the European context. Although the term 'European' is commonly used – as it is in the US too – to imply whiteness. This is something else that has begun to be challenged more systematically.

So how does whiteness look in the European context if these US categories don't suffice?

Well, I would say first that 'looking for whiteness' anywhere is never going to be the most productive approach. In fact, starting with 'whiteness' as something already defined and findable is likely to be misleading as it suggests an essentialism that's not useful. It's easy to be critical of the methodological nationalism of much US-based work in this area, but the best examples have illuminated the archaeological, ethnographic or theoretical labor involved in analyzing racial hierarchies in different locations. For example, I have found John Hartigan Jr's formulation of the concept of 'racial situations' to be tremendously helpful. It starts from the question: 'when and how do people make sense of racial categories in particular situations? What repertoires of meaning do they draw on, and why?' Now he was exploring these questions in the context of Detroit, but we can apply them anywhere and see where they lead. I have also found Matt Frye Jacobson's work invaluable as he has provided a model for thinking historically about whiteness as a category of belonging, of being fit for citizenship. It's not so much about what whiteness means in US history that is applicable elsewhere, it's the model of careful analysis within a specified framework – in this case, the national polity.

This is hard work, and we have to think carefully what it is we are looking for. Roger Hewitt has tried to define whiteness in a way that works in different countries. He agrees whiteness is usefully conceived through the historicized and gendered notion of citizenship, whether this is achieved through the status of settlers or natives. Whiteness does not necessarily arise from a conception of the ethnic majority or the dominant ethnicity, he suggests, but is 'augmented with the idea of 'born to rule' or 'standard by which all others are judged' or 'grid through which all things should be perceived'. Actually he was writing about the different approaches needed to research the effects of the immigration of Eastern Europeans – classed as 'white' – into countries like the UK where anti-immigrant discourse has been articulated in racist terms, and the immigrant assumed to be dark-skinned. And it's not as though all those who resent the new migrants – or the asylum seekers for that matter – can be classified as 'white' either. Since individual European countries have different patterns of economic migration, different understandings of multiculturalism, and so on, it does not make sense to have a fixed blueprint for identifying whiteness – if that makes sense.

From Beyond the Pale *to* Out of Whiteness *and your last book*, Who Cares about Britishness, *and thinking of them in terms of your career trajectory from a reporter on an anti-fascist paper, researcher of critical whiteness studies and to your work on nationalism and anti-fascism. How do you see this route – are you returning to anti-fascism and nationalism?*

Well first, I never thought of myself as doing something called 'Critical Whiteness Studies'. In fact I remember where I was when I first heard the term and how my heart sank. I had always approached whiteness as a relational category, part of a system of meaning about race, class and gender rather than something to be studied on its own. It was fundamentally a political project too, about taking responsibility for something that is happening in your name.

So *Out of Whiteness* was written to engage with the work on whiteness being done in the US, some of which took a very conservative turn in the mid 1990s. Les Back [co-author of *Out of Whiteness*] and I realized that we were quite alarmed by this development, so we decided to write something to clarify our own positions, and to go into questions of methodology and epistemology in more detail and depth. We developed a lot of our ideas through talking to each other over a period of five years or so. It was wonderful to work with someone who had come through a different route as a social anthropologist, and who also writes about music which has been such an important aspect of anti-racism. After this book I often felt quite reluctant to be drawn back into writing about whiteness itself – it can end up being too vague and abstracted.

One of our main critiques was that most of the literature was centered on the analysis of racism in the US as if the rest of the world did not have these problems and as if the US did not have a relationship with the rest of the world. It's been really productive to link up with people in other countries who are doing similar work on racism and white supremacy, and to have more of a global conversation about what it might mean to analyze whiteness in different countries.

But what was your question? About returning to anti-fascism and nationalism in my current work... well, the connecting themes have been pretty much the same. I lived in the US for six years, returning to London on the day after the bombings in 2005. New Labour's project to define Britishness was just getting going, and the backlash against multiculturalism was really underway. The question of national identity had become a contentious area again and I had always been interested in those struggles to open up what it meant to be British or English for that matter. Right now I am studying the British Army's recruitment of non-UK nationals – which came out of a project on postcolonial Britishness I did with the British Council – and it's giving me a different perspective on nationalism. But I have to say, this is also an area where war, racism, nationalism, postcolonialism and globalization are all mixed up. For one thing, it helps to know about the history of the British Army in relation to empire-building and colonial rule in order to understand the way it operates today. It also brings you to the heart of social welfare and citizenship. One of the things I am trying to do is to find a network of people in Europe who are working on different aspects of this. If we, for instance, look at the figure of the 'soldier' it raises all sorts of questions about entitlement, what it means to fight and kill for your (or anyone else's) country.

What commonalities do you see between the research analyzing whiteness and the research developing the issues of nationalism in a European context? Do they overlap, perhaps?

One of the touchstones of nationalism and national identity within Europe is the memory of the Second World War. Now that we are moving out of the living memory of the conflict, it is acquiring new strands of mythic status as revisionists get to work. I cannot speak about other European countries in detail, but I can tell you for example that the British National Party, which managed to get a member elected to the European Parliament this summer, has recently turned to this past to prove their credentials as loyal Brits under siege from foreigners. In their party political broadcast, shown on national TV, they do not use the language of black and white (even though membership of black and minority ethnic people is banned). The legality of the ban has been questioned and the BNP has been forced to allow all ethnic groups to become members of the party. They present themselves as admirers of Winston Churchill, and take pride from the defeat of Nazism (even though the BNP is known to have a neo-Nazi lineage). But what I found most striking was their footage of British war memorials, and their claim that only those who were descended from those who risked their lives in that war had a right to belong to the UK and enjoy the fruits of citizenship. As the camera pans down the names of English, Scottish, Welsh and Irish casualties, the narrator effectively excludes all those who came from elsewhere. There is no need then to use racial terms – like the old 'rights for whites' – as the point is made in more subtle ways. Of course there is no reference to Britain's colonial army fighting on many fronts around the world. It's a deliberate distortion of history, and it relies on grossly over-simplified accounts of British military prowess and civilian bravery derived from six decades of mis-remembering what actually happened.

One of the stimulating effects of discussing these things in a European setting is the way that differences and commonalities reveal overlapping trends. We can learn so much from each other, as long as we understand that our histories overlap but are not in any way identical.

How have you managed to combine the political projects of feminism and anti-racism, an academic approach to research, and your training as a journalist, particularly in relation to issues of whiteness and national identity?

I think I have managed to avoid any kind of formal training – I started working at *Searchlight*, the anti-fascist paper, as a volunteer because I wanted to be a journalist. Since then I've done various other jobs, including six years in a feminist NGO working on urban planning and design. In 1992 I managed to get an academic post, and have taught geography, sociology and women's studies in London and the US.

Now I have a research fellowship which is allowing me to draw on all these experiences. I like the element of investigation and tracking people down to interview them. But I am finding ethnographic work quite challenging because you have to be very focused. Cynthia Enloe gave me the best advice – she has been an inspiration to me, both because of what she writes and the way she works. When I asked her how I should go about this project, she said: 'Vron, you have to feel your way'. She basically reassured me that there was no prescription telling you how to do it. You start with a hunch and a motivation and then you follow it. Officially, I am interviewing recruits from Commonwealth countries, but how to use this material in order to write something that is not just descriptive and anodyne – that will be the hard part.

The temptation is to think that there is a proper way of doing interviews. I also asked Roger Hewitt for advice, as he has done a lot of ethnographic studies of racism. I was wondering if I was making the most of the situation and going about my interviews in the 'right' way. His advice was similar to Cynthia's: to 'be yourself', to 'follow your nose'. I think the most important aspect of ethnographic work is to be attentive to details and make the most of all your encounters, not just the ones with the people you are supposed to be interviewing. I think that might be more relevant to journalism though, as I find myself thinking about how to tell stories, bring issues to light, rather than collect 'data sets'.

Once I dropped in on a group of recruits who were practicing for a night firing exercise. While I was waiting for them a young officer came over to chat to me. He told me a bit about targets and techniques and so on, and then he said: 'we do find that people from Antigua and other Caribbean islands, they usually fail the first time. We have to spend a lot of time with them'. When I asked him why he thought that was, he said: 'Well, they blink a lot. And they move around and they can't focus. They don't listen to instructions'. Now this was really useful information, on many levels, but I wasn't actually interviewing him, we were just chatting. At that point he didn't know why I was there. When I told him he seemed put out that I wasn't interviewing the white British soldiers. If I had asked him outright about racism or about what he thought about the non-British recruits, I doubt he would have been so open.

I try to spend a lot of time hanging around. But I am learning a lot from simply listening to people – listening to how they talk. I feel like I am learning about these deep, deep racist attitudes across the country, but it's also fascinating to observe how racism, sexism and homophobia are being dealt with institutionally.

What does this approach bring to your work? Could you have written Beyond the Pale *and* Who cares about Britishness? *in a classic sociological approach?*

I organized a seminar where two speakers spoke about their research on white middle class families who chose to move their children to schools that were ethnically mixed and had a multicultural ethos. Both presentations were sociological and based on ethnographic research. It was interesting to see what was useful in that approach. But in order to have a real conversation, you had to sort of jump off the ethnographical data and engage politically with some quite difficult questions. Neither of the speakers felt comfortable talking about whiteness as a political category or how that might be constructed. Or about the relationship between a certain white, class, circumscribed identity and the material circumstances of people's lives. They hadn't asked those kinds of questions, but had gone around it by thinking about 'cultural capital'.

We didn't really get near half the questions the research posed. For instance, several people in the audience asked 'what do you mean by "mixed"?' There is a sociological answer which is technical, and which defined a 'mixed' school as having a significant enrollment of black and white pupils. But it leaves no room for thinking about the demographic group of people who have a black parent and a white parent and who might think of themselves as 'mixed'. So we came up against the limits of that kind of research that has proper research questions and findings but doesn't tell you much that you didn't already know or suspect. It simply maps out something and put it in different language. It doesn't challenge racism. To make real political change (and here I am using the theme of the seminar as an example) it might be more effective to work on either a particular school or engage more with how divisive the education system has been.

In terms of moving between being an academic and journalist...they present different opportunities, I suppose. In the academic world there is an envy that journalists are in a position to write a lot and reach an instant audience. And among journalists there's mistrust towards academics, because they use long words and talk in abstractions. I think the main thing is not to sacrifice complexity in favor of making things simplistic, easy to understand. *Who Cares about Britishness?* was specifically commissioned as a non-academic book, so I didn't use footnotes or engage with theoretical work to any great extent. But I wrote it with an academic teaching agenda in mind. There are lots of short pieces that I felt were illustrative of theoretical or conceptual issues.

The two things I consider to be really important in both professions are curiosity, having an open mind, and alertness – or attentiveness – in terms of being open to things going on around you, like visual imagery, conversations in public spaces, newspaper headlines. Sometimes I have picked up, for instance, a magazine on the train or in a waiting room – something I wouldn't normally see – and encountered material that could be used to illustrate something. This sounds like a fairly random use of artifacts and encounters, but that is what I mean about alertness – being open to what is happening around us in the present. It's important to have curiosity to go further – to see who, and when, and where. That is really how I try to work, I suppose.

So where is it going now? Where do you see these studies going – studies of Postcolonial Europe and Critical Whiteness Studies?

In Europe we are talking about the majority white population, who – broadly speaking – draw on similar sets of resources in terms of thinking about what it means to be white (and European). Again, though, the very different colonial pasts need to be taken into account. So, Austria didn't actually have its own colonies in Africa but had a colonial relationship to countries in south-eastern Europe, in the former Austro-Hungarian empire. I think there needs to be more transnational conversations about the historical memory of colonialism, looking at that particular question of how different countries' colonial pasts are being re-visited, reworked, forgotten etc.

Each country has a different relationship to its own colonial history; patterns of racism in the current period – questions of immigration controls, persecution of minorities, attitudes to Islam – all this needs to be analyzed within national contexts without losing sight of how Europe itself is constituted. It's taken for granted that our national identities – English, Welsh, German, Dutch, French – are assumed to be 'white' unless specified otherwise. We've seen how the idea of irreconcilable differences between Christian and Muslim cultures conveys deep-seated beliefs about the boundaries of European national identities – and how questions of gender and sexuality are central to that. Although there have been important battles in each country to assert the presence of black and ethnic minority citizens, they are invariably referred to as first, second or third generation immigrants, or allochthonous, or gastarbeiters.

'British' is more inclusive, partly because people have fought to make it so, but also because the term British did actually apply to colonized people too. It's astonishing that so many people forget that and don't take account of what 'British' might mean outside the UK, however, residual or nostalgic even. They have forgotten the 1948 British Nationality Act that gave British citizenship to everyone living in British colonies as well as the UK. But people still call themselves Black British or Asian British just to make it clear.

In the UK there has been a worrying focus on the white working class as a victim of the country's immigration policies. This needs a strong and clear analysis in response. For one thing it makes it seem as though this is a homogenous group, as well as a racialized one. Their class and race-based resentment is constantly represented as a rational, understandable response to decades of unfairness.

This is really divisive. It allows immigrants to be seen as the source of many social problems, particularly poverty and unemployment. The emphasis on whiteness, and the notion of being 'native' or 'indigenous' people is really alarming. Rather than try to change the terms of this discourse the government keeps repeating that it is important to listen, and to be fair. They can use this to justify greater and greater regulation of immigration and asylum policy as a result.

I think a discussion around the idea of the fear of white decline would be a productive way to go, particularly in this economic climate. It is certainly relevant in the US, Australia and Canada too. There's an urgent transnational conversation to be had there. It is imperative to think from different countries, from different national and regional locations. Since most of the literature on whiteness and white racism is from the US, it is not necessarily translatable. But we can take the best of it and then think it through from these different places as we develop our own work. It is really important to talk and to make other ways of connecting, making alliances as scholars and feminists and being open to learning from each other.

Vron Ware's bibliography:

Dr. Vron Ware is a research fellow at the Open University, London. She has done groundbreaking work on racism, (post)colonialism, feminism and whiteness published in books such as *Beyond the Pale. White Women, Racism and History* (2002, London and New York, NY: Verso Books), *Out of Whiteness. Color, Politics, and Culture* (with Les Back) (2002, Chicago, IL: University of Chicago Press) and *Who Cares about Britishness? A Global View of the National Identity Debate* (2007, London: Arcadia Books). She sums up her research interests as race and gender, whiteness, history and politics of antiracism, transnational feminism, postcolonialism, British/English national identity, Islamophobia, feminism in the Muslim-majority world, communicative citizenship, intercultural dialogue, cultural diplomacy, life-writing, landscape, place, social ecology, urban/rural divide, heritage. Her latest research explores the relations between militarism, nationalism and whiteness.

Index

Page numbers in **Bold** represent figures.

Abu-Lughod, A. 19
adoption: illegal 85–6
Africa 4, 16–17; Melilla 96
African cultural association: *Mfundi Kupa I Kribi-Itondi* 115
African culture 65–6
African emigrants 105–20, 127; Italy 48
Afro-Hispanic black diaspora 108–9
After Multiculturalism (Alibhai-Brown) 95
Agamben, G. 2, 32
Agbotom, A. 110
Ahmed, S. 74, 78, 88, 89
Akono, S. 105–6, 117–18; *Black Iris* 110–12; *The Weapons of my Disappointment* 112–13
Ali, M. 126; *Brick Lane* 100
Alibhai-Brown, Y.: *After Multiculturalism* 95
Álvarez, A.M. 8
Amir, K. 142
Andall, J. 127
Andrijasevic, R. 87
anti-immigration 5–6
art: black British artists 99
Asad, T.: *Formations of the Secular* 79–80
Asia 17; emigrants 75–80
Asian/British culture 75–80
asylum application: Austria 35–6
Atlantic world: Gilroy's terminology 13
Aulo: Song-Poem from Eritrea (Sibhatu) 131
Australia 17
Austria: Austro-Hungarian Empire 29, 30, 31, 35; Chechen immigrants 27–8; Habsburg Empire 30–2; Haider's letters 28, 29, 32–3, 34; imperial past 29–32; labor force shortage (1960s) 35; national treaty (1955) 32; newspapers 28, 34; political parties 36; public broadcasting (ORF) 42; state-of-exception 27–38
The Avis 66–7

Babylon system: reggae music 139–40
Back, L. 156
Balibar, E. 3, 29, 38, 50, 89; and Wallerstein, I. 37

Balkans 30–2, 37
Banton, B.: *Circumstances* 139
Bastian, J. 64
Bate, J. 65, 67
Bedminster, E. 66, 67
Bengal emigrants: Britain 100–1
Benjamin, W. 41, 110
Bennett, L. 139
Beyond the Pale (Ware) 153–9
Bhabha, H. 44, 124
bhangra music: Apache Indian 143
Blaagaard, B.B. 7
black diaspora 105–20; reggae music 137–51
Black Iris (Akonon) 110–12
black migrant subjectivities 114–17
blackness 5
Blair, T. 62
blogging 19–20; *Morgunblaðið* 13–14, 19
Boer and British conflict 17
border concept 2–4
border control 82, 86–7; Italy 46
Bosnia-Herzegovina 30
Bracke, S. 79
Brah, A. 128
Braidotti, R. 93
Brick Lane (Ali) 100
Britain: Asian culture 75–80; Bengali immigrants 100–1; Caribbean immigrants 139; citizenship 99, 160; fictional literature 93–120; migrant cinema 93–120; multiculturalism 8, 93–120; political parties 99, 157; racial discrimination laws 99; reggae music 140, 143, *see also* England
British and Boer conflict 17
Brown, W. 3
Bryan, A. 63–9
Bryson, V. 51
The Buddha of Suburbia (Kureishi) 142
Bunzl, M. 15
Buonaiuto, C. 7
Busek, E. 30

Cameron, E. 63

INDEX

Caribbean emigrants 99, 139
Caribbean islands 61, 63
Carinthia: Austria 27–8, 32–3, 36
Caritas regional immigration office: Contact campaign 49
Castelvolturno 43, 48–50; Catholic Church 49; street protests (2008) 48
Catholic Church 113; Castelvolturno 49; homosexuality 150
Certeau, M. 130
Chambers, I. 3
Chechen immigrants: Austria 33–5
Chechnya: First War 34; Second War 33–4
Chirac, J. 62
Christianity: slavery 148
cinema *see* migrant cinema
Circumstances (Banton) 139
citizenship: Austria 35–6; Britain 99, 160; Italy 47–8, 53
civilization 13, 16, 17
Close Friends (Wadia) 128–9
Coetzee, J.M. 153
collective unconscious 43
colonial identity formations: Iceland 11–25
colonialism 160; Austria 30; Austria's history 27–38; Denmark 61–70; Iceland 16–17; Italy 52–3; Nordic 6, 12, 62; St. Croix 61–70; Spain 115–16
Commission on the Future of Multi-Ethnic Britain 94
communist regimes 35
Concorso (Mubiayi) 129
Conrad, J.: *Heart of Darkness* 114
Contemporary British Women Artists (Fortnum) 99
conviviality: Gilroy's definition 94–102
Cooper, C. 143
Coppola, M. 8
Cosmofobia (Etxebarría) 97–9
Crapanzano, V.: defamiliarization 14
critical whiteness *see* whiteness
cultural insiderism: Gilroy's terminology 13
cultural knowledge: USVI 64–5
cultural mediators 49–50
cultural memory 7, 62–3, 65–7, 69–71
cultural origin 36–7
cultural racism: Balibar and Wallerstein's terminology 37
culture: Afro-Hispanic 108–9; British/Asian 75–80; Jamaica 137–51
Curti, L. 130, 132
Cyrus, S.: and Legge, J. 108
The Daily News 66–8

Danish colonialism: St. Croix 61–70
Davis, A. 148
De Lauretis, T. 86

defamiliarization 14
Deleuze, G.: and Guattari, F. 62, 69; history concept 69
democracy: Spain 108–9
Denmark: slave emancipation reenactment (1998) 63–7; USVI 61–70
Derrida, J. 123
diaspora: black Mediterranean 105–20; reggae music 137–51
dictatorship: Spain 108–10, 113
Diken, B. 88
Dismatria (Scego) 129
Documents Please (Mubiayi) 128
DuBois, W.E.B. 116–17

Easter Lunch (Ghermandi) 129
economy: Iceland 12; Naples and Caserta 54
education: Italy 45
El Hachmi, N.: *The Last Patriarch* 97–9
El-Ghibli (Ghermandi) 126
England: post-war 99–102
Enloe, C. 158
Equatorial Guinea 110, 114
Essed, P. 3
Etxebarría, L.: *Cosmofobia* 97–9
eugenics movement: Karldóttir's analysis 18
Eurocentrism 2–3
European Union (EU) 2, 96
Europism 3
exceptionalism 82
exclusion 41–56
explorers 17
The Fact of Blackness (Fanon) 115

Fanon, F. 43; *The Fact of Blackness* 115
Farah, C.A. 132
Farah, N. 2
female immigrants 73–89, 127–8; Italy 41–56
female migrant authors 121–35
female oppression 78–80, 98; reggae music 141
femininity 153–4; reggae music 143–7
feminism 14
Ferguson, R. 33
Fernando, C. 43, 44, 47
Ferrero, P. 55
film *see* migrant cinema
Fini, G. 55
Finnbogason, G. 18
football: European Championship 96
Formations of the Secular (Asad) 79–80
Forster, E.M. 153
Fortnum, R.: *Contemporary British Women Artists* 99
Fourth Plinth project: Trafalgar Square 95
Frankenberg, R.: white female study 15
fundamentalism 79–80

INDEX

Gangbo, J.M. 131
Garvey, M. 141
gender 8–9, 37–8, 110–14, 143–7, 146–51, 153–4; Iceland 11–25; reggae music 137–51
Geneva Refugee Convention 34, 37
German language 31–2
Germany: Iranian immigrants 80–4
Ghermandi, G.: *Easter Lunch* 129; *El-Ghibli* 126; *Queen of Flowers and Pearls* 131–2
Gheryb, M.: *Sleeping in the Open* 109
Gikandi, S. 43
Gilroy, P. 1, 27, 28, 43, 64, 87, 97, 126, 137, 138; Atlantic world 13; conviviality 94–102; cultural insiderism 13
Glenaan, K.: *Yasmin* 73–80, **76, 77, 78**
Glissant, E. 130, 132
global mobility 84–8
global terror 75–80
Gormley, A. 95
Gröndal, B. 18
Gronold, D. 7
Grozny: Russia 33
Guattari, F.: and Deleuze, G. 62
guest concept: Austria 37–8
Guinea: 1968 independence 106

Habsburg Empire 30–2
Haider, J. 8, 27, 32–3, 34, 36, 37; letters by 28, 29, 32–3
Hall, S. 94
Haraway, D. 155
Harrison, F.V. 15
Hartigan, J. Jr. 155
Heart of Darkness (Conrad) 114
Heritage, M. 141
Hewitt, R. 155, 158
Hipfl, B. 7
history: Deleuzian concept 69
homophobia: reggae music 140, 147–51
homosexuality 80–4; Jamaica 147–51
housing: Naples 45
Huggan, G. 2
human rights association: *Jolibà* 43
Hungary: Austro-Hungarian Empire 29, 30, 31, 35

Iceland 11–25; economy 12; gender 11–25; Icelandic Literature Association 16
identity 122–5; Austria 30; Icelandic 11–25; immigrant 73–89, 93–120; Italy 53; migrant Spain 105–20; USVI 62
Imagining the Balkans (Todorova) 30
immigrant work: care taking 51–3
immigrants 2; African 48, 127; Asian 75–80; Austrian 27–38; Caribbean 99; criminalization 84–8; female 73–89, 127–8; female writers 121–35; gender differentiation 37–8; Icelandic 19; Nigerian 43, 49, 50; second generation 8, 19; sexual politics 80–4; Slovakian 31; Sri Lankan 41–56; stereotypes 123–7; sub-Saharan African 107; Ukrainian 41–56, 84–8
immigration: Britain 75–80; Iceland 12, 19; legislation 86–7; policy 82–3; Spain 96–7, 97–9
imperialism 4
Iran: emigrants 80–4
Islam 19–20, 21–2, 75–80; female oppression 78–80; Muslim Association of Iceland 20; Muslim stereotype 98; prejudice 15; women 19–20, 75
Islamophobia 15, 74
Italy: border control 46; *camorra* illegal law 42; Campania Region 54, 55; economic hardship 54; education 45; female immigrants 41–56; immigrant exclusion 41–56; migrant literature 8; mixed-race marriage guidelines (2006) 53; Naples *see* Naples; North/South 54, 55; political parties 55; postcolonial literature 121–35; racist laws 55; reggae music 140, 143, 149–51, 150; temporary abode myth 44–8; Ukrainian immigrants 84–8; Ukrainian marriage 52–3

Jacobson, M.F. 155
Jamaica: reggae music 137–51
Jamaica culture 137–51; Empress Menem 144
Jolibà human rights association 43
Jones, C. 102
Journal of a Clandestine (Nini) 109

Karlsdóttir, U.B. 18
Khouma, P. 133
Kureishi, H.: *The Buddha of Suburbia* 142; *My Son the Fanatic* 76
Kuruvilla, G. 127, 130

Laforest, M.H. 7
Lafuente, S. 93–4
Lagaskaia, J. 47
Lago, D. 82
Lane, R. 99
language 109, 112, 114, 130–3; German 31–2; Jamaican 142; Somali 132
Larsen, A.F. 63, 64, 67
The Last Patriarch (El Hachmi) 97–9
Latin America 108
Lavapiés: Spain 97
law: racial discrimination 99; racist 55
Legge, J.: and Cyrus, S. 108
Levy, A.: *Small Island* 99–100
literary market places 125–7

INDEX

literature: African migrant 105–20; Afro-Hispanic 108–9; Asian British authors 99; black British authors 99; British authors 99; England 93–120; Italian 8; Italian postcolonialism 121–35; Spain 8, 93–120, 105–20; West Indian Renaissance 99
Livingston, D. 139–40
Loach, K. 76
Loftsdóttir, K. 6
Lombardi-Diop, C. 131
London: Trafalgar Square's fourth plinth 95

Maccarone, A.: *Unveiled* 73, 74, 80–4, **80, 81, 83**
Macías, F. 110–13, 113
Madrid: 3/11 terrorism 97
Magris, C. 29; Habsburgian myth 29
Mahmood, S.: *The Politics of Piety* 79
Makomé, I. 105–6, 114–19; *Spain and Black Africans* 115
Malcolm X 148
Malsani, G. 126
marginality 110–14
Mari E. 43, 49, 50
Marley, B. 150; destiny terminology 70
marriage: Milan guidelines (2006) 53; mixed-race 52–3
masculinity: reggae music 146–51
Mbembe, A. 43
Meadows, S.: *This is England* 101
media: Austrian newspapers 28, 34; Austrian public broadcasting (ORF) 34; blogging 13–14, 19–20; British newspapers 95; journalistic cultural memory 62–3; journalistic representation 61–70; migrant cinema 8, 73–89; *Skírnir* journal 16–17, 18, 21; Spanish newspapers 96; USVI newspapers 66
Meletti, J. 52
Melilla: Africa 96
Memmi, A. 115
memory: collective 29; cultural 7, 62–3, 65–7, 69–71; Deleuze, G. and Guattari, F. 69; singular 69; situated 67–8
Merolla, D. 124
mestizaje 108
Mezzadra, S. 82, 128
migrant cinema 8, 73–89, 93–120; Asian/British films 76; *The Unknown Woman* 74, 84–8, **85**, 89; *Unveiled* 73, 74, 80–4, **80, 81, 83**, 89; *Yasmin* 73–80, **76, 77, 78**, 89
migrant literature 8; female authors 121–35; publishing 125–6; Spain 105–20
migrant music: reggae 137–51
migration: Italy 123–5
Modood, T. 96
Mohanram, R. 17–18

Morgunblaðið 13–14, 19
Mubiayi, I.: *Concorso* 129; *Documents Please* 128
multiculturalism 15, 18–21; Britain 8, 93–120; Gilroy's definition 94; Iceland 11–25; Spain 93–120
music *see* migrant music
Muslim *see* Islam
My Son the Fanatic (Kureishi) 76

Naples 7, 41; class structure 45; Kiev-Piazza Garibaldi bus line 51–3; M1 bus line 48–50; Naples in color event 50; petit-bourgeois 54; Spanish Quarters **48**
Ndongo, D. 105–6, 110, 114, 117–18; *Shadows of Your Black Memory* 113
Nguema, T.O. 110
Nigerian emigrants: Italy 43, 49, 50
Nini, R.: *Journal of a Clandestine* 109
Nkogo, E. 110
nomadic subject 93–4
Nordic countries 6, 12, 62
North Africa emigrants 109
Norway 62
Notting Hill carnival 101–2
Notting Hill riots (1976) 142
Nsue, M. 110

objectivity 69
O'Healy, Á. 86
others concept 78, 124; Austria 37–8
Ottoman Empire 30–1
Out of Whiteness (Ware) 156–7
out-immigration 18–19

Papua New Guinea: White Women's Protection Ordinance (1926) 153
paradoxical inclusion 123
Pardo, E.S. 8
Parekh report (2000) 94
Passerini, L. 2
Penn, D. 143
Placido, M. 84
political elections: British local (2006) 96
political parties: Austria 36; Britain 96, 99, 157; Italy 55; Spain 106–7
The Politics of Piety (Mahmood) 79
Politics of the Veil (Scott) 79
Politkowskaja, A. 34
Ponzanesi, S. 8, 15, 124
postcolonialism: Europe 4–9, 21–2; Italian literature 121–35
prostitution *see* sex trade
Prutsch, U. 31
Punjabi, A. **76**
Puwar, N. 14

INDEX

Queen of Flowers and Pearls (Ghermandi) 131–2

race 110–14; Iceland 11–25
racial aggression 49; Naples in color event 50
racial classification 16, 18
racial discrimination laws: Britain 99
racialization 87
racism 5, 11–12, 14–15, 19–22; Austria 27, 28, 34–7; Italy 44, 45, 55; Spain 105–20; USA 156
racist laws: Italy 55
Rajoy, M. 107
Rappaport, X. 84, **85**
Rastafarianism 140–1, 144–5, 148, 150
Ravn, K. 63
refugee *see* immigrants
refugee definition: United Nations Convention 81
reggae artists: Anthony B 144, 145; Banton, B. 147; Capleton 148; Garnett Silk 144; Griffiths, M. 145, 146; Johnson, L.K. 141, 142, 146; Lady G 145, 146; Lady Shaw 147; Macka B 143, 144, 145; Marley, B. 150; Marley, R. 146; Mowatt, J. 144; Oumano 149; Outrage 149; Pato Banton 143; Ranking Ann 142–3, 145; Sister Carol 145; Sister Nancy 145; Sizzla 148; Top Cat 149
reggae music: female oppression 141; femininity 143–7; homophobia 140, 147–51; Italy 140, 143, 149–51, 150; masculinity 146–51; sexuality 147; UK 137–51, 143
religious fundamentalism 79–80
Rich, A. 154
Riquelme, J. 114
Ropero, L.L. 8
Russia 33; Chechnya conflict 33–4

Sabelli, S. 8–9
Said, E. 43
St. Croix: Danish colonialism 61–70; Danish slave emancipation commemoration 63–7
Sassen, S. 43, 50
Saviano, R. 50
Scego, I. 126; *Dismatria* 129; *The Strange Night of Vito Renica* 128
Schneider, R. 65, 66, 67
Scholl, S. 34
Scott, J.: *Politics of the Veil* 79
Seck, S. 109
Second World War 18–19
secular liberalism 79
Selvon, S. 99
sex trade 75, 84–8, 111
sexual politics 80–4
sexuality: Afro-Surinamese 68

Shadows of Your Black Memory (Ndongo) 113
Shonibare, Y. 95
Sibhatu, R.: *Aulo: Song-Poem from Eritrea* 131
Skírnir journal 16–17, 18, 21
Slav emigrants 31
slavery 61–2, 116, 154; Christianity 148; Danish emancipation commemoration 63–7
Sleeping in the Open (Gheryb) 109
Slovenia 32
Small Island (Levy) 99–100
Smith, Z. 126; *White Teeth* 142
Somalia 44
space 122–3; cultural 127–30; literary 127–30
Spain 8; African migrant literature 105–20; black females 111; black migrant subjectivities 114–17; colonialism 115–16; democracy/dictatorship 108–10, 113; dictatorship 108–10, 113; fictional literature 93–120; immigration 97–9; Lavapiés 97; migrant film 93–120; North African authors 109; political parties 106–7
Spain and Black Africans (Makome) 115
Spanish Empire 96
Spivak, G. 78, 79
Sri Lanka: female emigrants 41–56
Stanley, H.M. 17
Stephens, T. 148
Stephensen, M. 16
Stoler, A. 12
The Strange Night of Vito Renica (Scego) 128
Stråth, B. 89

Tabatabai, J. 81
terrorism 15, 77–8; Madrid 97
Tew, P. 99
This is England (Meadows) 101
Ticktin, M. 82
Todorova, M.: *Imagining the Balkans* 30
Tornatore, G.: *The Unknown Woman* 73, 74, 84–8, **85**
Trafalgar Square: fourth plinth 95
transport: Contact campaign 49; Kiev-Piazza Garibaldi bus route 51–3; segregation 48–50
Turkey 32

Ukrainian emigrants: female 41–56; Italian marriage 52–3; Italy 84–8
United Kingdom (UK) *see* Britain
United Nations Convention: refugee definition 81
United States' Virgin Islands (USVI): *The Avis* 66–7; cultural knowledge 64–5; *The Daily News* 66–8; Denmark 61–70

INDEX

The Unknown Woman (Tornatore) 73, 74, 84–8, **85**
Unveiled (Maccaroné) 73, 74, 80–4, **80**, **81**, **83**
urban space 127–30

Vienna: Austria 29
von Scholten, P. 63, 64, 68
Vorpsi, O. 125, 131

Wadia, L. 129; *Close Friends* 128–9
Wallerstein, I.: and Balibar, E. 37
Ware, V. 9, 96, 153–60; *Beyond the Pale* 153–9; *Out of Whiteness* 156–7; *Who Cares About Benjamin* 156–9
The Weapons of my Disappointment (Akono) 112–13
Wekker, G. 68

Werbner, P. 96, 102
Western Europe: British culture 75–80
white female identity: Frankenberg's study 15
White Teeth (Smith) 142
whiteness 6, 9, 66, 87–8, 153–60; femininity 153–4; Iceland 11–25
Who Cares About Benjamin (Ware) 156–9
Wodak, R.: Austrian national identity study 30

Yasmin (Glenaan) 73–80, **76**, **77**, **78**

Zamora, F. 110
Zapatero, J.L.R. 107

www.routledge.com/9780415686327

Related titles from Routledge

Gender, Race and Religion: Intersections and Challenges
Edited by Martin Bulmer and John Solomos

Gender, Race and Religion brings together a selection of original papers published in *Ethnic and Racial Studies* that address the intersections between gender relations, race and religion in our contemporary environment. Chapters address both theoretical and empirical aspects of this phenomenon, and although written from the perspective of quite different national, social and political situations, they are linked by a common concern to analyse the interface between gender and other situated social relationships, from both a conceptual and a policy angle. These are issues that have been the subject of intense scholarly research and analysis in recent years, as well as forming part of public debates about the significance of gender, race and religion as sites of identity formation and mobilisation in our changing global environment. The substantive chapters bring together insights from both theoretical reflection and empirical research in order to investigate particular facets of these questions. *Gender, Race and Religion* addresses issues that are at the heart of contemporary scholarly debates in the field of race and ethnic studies, and engages with important questions in policy and public debates.

This book was originally published as a special issue of *Ethnic and Racial Studies*.

December 2011: 234 x 156: 192pp
Hb: 978-0-415-68632-7
£80 / $125

For more information and to order a copy visit
www.routledge.com/9780415686327

Available from all good bookshops

www.routledge.com/9780415677134

Ethnic and Racial Studies

Ethnic and Racial Minorities in Asia
Inclusion or Exclusion?

Edited by Michelle Ann Miller

Ethnic and Racial Minorities in Asia explores the relationship between ethnic minority rights and citizenship in Asia. Occupying a prominent place on the global map of conflict, Asia is one of the most ethnically diverse and racially divided regions in the world. It is also the scene of some of the most contrasting state responses to ethnic and racial conflicts, ranging from violent military repression and coercion on the one hand, to offers of autonomy and other forms of self-rule aimed at granting minorities more equal and inclusive citizenship on the other.

This volume combines conceptual debates about citizenship with case studies of ethnic minorities from across the Asian region, with a particular emphasis on Southeast Asia. The contributing authors question the nature of citizenship in the broader sense of identity, belonging, and the rights and responsibilities of ethnic minorities in relation to sovereign nation-states. They examine a wide range of key issues including minority rights claims, ethnic and racial conflict, citizenship, constructions and representations of identity, post-colonialism and human security.

This book was originally published as a special issue of *Ethnic and Racial Studies*.

November 2011: 234 x 156: 160pp
Hb: 978-0-415-67713-4
£80 / $125

For more information and to order a copy visit
www.routledge.com/9780415677134

Available from all good bookshops

www.routledge.com/9780415679992

Ethnic and Racial Studies

Cosmopolitan Sociability
Locating Transnational Religious and Diasporic Networks

Edited by Tsypylma Darieva, Nina Glick Schiller and Sandra Gruner-Domic

This book approaches the concept of cosmopolitan sociability as a cultural or territorial rootedness that facilitates a simultaneous openness to shared human emotions, experiences, and aspirations.

Cosmopolitan Sociability critiques definitions of cosmopolitanism as a tolerance for cultural difference or a universalist morality that arise from contemporary experiences of mobility and globalization. Challenging these assumptions, the book explores the degree to which a 'cosmopolitan dimension' can be practised within particular religious communities, diasporic ties, or gendered migrant identities in different parts of the world. A wide variety of expert contributors offer rich ethnographic insights into the interplay of social interactions and cosmopolitan sociability. In this way the book contributes significantly to ethnic and migration studies, global anthropology, social theory, and religious and cultural studies.

Cosmopolitan Sociability was originally published as a special issue of *Ethnic and Racial Studies*.

September 2011: 234 x 156: 144pp
Hb: 978-0-415-67999-2
£80 / $125

For more information and to order a copy visit
www.routledge.com/9780415679992

Available from all good bookshops